FASHION
& TEXTILES
The Essential Careers Guide

Published in 2010 by
Laurence King Publishing Ltd
361–373 City Road
London EC1V 1LR
United Kingdom
Tel: + 44 20 7841 6900
Fax: + 44 20 7841 6910
e-mail: enquiries@laurenceking.com
www.laurenceking.com

A catalogue record for this book is available
from the British Library

ISBN: 978-1-85669-617-3

Designed by TwoSheds Design
Cover illustration by Marc Sandford @ Tangdc.com

Project Editor: Gaynor Sermon
Picture Researcher: Annalaura Palma
Copy Editor: Liz Dalby

Printed in Thailand

FASHION & TEXTILES

The Essential Careers Guide

CAROL BROWN

Laurence King Publishing

Contents

Foreword

Fashion has long been my drug, a potent elixir that – mixed with one part perseverance, two parts imagination and shaken with a dash of reality – has taken me on a crazy rollercoaster ride to a place where dreams can come true. Carol Brown's book is a must for anyone thinking of a career in fashion and textiles. It will provide you with the practical tools to navigate the various career appointments available within the industry, and inspire you. With ambition, anything is possible…

Antonio Berardi
Fashion Designer

Introduction

I wrote this book for students, graduates, teachers, lecturers, careers officers and anyone who already works in the industry and is seeking a change of career direction. I wanted to create a resource, teaching aid and self-instructional book that would encourage the reader to become actively engaged with the content, and I wrote it in response to the continual questions asked by students and recent graduates about future careers. This book answers those questions, identifying what particular jobs involve; how the industry works; how to find an internship; the value of work experience; where to find jobs advertised; what to expect and how to present yourself at an interview; how to create a portfolio; the importance of networking; how to write an effective CV and how to complete an application form.

The first five chapters provide an in-depth review of the broad range of career options in the fashion and textile industry as well as associated industries in the areas of design, media and retail, giving clear definitions of job profiles. Also included is an overview of a wide range of alternative career paths. Throughout you will find profiles and exclusive interviews with many well-known and influential international figures in the fields of fashion and textiles, providing professional and personal insights into particular careers.

All aspects of the job hunting process are analyzed in chapters six to eleven, with practical advice that will increase your chances of success in gaining employment. The final chapter focuses on the budding careers of recent graduates and up-and-coming designers, giving a taste of what to expect in the early stages of your career.

I hope that you will find this book to be a useful and inspirational guide to taking your first steps in the world of fashion and textiles.

Carol Brown

Chapter 1: Creative Opportunities

*T*here are many exciting creative opportunities on offer in the fashion industry, from being a designer in menswear, womenswear or childrenswear to acting as a designer in a specialist field: bridalwear, corporate wear, lingerie, swimwear, knitwear, millinery, footwear, accessories or printed or woven textiles. Other creative opportunities discussed in this chapter include: costumier, wardrobe mistress, fashion forecaster, colourist and fashion illustrator. This chapter explains the breadth of employment and career opportunities within the creative fields of fashion and textiles.

There are three main areas of design: haute couture, prêt-à-porter (designer ready-to-wear) and high street fashion, which is the largest area of design with garments often being designed and manufactured in their thousands. There are many opportunities in this highly competitive market due to the fast turnaround of ranges, the vast numbers of sales of garments and the speedy response of the industry to seasonal trends.

The fashion industry is constantly evolving, with developments in technology, an ever-changing global marketplace and the transience of emerging trends. There are two main seasons per year in the fashion calendar: autumn/winter and spring/summer. Each requires a new collection that promotes a forthcoming 'look', using new colour palettes and fabric ranges. Producing a new collection involves careful research into future trends, visiting fabric exhibitions and trade fairs and reviewing the success of the past season's collection and the work of competitors, in order to produce a directional and appealing collection.

The Role of the Fashion Designer

The role of a designer varies from company to company depending on the size and type of business. In a larger company the designer may concentrate on one of the following areas: analyzing and predicting trends in fabrics, colours and garment shapes; producing concept and mood boards; sourcing fabrics, developing ranges and working with buyers and manufacturers. However, in a smaller company the designer may be responsible for every stage of creating and developing garment ranges from the initial concept of the design through to the production of garments. They may also be responsible for the manufacture of the blocks through to the patterns, supervising the making-up of samples and overseeing the manufacture of the garments.

Antonio Berardi with a model, autumn/winter 2008-2009

Antonio Berardi: Fashion Designer

Antonio Berardi was born in the UK but now works in Milan, and is recognized as a key figure in today's fashion world. He studied fashion design in Lincoln in the UK and then worked as an assistant at John Galliano's studio before he gained a place on the BA (Hons) Fashion course at Central St Martins, London, in 1990. After graduating from St Martins in 1994, Antonio won a contract to design a high-street collection for a Japanese company. This contract assisted him in financing his own label.

In 1999 he moved from the London catwalks to Milan and by 2000 he was appointed Head Designer by Extè, who also became producers of his own collection. In 2006 he moved his focus to Paris where he presented his spring/summer collection, which was well received.

Antonio's work has achieved an impressive international following, as indicated by the popularity and the success of his collections, which are now available across Europe, America and the Far East. His work is regularly featured in top international fashion and lifestyle magazines such as *Vogue*, *Harper's Bazaar*, *Elle*, *i-D*, *Numero* and *Marie Claire*.

An Interview with Antonio Berardi

How would you define your style?
There are two parts to my style: elements of Sicilian culture – romantic, ultra feminine, frou frou, Baroque – and the other element is British: Royalty, Rock 'n

Roll, Madonna–whore; creating a play against masculine and feminine.

What inspires and influences your designs?
Absolutely everything – films, music, literature – it may be a line in a book that is so evocative. Everything and anything!

In your opinion, what makes a successful fashion designer?
It is important to stay true to your vision; it's about believing in yourself and what you do. Most people tend to have a vision; to be successful it's about creating something that's totally yours.

What is the key to your success?
Perseverance and never giving up, continuing to do what I do.

What is the most difficult part of designing a collection?
Editing the collection, narrowing it down, making sure there are not too many things going on, having clarity of vision.

When and why did you start your own business?
After showing my degree collection at Central St Martins, my work received a lot of publicity. A La Mode and Liberties in London bought my collection and people wanted more, so I took out a £500 bank loan and that was it.

What is your greatest achievement to date?
Receiving an Honorary Degree from the University of Lincoln, UK.

What has been your biggest career challenge to date?
I produced some work for Emilio Pucci; there was little money available and it was a challenge to make it work, but it was a challenge that paid off.

What next?
A period of growth – attracting investors and making the label a brand with accessories, international stores and menswear. Consolidating what I have been doing.

What advice would you give to an aspiring fashion designer?
Never say never!

To be a successful fashion designer you need to be creative with a good working knowledge of the technical process of garment development, as well as range-building. The designer usually works very closely with buyers, product developers, garment technologists, sample machinists and manufacturers (often based overseas). This is to ensure that designs are reproduced accurately to the garment specifications.

The majority of designers study fashion design at college or university. There are many fashion- and textile-related courses offering a varying degree of specialism. Some courses offer a broad programme; while many others are subject-specific, focusing on a specialist area of design, for example costume design, surface patterning or fashion marketing.

Graduates usually enter a company in a junior role as an assistant designer, supporting the designer and design team, and, with a successful work record and one or two years' experience working in this position, progress to a position of designer and then senior designer.

Womenswear Designer

Womenswear is one of the largest sectors of the fashion market. Whether working for a fast-moving high street design brand producing casual jersey ranges or in the luxury market sector producing tailored modern classics, a womenswear designer must have an excellent understanding of trends and be able to translate customers' requirements. In the planning and development of garment ranges they must give consideration to season, silhouette, colour and fabric range, creating ideas appropriate to the target market.

Employment opportunities will vary from company to company. You may work for a small, independent fashion label, possibly as the sole designer, managing all aspects of the design process from the initial concept to the execution of the finished product. Alternatively, the position may involve working in a larger company within a design team and having a creative input into each range, from researching design concepts in line with the brand ethos to designing the collection within the parameters of the range plan, producing mood boards, selecting fabrics and trims or developing products from specification sheets to final sample approval. Other positions within companies may include organizing a design office's administration relating to each design range or ensuring all pre-production checks have been completed on sample collections before shipment, alongside a contribution to designing a seasonal range. No two design positions are the same.

Typical Skills Required

===

✖ *The ability to work to a design brief with understanding of the customer and their lifestyle*
✖ *An instinctive feeling for fashion and ability to identify emerging fashion trends*
✖ *Strong creative skills with a good knowledge of design*
✖ *An understanding of fabrics and manufacturing techniques*
✖ *Commercial awareness*
✖ *Proficiency in Adobe Photoshop and other CAD software*
✖ *Ability to work under pressure, to meet deadlines to produce new collections each season or mid-season*

Menswear Designer

In recent years there has been a huge growth in the menswear market due to the accessibility of menswear labels in the high street and the growing sales of menswear magazines and journals promoting men's fashion, style, music, health and lifestyle. There are now more varied menswear styles available than ever before. These range from casual and sportswear to classic tailored and more refined styles and are available in many high street outlets and designer boutiques. Men now demand a greater variety of styles from which to choose including edgier looks, functional clothing with sportswear overtones, casual clothing and tailored suits with great attention to cut and detail.

Typical Skills Required

===

✖ *Possessing a good understanding of the customer base and competitor market*
✖ *Ability to work within a clearly specified design brief*
✖ *Strong design skills supported by good technical knowledge and understanding of manufacturing techniques*
✖ *Good communication skills*
✖ *Ability to work in a team, as well as independently*
✖ *Proficient with CAD software, such as Adobe Photoshop*
✖ *Ability to spot a trend*
✖ *Capacity to work to tight deadlines to produce new collections*

===

Bespoke Tailor

Tailoring is a significant and valued career option. Bespoke tailoring involves making clothes to the specific requirements of the client from the type of suit, jacket or coat, to the cut and fit and the choice of fabric, style, finish and detailing. A personal pattern is made to fit the precise body measurements of the client, and traditional sewing techniques are applied. In this respect, tailoring is a craft: the suit is completely handmade, including all the finishings.

Usually tailors are trained through apprenticeship schemes, followed by on-the-job training working alongside a master tailor. Many successful tailors have trained in fashion design, then completed work placements in tailoring and afterwards continued their training by working through an apprenticeship scheme and mastering the skills required to work full-time in the tailoring trade.

Typical Skills Required

✖ *Knowledge of design, fabrics and tailoring techniques*
✖ *Accuracy and the ability to draft and cut a pattern to precise measurements*
✖ *Excellent skills in traditional hand sewing and construction methods*
✖ *Keeping up to date with emerging fashion trends*
✖ *Strong creative skills*

Corporate wear clothing by
Simon Jersey Ltd., UK

Corporate Wear Designer

Corporate wear design is one of the least popular choices of design areas due to lack of understanding of what this area of design involves. Corporate wear is a specialized area of the clothing industry which concerns the development of garment ranges covering a wide variety of professions including medical, healthcare, airline, catering and security, as well as safety wear, receptionist uniforms, business suits, retail service outfits, office wear and general workwear.

Corporate wear companies usually carry and supply a general stock range, which can be modified and adapted as required through in-house personalization. This includes the addition of embroidered and printed logo designs and motifs or screen-printing with colourful artwork to meet the individual requirements of the client.

When designing corporate wear the garment range must reflect the corporate identity of the company, making the right impression and adhering to the company's brand. Garment designs must be comfortable, functional and practical, as they are usually worn every day. They must be designed to be suitable for a wide range of ages and figure-types, using easy-care fabrics and adhering to the health and safety standards and regulations for clothing at work.

Many corporate wear designers are employed from clothing and technology backgrounds and have a good understanding of the technical parameters within this market sector.

Typical Skills Required

==

✖ *Ability to work to a specific brief*
✖ *Excellent understanding of customer profile*
✖ *Knowledge of design, fabrics and manufacturing techniques*
✖ *Understanding and awareness of commercial viability*
✖ *Ability to work to deadlines is essential, along with the ability to work under pressure to produce new ranges*

==

Childrenswear Designer

Childrenswear is an extremely competitive market with many labels having strong fashion influences. There are many smaller independent retailers specializing in childrenswear. However, many of the larger retailers have now expanded into this area, producing ranges of active wear, casual wear, sportswear, party wear, school uniforms and also specialist branded clothing.

Branded clothing is a very specialized area of the market, with garments featuring well-known characters linked to merchandise and licensing trademarks. This involves the design team developing an established brand through the use of imagery: examples include Winnie the Pooh, Disney Princess, Spider-Man and Power Rangers.

The role of the childrenswear designer involves research into its customers, competitors and market level as well as knowledge of fashion trends. Mood boards are produced incorporating imagery and colourways, communicating design ideas from the research obtained to produce childrenswear ranges that are appealing, practical and competitively priced.

Left: Bright clothing and lively prints from the spring/summer 2009 collection of Spanish childrenswear design label Tuc Tuc

Right: Bright stripes and denim co-ordinates from the autumn/winter 2008 range by Tuc Tuc

Childrenswear designers need to recognize the restrictions of the market, understanding and following the codes of practice for the design and manufacture of childrenswear (available from any childrenswear design association). Safety considerations include securing buttons, fastenings, bows and trims, careful use of drawstring cords and sensible choice of garment packaging.

Employment opportunities include assistant childrenswear designer, designer and senior designer, freelance design positions, licensed childrenswear designer and graphic designer/artworker and forecasting for the childrenswear sector.

Typical Skills Required

✖ *Good knowledge of the childrenswear market and its competitors*
✖ *Proficient CAD skills in software such as Adobe Photoshop*
✖ *Knowledge of, and ability to interpret, fashion trends*
✖ *Ability to produce sketches and present design ideas*
✖ *Ability to liaise with customers to plan and develop designs*
✖ *Excellent range-planning skills*

Adidas Woman's performance wear autumn/winter 2008–2009

Sportswear Designer

In recent years the industry has seen a huge growth in the sportswear market, ranging from active performance sportswear through to leisure sportswear and outdoor clothing. This is a hugely competitive market that has experienced great demand for very stylish, highly branded clothing that is practical, yet also has design appeal.

Active wear and performance sportswear needs to be highly functional, protective and designed for safety. It makes use of durable fabrics that are comfortable and designed for specialist, niche sports. These fields include: diving, surfing, sailing, snowboarding, skiing, motorbike riding and competitive swimming.

Leisure sportswear activities include: football, rugby, cricket, golf, running, cycling, swimming, tennis, yoga, dance, aerobics, gymnastics and fitness. These designs need to be non-restrictive, allowing for freedom of movement, yet offering support, protection and comfort.

The outdoor clothing market caters for outdoor leisure pursuits. Garments include: fleece jackets, gilets, waterproof and insulated jackets and over-trousers, and insulated vests, designed for pursuits such as walking and trekking, climbing, camping, backpacking, mountaineering, travelling and fishing.

Overleaf: Co-ordinating bikini collection from the swimwear design range by O'Neill

Companies range from small, specialist family-run firms to large-scale enterprises catering for all aspects of sportswear. Designers choosing to work in the sportswear field require excellent technical awareness and understanding of the practical requirements of the garments.

Typical Skills Required

===

✖ *Good understanding of the latest technological developments in sportswear and the specialist target market*
✖ *Knowledge of the suitability and practicality of fabrics and advanced materials for specialist areas*
✖ *Understanding, awareness and appreciation of trends*
✖ *Understanding of relevant digital technology and software*
✖ *Problem-solving skills in both the creative and technical approaches to design*
✖ *Good understanding of technical processes and construction methods: flat-locking, blind-stitching, gluing and binding, laser-cutting, rapid prototyping*

===

Feminine printed lingerie design from Intimissimi's catwalk collection

Lingerie Designer

Another area of the industry that has seen rapid growth in recent years is the lingerie market, with many trade shows established exclusively for this market: The International Lingerie Show, USA; Mode Lingerie Show, Hong Kong; and Harrogate Lingerie and Swimwear Exhibition, UK.

The term 'lingerie' includes bras, knickers, shape-wear, vests, corsetry, under-slips, nightwear and loungewear, produced in a wide range of fabrics from silk to cotton and innovative stretch blends. Designs range from sporty to classic, romantic, bridal, exotic and maternity and nursing bras. Many designer ranges have been developed, including: Victoria's Secret, Agent Provocateur, Ultimo, La Perla, Guia and La Bruna. There have been many celebrity ranges introduced to the market including the Elle Macpherson Intimates range, designs by Caprice and Love Kylie Princess by Kylie Minogue.

The role of the lingerie designer involves researching new silhouettes and keeping abreast of changing trends to design garment ranges considering design appeal, comfort, fit, quality and function. During the design process the designer works closely with the technical team, which may comprise a garment technician, design co-ordinator and sample machinist to produce the first sample garments within the price target.

Areas of employment within the lingerie sector include lingerie/nightwear designer for the high street or luxury lingerie market, independent lingerie designer, lingerie buyer and lingerie retailer.

Typical Skills Required

==

* ✖ *Good understand of current market trends in specialist and target market*
* ✖ *Knowledge of design, pattern cutting and manufacturing for both structured and non-structured lingerie*
* ✖ *Understanding of the brand*
* ✖ *Strong sourcing skills with excellent knowledge of fabrics and trims*
* ✖ *Good commercial understanding of designing within a price target*

==

Bridalwear Designer

Today the bridalwear market caters for every style of wedding dress conceivable, from the contemporary to the alternative, including theatrical and themed designs through to the traditional 'big white dress', or from bespoke wedding dresses to commercial ranges that are mass produced. Most bridalwear companies also produce special-occasion wear, outfits for the mother of the bride and bridesmaids' dresses.

Ian Stuart: Bridalwear Designer

Ian Stuart trained in the UK and specialized in bridal and eveningwear design, winning several student awards. He started his training working for Belville Sassoon, one of London's finest couture houses, extending his knowledge and developing greater understanding of cut, proportion, balance and wearability. Ian continued his career working for various labels designing bridal and eveningwear collections in London and then in New York, which were sold throughout the world.

With ten years of couture knowledge and industrial experience Ian then launched his own label – Ian Stuart Bridal Gowns. His designs concentrate on creating individual collections of exquisite gowns, providing brides-to-be with individual romantic designs inspired by theatre, music and costume, which are contemporary in design with an emphasis on beautiful, intricate detailing.

Ian has won numerous prestigious design awards. In 2002 he was awarded Design Excellence in the Bridal Industry – Style Innovator (USA) – and in 2004, 2005, 2006 and 2007 he was awarded the Bridal Buyer Awards Best Bridal Designer and Designer of the Year (UK) and the Bridal Buyer Awards Outstanding Contribution to the Industry in 2008 (UK).

An Interview with Ian Stuart

When did you first become interested in bridal and eveningwear design?
I studied a general art and design course and then studied a Higher National Diploma course in design. I had never considered a career in fashion, but I loved drawing and illustration. I also became interested in theatrical costume, but was more interested in the glitzy side of the design than the historical aspects. In my fourth year of study I produced a bridalwear collection and then worked for many designers in the UK and USA including Belville Sasoon, London.

When and why did you start your own business?
I wanted to move away from the constraints imposed on me by working for other designers, cutting corners to please others. I wanted to try new things,

designing something different and innovative, and for the first time in my life I am really designing what I want to. We now sell to twenty-seven different countries including Japan, Russia and France.

How would you define your work?
I would define my work as diverse, quite humorous, diva-ish; designs with an edge to them.

What or who has been the greatest influence on your work?
I am a Cecil Beaton fan and I also love the work of Christian Dior, Norman Hartnell and Balenciaga.

What is the secret of your success?
Showing internationally has promoted and raised the profile of British bridalwear abroad. Everything I disliked that my past employers implemented I did the opposite; this is part of my success. Be free with your designs, have your own look, why try to be something you're not? The designers that are the strongest are people that have their own signature and have their own look.

Remember to do what you're good at and go with your gut feeling!

What is the most difficult part of designing a new collection?
Getting started: once started I am then on a roll and I work better under pressure. Much of designing a collection involves administration; working with suppliers and manufacturers.

What has been your greatest career challenge to date?
Starting the business: the fear, emotion and excitement and so many things to do. When you have your own business every day there are new challenges. Launching our new social occasion collection was like starting all over again and wondering whether people would accept it.

What makes a successful bridal and eveningwear designer?
Being prolific in your ideas and coming up constantly with new collections. There is a definite formula that sells a dress, but it's about putting your signature on it and coming up with a new look, introducing new fabrics and constantly developing your ideas.

What advice can you give to a graduate who wants to design and establish his or her own label?
Send your CV out with pictures of your work, your final collection, to anyone you are interested in working for. Badger them until you are offered an internship or get a foot in the door. Be prepared to start at the bottom and work up and be passionate about everything you do.

What next for the Ian Stuart label?
I would love to have a perfume, a shop selling our eveningwear and also to develop an accessories range.

Positions in the bridalwear industry vary from working for a small, independent company, producing one-off individual designs, to working in a large company that produces vast quantities of bridalwear for a commercial market. The effective running of an independent studio involves the design and production of individual, bespoke gowns. The designer works closely with each individual client, meeting for an initial design consultation to the final fitting and collection of the gown. This work involves sourcing of fabric ranges, through to pattern cutting, manufacturing and hand-finishing trims.

A bridalwear designer should have a good knowledge and understanding of boning, corsetry, fine fabrics and an eye for detail. If you are interested in working in the bridalwear sector it is useful to gain as much knowledge as possible, through work experience, of fitting garments, completing alterations, manufacturing and hand-finishing garments.

Typical Skills Required

===

✘ *Knowledge of design, pattern cutting and manufacturing*
✘ *Excellent knowledge of fabrics and trims*
✘ *Strong sourcing skills*
✘ *Good communication skills to be able to work in a team or with the customer*

===

Textile Designer

The term 'textile design' includes the creation of woven, knit and print fabrics. Textiles are designed and produced for clothing, accessories and branded merchandise, and are also used for interiors in the design of fabrics for soft furnishings – curtains, bed linens, throws, cushions and hangings – or alternatively designs for wallpapers, upholstery fabrics, carpets, rugs and lifestyle products.

To work in the textile industry designing fabrics you must have a good understanding of the processes in fabric development from the design of the fabric through to construction and production processes.

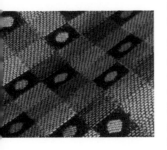

Susan Ritchie, co-founder of TANA BANA Design Services, USA, discussing fabric swatches and colourways with Srinivasan Jayapal

Fabric samples by TANA BANA Design Services, a full-service textile design studio, which offers design and production solutions to manufacturers and distributors worldwide

Woven Textile Designer

Woven textiles are designed and produced for garments or interior and home textiles – curtains, bed linens, cushions, throws, carpets and textile flooring covers – and also industrial uses, including packaging, public services or military clothing and textiles for the medical profession (garments and pressure dressings).

Planning and developing woven fabrics involves designing and working with colour, balance, shape, form, texture, construction and fabric finish to create fabric ranges. A career as a woven textile designer involves working closely with mills, yarn suppliers, customers and retailers. To work in the textile industry designing fabrics you must have a good understanding of the processes of fabric development, from the design of the fabric through to the construction and production processes.

Areas of employment include working as a designer for fabric manufacturers, fashion forecasting houses, garment manufacturers and interior companies. Other jobs in this sector include: textile buyer, studio artist or consultancy work.

Typical Skills Required

==

✖ *Excellent technical understanding of construction techniques with the ability to develop new and interesting fabric structures*
✖ *Good understanding of colour and texture*
✖ *Awareness, understanding and appreciation of trends*
✖ *Ability to liaise with customers to plan and develop designs*
✖ *Understanding and proficient use of CAD*

==

Sophie Steller:
Textile Design Consultant – Knit

Sophie Steller established her Textile Design Consultancy in 1996 working with a team of in-house designers offering a range of services from creating knit swatches for the women's, men's, children's and accessories markets to consultancy projects, technical knit expertise, a colourway service and trend guidance to an international clientele based in the UK, Europe and the USA.

An Interview with Sophie Steller

How did you get into this line of work?
Having graduated with a degree specializing in knitwear I knew I wanted to work in the commercial end of fashion and applied for many jobs. I was fortunate enough to get my first job as a knitwear design assistant for the Burton Group central design team a couple of months after graduating.

Before establishing your own consultancy what industrial experience did you have?
I worked in many different areas related to knitwear design, working for trend and design development for the many brands under the Burton Group umbrella, followed by more specific product development knitwear design jobs for the Alexon Group. I then moved to New York and worked at designer level for Joseph Abboud developing product, and then finally working as a men's knitwear designer for American Eagle. I took this job through into my consultancy and remained a freelance consultant for American Eagle for over 10 years.

When and why did you start your own textile design consultancy – The Sophie Steller Studio?
After working in the industry for about eight years and having spent four of those years in the US, I wanted to live back in London and decided to use my return to London as an opportunity to continue to work freelance for a few US brands and evolve this into a consultancy business.

What is the concept behind your consultancy?
To offer a full range of knitwear-related services to the fashion industry and to offer the ability to cover any specialist area of knitwear product development from yarn and colour through to fabric and silhouette concepts and technical recommendations.

What type of services does the consultancy offer?
The business divides itself into three aspects. We have the swatch studio, which produces unique, one-off knitted concepts that are sold at trade shows and direct to wholesale and retail. We also charge the studio out as a sample service for clients to use the studio to create their own unique ideas, or develop ideas through colourways or additional stitch and pattern ideas. Finally, I work as a knitwear design consultant, offering a variety of services, which include colour prediction, yarn and fabric development, sketching and line creation. I also offer technical services and market knowledge.

Who are your clients?

We have a broad international client base, from yarn spinners and knitwear manufacturers in Asia to wholesalers and retailers in the UK, Europe and the US. We consult for and sell to all levels of the market, from high-end designer to mass market, in menswear, womenswear and childrenswear, plus accessories.

What type of machines do you use for sampling?

As a studio we try to offer a mini version of what can be achieved at factory level, particularly with China production in mind. We knit on hand flats on 12-, 7-, 5- and 3-gauge, plus on domestics in 9-, 7- and 3-gauge, offering all aspects of stitch and pattern creation. We wash all our fabrics to create the best possible handles, but in terms of linking samples together we only need to create 'mock up' concepts.

What inspires and influences your designs?

We are continually looking for inspiration. We are known as a commercial studio so what is happening on the catwalks and at retail are important. Cultural influences such as film and music are also important.

What advice would you give to someone who wants to be a textile designer specializing in knit?

Make sure you are passionate about it and you are realistic about what being a knitwear designer really means. It is a specialist field and if you are good at it you'll be in demand because the UK offers the best training for knitwear design in the world. However, it is not the highest paid of design jobs, is very technical and demands a high level of perfection: to succeed, a passion for yarn, colour and hands-on knitting is essential in order to get a good job and also gain satisfaction from what you do. Being a knitwear designer is as much about personal satisfaction in creating good fabrics and ideas as it is about any financial gain.

I would also recommend that any knitwear designer who would like to start their own business gain as much industrial experience as possible before becoming self-employed, leaving it at least four to five years before they work for themselves.

Knitwear Designer

Above: *Recycled wool jacket by Davina Hawthorne*

Right: *Stunning green cable-knit dress by Antonio Berardi – autumn/winter 2009*

The role of the knitwear designer in industry varies depending on the size of the company, the type of garments produced and the manufacturing techniques applied to the garment ranges. A knitwear designer's job usually involves producing sketches and design ranges for presentation to customers, making up sample designs, maintaining up-to-date knowledge of new and developing design concepts and working closely with customers, clients, suppliers and factory staff to ensure that projects are completed on time. It is important to have a good technical understanding of flatbed knitting and industrial knitting production, knowledge of pattern cutting and grading patterns, garment construction and manufacture techniques, and to be able to assist in sorting out production problems relating to design, garment construction and manufacture.

Knitwear designers work in womens-, mens- and childrenswear. Other opportunities are also available in the specialist areas of accessory design and interior and product design, producing knitted fabrics for blinds, throws, cushions and soft furnishings or designing knitted fabrics for industrial interiors. Important considerations for designing knitwear include: season, customer needs, the technical capabilities of the knitting machinery available, yarn types (natural, man-made or combination), colour palette, texture and weight of yarns, stitch structure and the durability of the fabric produced, trend information, method of manufacture and cost.

==

✖ *Excellent technical understanding of knit construction with the ability to develop new and interesting fabric structures*
✖ *Knowledge of yarns, yarn development and stitch structures*
✖ *Good understanding of colour and texture*
✖ *Awareness, understanding and appreciation of trends*
✖ *Ability to liaise with customers to plan and develop designs*
✖ *Understanding of market level*

==

Print Textile Designer

To be successful as a print designer you must have a good insight into and understanding of the design process and the importance of surface pattern design from repeat to half drops, placement prints and border designs. An excellent understanding of colour is required to enable you to produce alternative colourways, re-colourings and co-ordinates that work well as a design range, supported by a good understanding of graphics.

Areas of employment for textile designers include: working for fabric manufacturers, fabric printers, and fashion forecasting houses, garment manufacturers and interiors companies. The work will vary from position to position but may involve producing sketches, sample designs and ranges, which may be created using specialist CAD software or worked manually. A textile designer working in industry liaises closely with technical print staff working to a project brief, meeting the clients' and buyers' requirements.

Many textile designers who establish their own businesses or work as freelance practitioners producing textiles gain contracts through commercial agencies (see Resources). Their work often involves producing small to medium production runs in many areas of design from fabric printing for the textile and clothing markets to producing fine-art textile pieces or alternatively paper-based products – greetings cards, wrapping paper and packaging.

Typical Skills Required

==

✖ *Good understanding of the principles of design*
✖ *Excellent eye for colour and texture with the ability to re-colour prints*
✖ *Understanding of processes and production techniques*
✖ *Ability to design by hand or digitally*
✖ *CAD-literate*
✖ *Good understanding of printing techniques and new applications*

==

Zandra Rhodes: Fashion/Textile Designer

Zandra Rhodes has achieved a fantastic international reputation for her innovative design work in the fields of fashion and textiles. A graduate of the Royal College of Art, UK in 1963, she is renowned for her unique approach to her work exploring pattern and colour. Her designs are print-led due to her first love being textile design, with the garment following the organic flow and the movement of the print design. She is a prolific designer who has produced designs for individual clients, including Diana, the Princess of Wales, and other royals, along with many celebrities. Her work has included regular fashion collections and costume designs for the opera *The Magic Flute,* and she designed many costumes for Freddie Mercury of the rock group Queen.

Zandra's work has been internationally exhibited and has been purchased by many museums for their collections – the Victoria and Albert Museum, London, UK; Musée de la Mode et du Textile, Paris, France; the Royal Ontario Museum, Toronto, Canada; the Phoenix Art Museum, Phoenix, Arizona, USA. Throughout her career she has received many awards, including the Hall of Fame Award by the British Fashion Council for her outstanding contribution to the British Fashion Industry.

Far left: *Zandra Rhodes Garment Collection – 'Mexican Sombrero' print on orange silk chiffon*

Left: *Zandra Rhodes Garment Collection – 'Indian Feather Border' print*

Right: *Zandra Rhodes and Francis Ben reviewing a newly painted fabric in a design/print studio*

An Interview with Zandra Rhodes

How would you define your work?

I consider my work to be colourful, directional, original, recognizable, fantasy and heavily patterned.

Who or what has been your greatest influence on your work?

My mother has been one of the biggest influences; she taught me to believe in myself. Travel has also been a huge inspiration to my work; getting away from my daily surroundings, working in my sketchbook constantly, finding time to play around with ideas, freeing my mind and going from there. Going back to nature has always inspired my work.

When and why did you start your own business?

I never got offered a job where someone wanted to employ me; no one saw me in that position. So I worked for myself and created my first solo dress collection in 1969, which was worn by Paloma Picasso and Natalie Wood.

What is the most difficult part of designing a collection?

Coming up with the most original idea, an idea to hang the collection on; making decisions about a theme.

What has been your most enjoyable commission to date?

The last one that you really get your teeth into. Designing for Mozart's *The Magic Flute* and Bizet's *The Pearl Fishers* were great vehicles for my textiles.

What is your greatest career challenge to date?

Continuing to be inspired and adding to one's work, even when the world isn't going with you. Only history is going to tell the value of your work, when it is fully recorded and then it's discovered.

What makes a successful textile/fashion designer?

The concept of a print, how they should look made up into a dress. Celia Birtwell has done that, Duffy – Matisse – have created wonderful, wearable fabrics. I adore the work of Lucien Day in his furnishings.

What advice can you give to an artist or designer that wants to launch his or her own business?

Always stay true to yourself. Don't give up. Surround yourself with encouraging friends. When the hard knocks come your friends will encourage you to keep going. It takes about ten years to be an overnight success.

Kim Parker: Textile Designer/Artist

American textile designer and artist Kim Parker is internationally recognized for her bold floral and organic prints, brilliantly rich in colour and design. Kim is a self-trained textile designer and artist who established herself by launching her own label selling her designs to a range of clients, including Anna Sui, Diane von Furstenburg and Spode, which is the exclusive manufacturer of Kim's tableware ranges.

Kim has received many design awards. Her work includes designs for fabrics, dinnerware, giftware ranges, bedding, fabrics, designer rugs, wall hangings, stationery, greeting cards and collections of artwork, which have been sold throughout the world.

An Interview with Kim Parker

What type of formal training did you have?
I never actually had any formal training in design. I trained as a classical flautist and graduated with a degree in Flute Performance. Since childhood I was passionate about drawing and creating dense patterns in vivid colours. In my music career I was always painting in between performances.

Who or what are your biggest inspirations artistically?
I grew up with art books, and was always attracted to the painters who combined rich colour and pattern such as Vuillard, Bonnard and Matisse. I also love the German Expressionist painter Emil Nolde.

Music is equally important and inspirational. Having performed many of the great classical orchestral works, I have always been extremely fond of Maurice Ravel. I also listen to Mozart when I work.

How would you describe your work?
I would describe my work as organic. It is not pre-planned. I don't think in repeat when I paint, I just leap into the process and am guided by mood, colour and inner rhythm. My work has also been called 'exuberant' and 'lyrical'. Colour has been a healing force in my life ever since I was a child. Working with an exuberant palette heals and lifts my spirit.

What is your greatest career challenge to date?

Without question, my recent book on art and design, *Kim Parker Home: A Life in Design*. It took me years to assemble and write this book, and even once it had been handed over to my publisher, so much more work was required. The assembling and refining of the book's visuals and text spanned more than two years, and was an exhaustive, passionate undertaking, but an extremely valuable and enlightening process.

What has been your most enjoyable commission to date?

Designing my 'Emma's Garland' dinnerware and giftware collection for Spode was a joyful experience. Painting within the confines of each template whether dinner plate, cup, vase or teapot was precious. I liked having a finite shape to create gardens inside of. I handpainted an individual pattern for each shape, not repeating the same design from form to form. The process was truly joyful, creating a mix of designs that would allow the consumer to create their own table setting from a rich assortment of pattern.

What is the key to your success?

I think success is about connecting to what you love doing, taking risks, being patient with each step of development. I have always been passionate about working with colour and pattern. By no means was it overnight success for me. I don't believe there is any one 'formula' for success. But I do believe that each person has his or her own path and gift, and should navigate with love, passion, hard work, patience, determination and integrity.

What advice would you give to an aspiring textile designer?

My advice would be to connect to your gift and steer clear of others who want to mould or change your vision. If you are passionate about what you are doing, then you're doing the right thing. Believe in it. It's important to stay open and explore all possibilities that come to you. Each one of us has been given a special gift that is uniquely our own: find that connection and nurture it passionately.

Costume Designer

The role of the costume designer, or costumier, varies greatly depending on the size and the type of company they are working for, which can range from designing for the theatre, film, stage, opera and ballet through to working on commercials for television or producing costumes for contemporary and historical period dramas.

The skills required for all productions include excellent research ability, with an aptitude for analyzing and being able to visualize a concept, and translating an idea from two-dimensions into a three-dimensional design. The work involves a good understanding of flat pattern cutting and modelling on the stand, with the ability to combine the two methods where necessary. A fantastic book of industrial contacts is required to be able to source appropriate fabrics, trims and construction materials to create the look required.

On larger-scale productions the costume designer works closely with directors, producers and choreographers of the film, play or drama, and also heads up a production team. This will comprise design assistants, a wardrobe supervisor, wardrobe assistants, seamstresses and wig makers. To achieve success in a production, excellent research skills, knowledge and understanding about the characters, the actors' movement and an understanding of the stage and set dynamics are required.

Occasionally costume designers are employed full-time as residential costumiers by a company. However, whether for television, film or theatre, it is more usual for a costumier to be employed on a freelance basis working to commission, contracted through an agent. Usually the role of the costume designer requires flexibility in the hours worked, depending on the type of production, times of rehearsals and fittings.

Many costume designers study specific courses in theatre and costume design or fashion design. Alternatively some designers train through a production company, working their way up from wardrobe assistant or costume assistant to costume designer. There are many opportunities to gain experience working with local theatre groups, helping with small-scale productions, working alongside the wardrobe mistress and developing costume designs for local amateur productions.

Typical Skills Required

==

- ✖ *Good knowledge and understanding of fashion history*
- ✖ *Strong research skills with the ability to interpret ideas*
- ✖ *Ability to sketch ideas*
- ✖ *A good eye for detail and accuracy to produce authentic looking garments*
- ✖ *Pattern making and garment fitting skills*
- ✖ *Ability to improvise and be innovative*

==

Wardrobe Assistant

The job of a wardrobe assistant involves working alongside the costume designer and the production team, maintaining a working wardrobe for theatrical, TV or film production companies. The work entails monitoring stock; adapting, repairing, altering and fitting costumes; maintaining accessories and packing costumes. Many local amateur dramatics societies keep a costume wardrobe and are always in need of assistance, particularly around festival periods. Completing a work placement with a local group will provide insight into the management and workings of a costume wardrobe. Positions of employment are available in local and national theatres, television and film productions.

Typical Skills Required

===

✖ *Excellent sewing and alteration skills*
✖ *Ability to adapt and fit a garment*
✖ *Creative skills supported by practical knowledge to adapt and develop a new design*
✖ *Good management and organizational skills*
✖ *Ability to organize and store garments and accessories appropriately*

===

Enzo Pirozzi: Costume Designer

Enzo Pirozzi studied at the Fashion Academy in Rome, specializing in fashion and costume design. He has worked for many years as an independent designer in film, theatre and television. Throughout his career Enzo has also worked in fashion showing his own collections at AREA (an independent fashion fair in France), Paris prêt-à-porter and Alta Moda Roma and he has also established an independent fashion studio, Arte & Mise, in Naples where he sells his collections and organizes arts events.

An Interview with Enzo Pirozzi

What made you go into costume design?
I was born in a trunk – my dad runs a high-fashion tailor's in Naples. I was brought up among fabrics and clothes. I have always been in love with everything connected with making clothes. My other main passion is the theatre, so it was natural for me to go into costume design.

How important is it to have formal training?
I think having formal training is essential. I studied at the Costume and Fashion Academy in Rome, which gave me the chance to study the history of art and theatre. The most exciting experience that the Academy offered me was the possibility of creating and putting into practice what I was studying.

What is the most difficult part of designing a costume?
Successfully representing the ideas of the director and embodying the peculiar aspects of a character in a costume, but without being predictable and always in keeping with my style.

What is the most important aspect of designing and producing costumes?
The most important aspect is making actors feel comfortable in their costumes. The costume should help and complete the characters but never overwhelm

Left: *Enzo Pirozzi designing costumes for a production*

Right: *Atmospheric stage set and costume designed by Enzo Pirozzi*

them. It is very important to create a good, respectful relationship with the actors. Actors have to communicate through the costume, and it is my job to enable them to do this.

Can you describe your design process in a few sentences?

First of all I read the play and then have meetings with the director and the set designer. Only when I get the point of view of the director and understand the complexities of the characters can I start working on the costumes. The creative process includes drawing many sketches, flicking through art books, listening to music, watching films, and having a stroll on the beach. And then finally, when I have my project, I show it to the director. On the first day of rehearsal the costume is very roughly constructed. My presence at the rehearsal is vital for me; I need to get to know the actors and their acting style.

What is the most challenging part of your job?

Getting to a point where there is a perfect balance between the costumes, the direction and the set design. This can be very hard when you are as meticulous as I am with every detail and yet there are 14 characters on stage!

What is your dream project?

Actually I have two dream projects! As a fashion designer I dream of showing my collection at the Paris Fashion Week and as a costume designer, it is to produce the costumes for an opera at the Paris National Opera.

What advice would you give to someone seeking employment as a costume designer?

First of all, study – it is not a job that you can improvise. It is also vital to be flexible. You should be a creative person, a good artisan, cultured and with good taste. You should be ready to make some sacrifices because it is a hard career and you need lots of patience. Try starting as an assistant to an established costume designer: experience from working on the job is the best way to learn.

Right and opposite: *The accessories market is a huge growth area within the fashion industry, and includes footwear, millinery, gloves, belts, bags, glasses and jewellery*

Accessory Designer

Accessory design is an area of the industry that has seen recent growth. Every season, accessories are heavily promoted in fashion supplements and magazines, and on the international catwalks. Designer collections are accessorized through the use of bags, leather goods, scarves, belts, gloves, ties, scarves, hair decorations, watches, sunglasses and costume jewellery.

Good accessories can make an outfit; they can update existing outfits or change them completely and can be worn to dress up an outfit and make a big fashion statement. Accessory designers are employed by fashion and retail companies and the film industry or, alternatively, they may work freelance producing their own ranges for independent clients. Many small, independent labels have sprung up and their designs are sold online or merchandised to independent retailers and the larger department stores.

If you are interested in a career as an accessory designer it is useful to complete a fashion course or a specialist fashion accessory programme introducing you to the various types of materials, the design and technological processes and the construction methods required, supported by business and consumer studies.

Typical Skills Required

===

- ✖ *An eye for forthcoming trends*
- ✖ *Ability to sketch by hand or CAD*
- ✖ *Aptitude for developing patterns and sample ranges*
- ✖ *Good technical understanding of materials and equipment in specialist areas of manufacture*
- ✖ *Ability to oversee production*

===

Footwear Designer

Above: Footwear design range by Gemma Anne Valance, De Montfort University, UK

Below: Black top-stitched boot design by Kevin Guildford, De Montfort University, UK

Footwear design has grown in popularity due to the success and fame of designers such as Manolo Blahnik, Jimmy Choo, Patrick Cox, Giuseppe Zanotti and Miuccia Prada. Footwear designers can work in many areas of the industry from haute couture to designer, high street fashion, technical athletic, fashion sports, outdoor, hiking and workwear, beach footwear and orthopedic markets.

The footwear designer usually works within a design team on the development of all aspects of a footwear range from the design through to production and the merchandising of the product. Depending on the size of the company, the design team may consist of a footwear designer, assistant footwear designer, footwear technician, production manager and marketing manager. When developing a range, the design team will work closely with last, heel and sole factories, and will also source materials from a range of suppliers including tanneries and textile firms for trims and finishes. As a footwear designer it is important to have awareness of the key looks for the season, the forthcoming trends and what is happening globally in fashion, as well as knowledge of competitors.

To be successful in this specialist field of design it is important to be able to design directional footwear ranges to suit specific target markets, producing illustrations and technical drawings for new design concepts. You must have a good working knowledge of materials, pattern cutting and footwear construction techniques. Most designers train through studying a degree specializing in footwear and start work in the industry as a junior design assistant, progressing to a position as designer.

Typical Skills Required

==

- ✖ *Ability to analyze trends in fabrics, colours, textures and shapes*
- ✖ *Ability to sketch by hand or using CAD*
- ✖ *Aptitude for developing patterns and sample ranges*
- ✖ *Good technical understanding of footwear techniques*
- ✖ *Ability to source suppliers and oversee production*

==

Hat Designer/Milliner

A recent revival in the wearing of hats as a fashion accessory has led to a growth in this industry. There is now a demand for hats of all shapes and sizes and a hat designer can find employment in producing mass-market designs for high street outlets, catalogues and sports retailers. Milliners, who usually work in the couture sector, produce short runs or one-off bespoke designs for individual clients and may find employment making hats for special-occasion wear, bridalwear, theatre productions, film and television, and costume dramas.

The technical process of hat construction involves pattern making, cutting fabrics, hat pressing or blocking, hand- and machine-stitching, lining and trimming. For the mass market, hats are usually pressed into shape using industrial machinery. Hats produced in small runs, for the couture and bespoke markets, are usually shaped by moulding the form on a wooden or aluminium block. Many independent designers use a method of free-form sculpting, moulding the hat by hand without a block. Hat designers and milliners usually work using a wide variety of materials.

Many milliners choose to work freelance under their own label producing bespoke millinery designs for clients' individual specifications. To be a successful freelancer you must have excellent design and production skills, knowledge and understanding of traditional and contemporary millinery techniques, an eye for fine detailing and excellent business acumen and communication skills (see Starting in Business, page 197).

Typical Skills Required

==

✖ *A good technical understanding of millinery techniques, including hand sewing skills*
✖ *A creative imagination and excellent artistic skills*
✖ *An understanding of proportion, balance, line, composition, colour and detail*
✖ *Ability to analyze and understand trends, including developments in silhouettes, fabric and trims*
✖ *The skill to develop patterns and sample ranges*
✖ *The capacity to oversee production*

==

Fashion Forecasting

Fashion forecasting is a very competitive business that involves researching and predicting international seasonal trends 18 to 24 months in advance of the marketplace. Trend information is used in the fashion, textiles, interiors, cosmetics and product design industries, and usually gives guidance on thematic stories, colour palettes, styling, detailing, fabric, print, yarns, trimmings and graphic design.

Céline Robert: Milliner

French milliner Céline Robert studied sculpture, art history and sociology at the Beaux Arts in Paris. Her grandmother, who was a milliner by trade, inspires her work. Céline works like a sculptor, moulding and manipulating fabrics to explore new silhouettes, from large designs to neat, head-hugging cloche-style shapes.

An Interview with Céline Robert

How did you become interested in millinery?
My grandparents were in the fashion trade, with a business located in Paris, and at the height of their activity they had up to 17 employees. Even after they retired their house remained a workshop, with my grandmother continuing to make draped turbans for a few privileged clients. So it was a trade of which I had always been aware; it formed part of my education. Other parts of that education included the clay worked by my ceramicist mother and the stained-glass windows made by my other grandmother.

What interests me about hats is the social statement of shape and form. I trained as a sculptor at the Paris Beaux Arts: a hat, because of its fanciful nature and its form can also be a sculptural work, but when it is worn it takes on a meaning, personal to its wearer, becoming a 'social form'.

How would you define your style?
My work consists of hot-moulding on the material. I like the process of searching for shapes and for specific volumes, especially where you only have a real perception of how the hat will work when it is worn since the overall effect has to include the face and the shape and form of the body.

Can you describe your design process in a few sentences?
I work freehand, directly hot-moulding on natural materials. For other materials I use the 'cut and sew' method. Each collection is a story, which begins at the end of the previous one – often with a piece that creates a link taking the process forward to a new form or expression. The principles of creation come either from a visual image, or from handling the materials, especially if it is the first time I have used them and I can learn how they will respond.

Where do you get your inspiration for your designs?

Creativity must be nourished constantly. It is important to view everything around you with a sharp eye, looking at nature, architecture and the fine arts; everything and anything that can lead to a triggering of associations of materials, types of construction, combinations of colours and so on.

What advice can you give to an artist or designer who wants to launch his or her own business?

The most important thing is to experiment, even if you make mistakes and ruin materials, but know that by doing so you can learn from those mistakes, discovering the creative potential of those materials; don't be afraid to experiment, even if it costs you money. It is also important to have your own identity to offer combined with, in the case of hats, a generous and positive view of your clients' own personalities.

What makes a successful milliner?

After careful and creative work, probably the press and PR.

What is your vision for your label?

Today it is a label that is recognized, and that is its strength. But it is also its weakness because models that are too marked also limit the numbers that can wear them.

As a small design and production unit of just seven people we can, however, be very reactive and flexible in our creative offers. This enables us to develop the label, but also to work on other lines sold under licence or through exclusive commercial partnerships. The aim is to upgrade each collection season by season and to include one-off pieces. It is a challenge to move each collection forward, but the need to do so also provides a business weakness for us, despite our twenty-year long experience.

The larger forecasting companies employ a range of people including: in-house designers, researchers of market trends, communication and marketing experts, cultural and lifestyle consumer researchers, colourists, fabric and yarn developers, graphic designers and illustrators. They work as a team to analyze emerging trends and present the information in various forms: prediction books, video links and on-line trend sites.

Trends are predicted through the careful analysis of catwalk, street fashion and retail trends, fashion directions of the previous season, demographics, consumer lifestyle analysis and social and economic changes. They provide the client with critical insight into the global market. Some companies work with sociologists and psychologists who assist in the analysis of consumer trends and lifestyles. This information is translated into carefully designed seasonal fashion trend books offering directional colour palettes, themes, images and fabric stories for the development of seasonal product categories. Many of the trend books contain samples of fabrics, yarns and trims with references to colour guides (such as PANTONE®, considered a colour authority), providing accurate cross-referencing for consistency of colour matching globally.

Many prediction companies produce series of individual trend books aimed specifically at various branches of the industry. The trend information is used by major high street designers, retailers, stylists and buyers. Alongside the publication of trend books, many forecasting companies offer regular online trend updates, which are available on a subscription basis.

Trend consultancy services offer statistical data, providing a wide range of market analysis, publications and reports, often in conjunction with online forecasting services and runway reports. Other services offered often include the live presentations of trend reports at trade fairs and conferences and also the publication of regular newsletters providing mid-season updates and business news. There are many international forecasting companies, a complete list of which can be found on page 247.

Directional trend information providing thematic, fashion and colour guidance from Peclers, Paris

Employment in the field of fashion forecasting is very competitive. However, there are opportunities in large design studios, textile companies and prediction companies as researchers, writers, designers and illustrators. It is worth approaching forecasting companies to present your portfolio as they are always searching for something new. Many of the positions are freelance.

Designers from graphics backgrounds are often required to produce the graphics for the trend packages, working to the company's brand. The best way to get a foot in the door is to complete an internship, which will give you a greater understanding of the variety of jobs on offer within this specialist area.

Typical Skills Required

===

- ✘ *Good knowledge of the international marketplace*
- ✘ *Understanding of trends: film, theatre, television; fabric, yarn and trims*
- ✘ *Ability to spot a trend in advance*
- ✘ *Excellent research skills*
- ✘ *Good written and verbal communication*
- ✘ *A good eye for colour and texture*
- ✘ *CAD skills*

===

Colourist

The position of 'colourist' varies from company to company, whether it is working in a forecasting company or a fabric or yarn manufacturer, printed textile company or colour laboratory. In a forecasting house a colourist would work closely within the forecasting team, advising on colour stories for trend predictions. They would produce inspirational concept boards, evoking moods, trends and ideas and offering colour palettes reflecting themes for the forthcoming seasons.

The Pantone® colour system is recognized worldwide and is used for identifying, communicating and accurately matching colour

Other employment positions for colourists include working with fabric and yarn manufacturers advising on fabric colours, measuring the colour of a garment, fabric or yarn and checking the quality of the colouration and fastness of the dye. This work is highly technical and it is useful to have a science or chemistry qualification due to the continuous advancements in the development of new fibres and fabrics.

All colourists should have a good understanding of the complex area of colour theory, a working knowledge of the PANTONE® colour system and a good understanding of the relationships between colours.

Typical Skills Required

===

- ✘ *Awareness of the impact of colour and the influences that inspire seasonal developments*
- ✘ *An excellent understanding of colour theory*
- ✘ *An understanding of the Pantone® colour system and other similar systems*
- ✘ *Ability to produce inspirational mood boards*
- ✘ *CAD-literate*
- ✘ *Ability to keep accurate records relating to colourways*
- ✘ *Good understanding of technological processes in dyeing*

===

Fiona Jenvey: Fashion Forecaster

Fiona Jenvey is Chief Executive and founder of Mudpie fashion forecasting agency, whose services include the publication of seasonal trend prediction packages, trend presentations at global trade events and working with manufacturers around the world, offering a consultancy service. Fiona originally set up Mudpie designing collections, and in recent years the company has grown into a highly established trend agency.

An Interview with Fiona Jenvey

What is the concept behind Mudpie?

We have three brands: Consultancy, Trendbooks and Mpdclick. Mudpie is focused on providing the industry with good-quality design in the best format for the user. Mudpie is able to provide consultancy clients, such as Marks and Spencer, New Look and Primark, with specific design solutions that perfectly suit their current design and trend needs. Such needs can range from colour development right through to seasonal concepts and final production-ready artwork. Our trend books are sold worldwide and provide designers with readymade ideas for complete garment ranges on a seasonal basis. We publish five books covering women's, men's and kids' fashions. These products are colour-, garment-, print- and graphic-driven which makes them a complete solution. Budgets are very tight in the clothing business today; Mudpie trend books save designers time, resulting, ultimately, in saving costs. Mpdclick is our newest concept and is the online trend solution for the designer or retailer that wants up-to-date information on a daily basis. We cover retail, popular shops in various major cities, street fashion, trade fairs and fashion shows.

What is the key to the success of Mudpie?

I would say that the heart of a successful trend service is the research. It is important to understand that the client is investing large sums in realizing collections based on our information. Additionally, our biggest factor in success has been the complete understanding of the needs of the designer and buyer. This knowledge is unique to us because Mudpie has worked successfully with the smallest importers, multiple retailers and major brands.

Where do you promote Mudpie trend books?

We promote our trend books via our international partners who sell them in over 50 countries. Our key markets are the USA and Europe, but we are currently seeing huge growth within the Asian and South American countries, and expect to see a further increase over the coming seasons. We sell our books at key industry events.

Who works within a typical forecasting team at Mudpie?

I head up a research team, which is made up of designers and trend analysts. We then have a team of fashion designers, graphic designers and fashion writers who create commercial interpretations of the trends for our trend books and online service.

Above: Sample trend from MPK, male forecasting trend book by Mudpie providing garment ranges, graphics and print ideas

Right: Fiona Jenvey, Chief Executive of Mudpie, publishes a range of fashion forecasting books

Are most positions within forecasting companies freelance or permanent?
We are unusual as most of our creative jobs are permanent, although we do have freelance opportunities. The quality of research is very important to us so we prefer to have an in-house team. Every season the trend 'develops'; if you have the same core team working on the project it allows the trends to flow.

What do you look for when employing or commissioning a designer?
The most important thing is that they fit in with the rest of our team. After that they need to be able to balance creativity with commerciality, and be able to use programs such as Adobe Illustrator and Corel Draw. Good drawing skills are useful, particularly for illustration, and good colour sense is also very important

Which international events do you attend?
Speaking is very much part of our business and is something that we get invited to do at most major shows as well as trend seminars. I conduct seminars in New York (Fashion Institute of Technology), Los Angeles, São Paulo, Bangkok, Montréal, Munich, Amsterdam, Paris and London. These promote our trend books and online service.

What is the key to your career success?
Expertise has to be the most important factor as our clients must be able to rely on our information season after season. To build a trend business you have to be able to build a good, committed and well trained creative team. Good contacts are important; Mudpie has contacts all over the world, which I have built up during my travels. Finally, hard work is a big factor. The travel sounds glamorous, but it can be very tiring; when I do a seminar I always speak without notes and do an open Q and A at the end, which can be hard. I have to be able to perform regardless of an overnight flight and a different time zone.

What is your greatest career challenge to date?
I would have to say having two young children, travelling and managing a business employing 30 people and with over 50 partners around the world.

What advice would you give to someone who is interested in a career in fashion forecasting?
Of course you need to have talent, but to really make it you have to consider your career to be a way of life rather than just a job.

Fashion Illustrator

Fashion illustration is used to illustrate garment designs for advertising and editorial in newspapers, fashion journals, fashion forecasting packages, designing packaging or in the context of a fashion house. Most fashion illustrators are employed on a freelance basis, gaining commissions through an agent and working to a brief, deadline or production date stipulated by the client.

As a fashion illustrator it is important to have the ability to work using a wide range of media and techniques: gouache, watercolour, acrylic, spray paints, pencil crayon, pen and ink, marker pens, pastel, airbrush, collage and photomontage techniques, as well as photography techniques, embroidery threads, CAD and mixed media. Many illustrators use a combination of techniques to achieve maximum impact in their work.

It is important to develop an individual style that is adaptable and versatile through practise and exploration, and to be able to illustrate garment ranges and individual designs portraying the mood of the clothing, giving a sense of

Below: *Design sketched by David Steinhorst, demonstrating his ability to communicate ideas for a range of detailed separates through the fluency of line and shape*

Opposite: *Fashion collection designed and illustrated by David Steinhorst*

the style of the look. The work should be visually exciting through the quality of line, the application of colour, the composition and the media applied.

Work is usually commissioned through an agent. Before approaching an agent you should prepare a professionally presented portfolio showcasing the full breadth of your work, enabling the agent to understand and appreciate your full abilities. (See page 155.)

Typical Skills Required

===

✖ *Ability to work in a broad range of media and styles*
✖ *CAD-literate*
✖ *Ability to reflect the style of the clothes*
✖ *A strong sense of colour, image and design*
✖ *Ability to collaborate with clients*

===

Anna Kiper: Fashion Illustrator

Anna Kiper is an Assistant Professor in the Fashion Design Department at the Fashion Institute of Technology, New York, and an Instructor at Parsons School of Design, New York, teaching portfolio development and advanced fashion drawing. Since graduating in 1987 with a Bachelor of Fine Arts, Fashion Design Major from Moscow College of Arts and Technology in Russia, Anna has worked for numerous design companies. These include Calvin Klein, CK Division, New York; Pat Tunsky, Inc (Fashion Forecast, Trend and Colour Service); Mondi, Munich, Germany; and Art Space, New York. She has worked as a designer, sketching and creating ranges for womenswear, eveningwear, bridalwear, sportswear and denim collections. She has worked as designer–illustrator, creating moods, themes and colour stories, developing concept boards for styles, fabrics and trims, designing and sketching apparel and accessory collections. She has also sourced antique fabrics for couture collections and created illustrations for publications such as *Quest* magazine, *WWD*, *Gotham* magazine and *Wedding Style*.

An Interview with Anna Kiper

How did you become a fashion illustrator?
When I moved to the US in the late 1980s, I began not only creating and illustrating my own designs, but taking on illustration projects from other designers. Until now, most of my work focus has been on design, not illustration.

Left to right: *Fashion illustrations by Anna Kiper*

How did you develop an interest in illustration?
I always loved fine arts and spent a lot of time painting and drawing. Since the age of 12 I knew I wanted to design and illustrate costumes.

How would you define your style?
My fashion figures are very modern and dynamic. I try to create unusual compositions; I play with negative and positive spaces on the page as well as line qualities.

What techniques do you apply to your work?
Actually, I use different styles and techniques. My favourite media are felt tip markers, pen, ink and bamboo sticks, watercolours and collage techniques.

Where, how and when do you find inspiration for your work?
My inspiration has many sources – architecture, interior design and craft. My favourite costume designers from the Art Deco period have Russian roots. I always admired dramatic compositions and colour palettes of Bakst, Benua and Vrubel.

What in your opinion makes a successful fashion illustrator?
An illustrator, like any creative person, should constantly reinvent themselves.

What advice would you give to someone who wants to become a fashion illustrator?
An aspiring fashion illustrator should start with fine art training. Keep an open mind and seek new inspiration sources in various forms of arts.

Chapter 2: Technical Opportunities

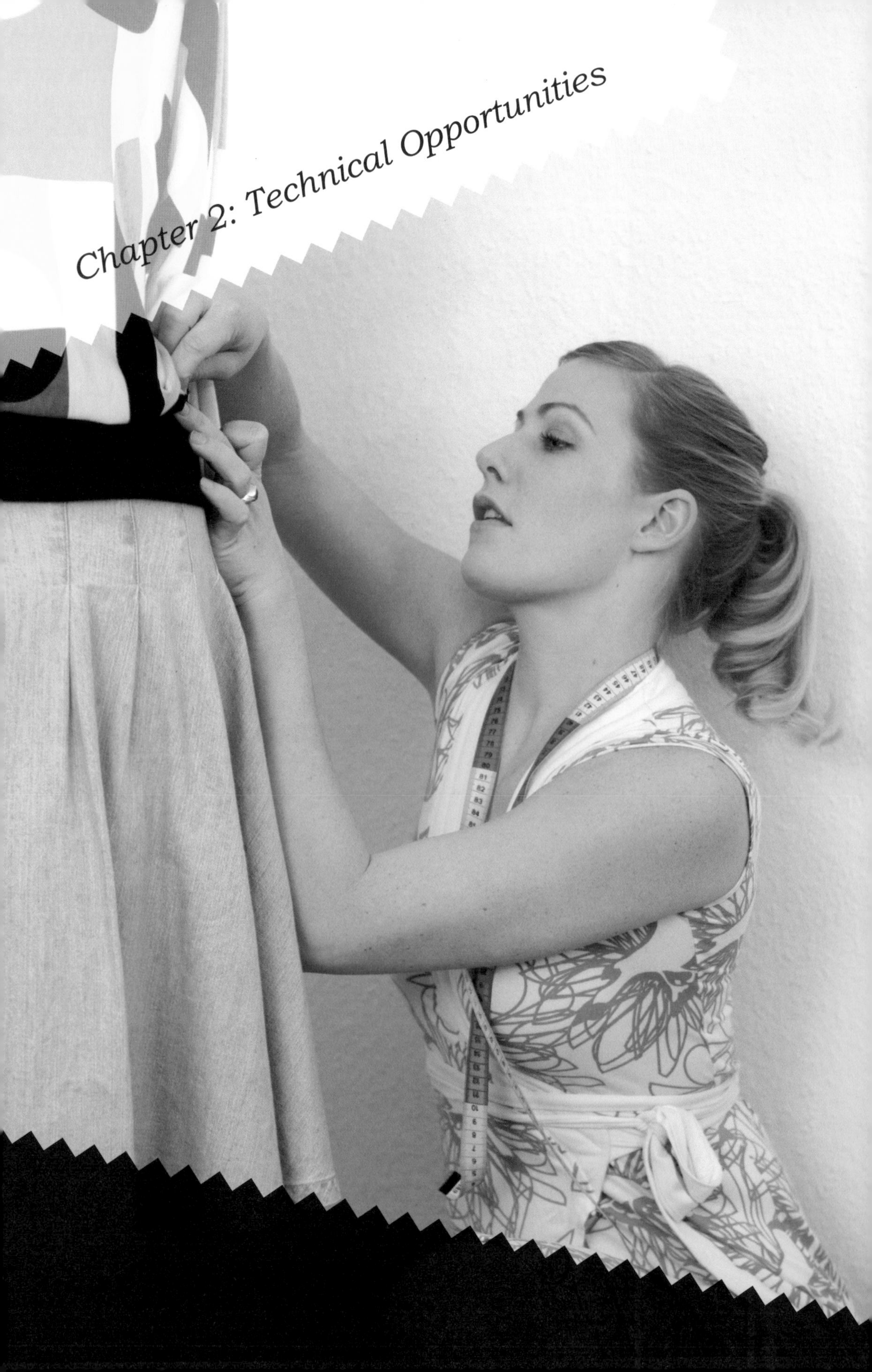

*T*echnical opportunities related to fashion and textiles are often overlooked as potential career paths in the fashion and textile industry. But there are many exciting technical opportunities available, with good employment prospects. Behind every fashion collection that appears on the catwalk and every collection of interior design or dress fabric, there are many very skilled jobs and specialist processes – from the design, sampling and the production of the fabric, to the cut, sizing, manufacture, labelling and packing of the garments or textiles. There are rigorous quality-control checks, making sure the fabrics, yarns, garments or products are fit for purpose.

This chapter discusses the many technical opportunities within the fashion and textile industry. There are many opportunities to train within the industry or alternatively there are many textile technology courses available offering study in the theory of textile technology, current industrial practices, colouration technology, technical textiles, yarn and non-woven technology and an introduction to the CAD software that is used within the fashion and textile industry. Clothing technology courses offer study of the product, pattern technology and manufacturing processes, alongside an introduction to the specialist use of CAD software and its applications. Today most programmes of study have well-established industrial links providing excellent work placement opportunities.

Production Manager

A specification sheet (spec) records all the garment details, enabling the garment to be manufactured to the exact size and specifications required.

The production manager oversees all aspects of the production of a garment range, from prototype sampling to the finished garments. Due to overseas production, there are many opportunities for a production manager to travel, and languages are a huge advantage. Responsibilities include reviewing the technical-, quality- and delivery-control of products, and the negotiation of prices with factories overseas.

A production manager works closely with the design team, which usually comprises a designer (or designers), pattern cutter, pattern grader, sample

Pattern cutter checking the fit of a garment on a mannequin

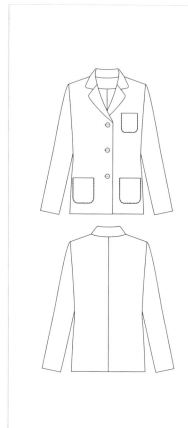

SPECIFICATION SHEET

GARMENT DESCRIPTION: WOMEN'S BLAZER
STORY/SEASON: AUTUMN/WINTER
STYLE NUMBER: XXX
SUPPLIER: XXX

Garment measurements	S	M	L
CB length	26	27	28
Bust	39	41	43
Waist	32	34	36
Shoulder	15	15.5	16
Armhole	9	9.5	10
Cuff	9.25	9.5	9.75
Sleeve	31	32	33
Neck circumference	15	15.75	16.5

Trim description	Quantity		
Copper buttons	3	3	3

Material consumption			
Satin lining JX433	1.25 yards	1.5 yards	1.75 yards
Medium-weight worsted wool FB8765	2 yards	2.5 yards	3 yards

Construction notes
Seam allowance: 0.5 inches except for collar and cuff (0.25 inch)
Sew exactly as per sample

machinist and garment technologist; together they ensure the best quality garment is being produced within budget in the allocated timeframe. The production planning of a range involves organizing and overseeing the time allocated for a production run and reviewing how the garment is assembled, as well as ways of improving production efficiency to meet the delivery dates.

Production managers are usually formally trained with a qualification in garment or textile technology. After formal training, the entry level is as junior garment technologist, with opportunities for promotion to more senior positions.

Typical Skills Required

✖ *Knowledge of all garment production processes*
✖ *Experience and knowledge of modern production systems*
✖ *Ability to plan and organize the production line to meet the required deadlines*
✖ *Good time-management skills*
✖ *Ability to multi-task and work under pressure*
✖ *Ability to work to a given brief and meet deadlines*

Pattern Cutter

When designing and constructing a garment, the pattern needs to be accurate and precise in measurements, fit and balance to give the correct look. A pattern cutter produces patterns from original sketches and garment specification sheets, listing all the garment's finished measurements. This ensures the pattern cutter cuts the pattern according to the instructions and information given. For example on a coat, some of the measurements listed would include the centre back length (CB length), chest measurement, waist, back neck drop and front neck drop.

The role of the pattern cutter is to cut an accurate pattern using flat pattern cutting methods or CAD tools to produce computer generated patterns, grading spec sheets and first patterns. To be a successful pattern cutter you must be able to work closely with the designer and the design team.

Job prospects are good, with accurate pattern cutters always being in demand.

Opportunities in industry include working in a design team as a pattern cutter, initially entering as a junior pattern cutter and rising to pattern cutter, senior pattern cutter or working for a pattern maker – a company that offers pattern cutting and grading services to the industry with the ability to draft a wide range of styles including womens- and menswear, childrenswear, sportswear, street wear and outerwear. Alternatively, many pattern cutters work freelance, offering a pattern and grading service and working on contracts for designers, manufacturers and retail chains. Some companies offer pattern cutting services from producing patterns to first samples and small production runs.

Most pattern cutters receive formal training through study on a fashion and technical production course and start work in the industry as trainee pattern cutters.

Garment pattern designed and cut by the pattern cutter

Typical Skills Required

==

✘ *Good understanding of computerized pattern-making software*
✘ *Ability to work to a given brief and meet deadlines*
✘ *Capable of working under pressure*
✘ *Ability to produce high quality and efficient patterns*

==

Sally Jane Botwright: Pattern Cutter

Sally Jane Botwright was introduced to the 'rag trade' by her father Peter, founder of Wested Leather, where she worked part-time dealing with sales and assisting with made-to-measure orders. At 16 Sally studied on a one-year City and Guilds textiles course and for a further two years on a fashion and design course.

On graduation she worked as an assistant pattern cutter for a small mail-order company, copying patterns for factories and carrying out quality control on first samples. After 18 months Sally secured a job with the designer Nicole Farhi, pattern cutting and toiling, and also dealing with factories in India for French Connection. Sally has also worked freelance for several companies, including Jasper Conran, creating toiles and patterns for bridalwear, eveningwear and prom wear. In 2008 she and Glen Robinson launched Robins & Wright Ltd., an internet pattern cutting service, which was an overnight success.

An Interview with Sally Jane Botwright – Pattern Cutter

How did you get into this line of work?
I was born into the rag trade as my father had a factory producing leather, suede and sheepskin garments for film, television and the general public. However, as my passion is for women's light clothing I chose not to enter full-time into the family business.

What training and qualifications are required to become a pattern cutter?
I went to college for three years to study fashion, art, textiles, pattern cutting, grading, production process engineering and designing.

Do you create all patterns using flat pattern cutting methods, or do you model on the stand, or use a combination of methods?
I do both depending on what I am creating. I work at the high end of the fashion trade, which tends to like to see the design taking shape on the stand. Therefore I tend to do a half toile first in calico or jersey, get approval, make the first pattern and then have a full toile made up in our sample room, produced in a similar fabric to that required for the final garment.

Do you use traditional or computerized methods to produce patterns?
I have used both methods in the past but I prefer using traditional pattern cutting methods.

Can you describe your average working day?
My day can be quite varied. A typical day starts with discussing sketches with the designer before I start pattern cutting. I then start creating the design in toile form in calico or jersey on the stand, discussing any manufacturing problems that may arise with the designer. A design can look great on paper but does not always work in 3D. Once the initial toile is passed, then I start to create my pattern, which, once completed, is taken to the sample room to be cut and produced by the sample machinist. Sometimes part of my day includes a fit meeting, when the designer and I meet to look at the design and fit of the toile, making any note of amendments. Another part of my day is spent

working closely with my sample machinist making sure that all pattern needs can be met.

Which companies and labels have Robins & Wright worked with?

We have worked with a wide range of companies, mainly independent labels in the ready-to-wear, leisure wear and bridalwear sectors.

What is the key to the success of Robins & Wright patterns?

Robins & Wright has been successful because we offer companies an accurate first pattern cutting service; most companies have to employ a pattern cutter and machinist in order to create a toile and first pattern. By using our company they send us a sketch and we send back a toile and a pattern for a one-off fee. They can go straight into fitting. It saves them the expense of agency staff and takes the stress out of creating a collection.

What makes a successful pattern cutter?

Talent. You have to have a natural eye for fit and form. A good pattern cutter can bring a simple drawing alive. A good understanding of the body and fit is also a factor. You have to understand how the body moves and where extra tolerance is needed to ease movement and create comfort. You also need to know your fabric and how one can react differently from another. There are many factors, but with experience it all comes naturally.

Modelling on the stand to produce a toile, Robins & Wright Ltd.

What advice would you give to someone who wants to be a pattern cutter?

Many of my friends did the course but found it hard to find their first job and gave it all up. The first job is hard to find, but keep trying because eventually someone will say yes and then the world is your oyster. I would say that it is a very rewarding job and great fun. The world of fashion is a very glamorous one. To be part of a fashion show is a fantastic experience.

Pattern Grader

Pattern grading is the sizing up or down of a pattern to fit a range of sizes – worked manually or using CAD.

Grading is the process of increasing or decreasing the size of the original pattern to produce other size patterns. For example, if a pattern is produced in size 10, then additional patterns can be made by sizing the pattern up, to produce patterns in size 12, 14, 16, 18 and so on. This work requires extreme accuracy.

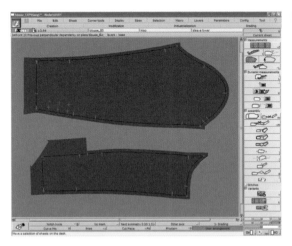 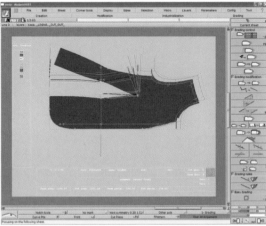

CAD applications such as Lectra's Modaris system, above, enable the designer to create lay plans and quickly and easily grade patterns

In some companies the pattern cutter will both cut and grade the pattern; however, in larger organizations a separate pattern grader will be appointed. Pattern grading can be worked manually or using a computer package to size patterns up or down, as required.

Most pattern graders complete a fashion/clothing technology course giving a good grounding in garment design, pattern cutting, pattern grading, garment manufacture and fabric technology. After formal training, entry into employment starts at pattern grading assistant level, rising to pattern grader and then senior pattern grader. Alternatively, some pattern graders train through apprenticeships in industry.

Typical Skills Required

==

✖ *Great accuracy and attention to detail*
✖ *Good understanding of computerized pattern making software*
✖ *Ability to work under pressure*
✖ *Ability to work to a deadline with speed, accuracy and proficiency*

==

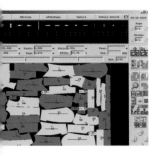

Lay Planner/Cutter

The lay planning process is designed to make sure that there is minimum fabric waste during the garment cutting process.

All companies and labels work to a budget and each stage of the design and manufacturing process is carefully calculated to produce the garment range at the most cost-effective price possible. The job of the lay planner involves producing the best fabric lay to ensure the most economical use of the fabric. This can be completed manually or calculated by CAD software.

Many lay planners/cutters receive formal training, studying courses in fashion technology; alternatively, companies also train lay planners on the shop floor.

Typical Skills Required

✖ *Knowledge and understanding of fabrics*
✖ *CAD-literate*
✖ *Great attention to detail and accuracy*
✖ *Ability to work to deadlines*

Manufacturing a garment using an industrial lockstitch machine

Sample Machinist

A sample machinist works closely with the designer and pattern cutter to produce and develop prototype sample garments, which must be accurate in construction, detail and finish, ready to present to the design team and buyers. A sample machinist must be able to translate the working drawing/specification sheet, which lists all the garment's finished measurements, flat sketches and construction details, into a sample garment.

Sample machinists usually start their career as machinists trained on the shop floor and, with experience and training, progress to sample machinist. To be successful in this work you must have a good understanding of a wide range of fabrics and be able to analyze fit, making the necessary alterations on the sample garments.

Typical Skills Required

===

✖ *Excellent technical skills and knowledge of manufacturing techniques*
✖ *Quality workmanship and ability to work with a wide range of fabrics*
✖ *Good attention to detail*
✖ *Ability to work to a deadline*

===

Machinist

Many companies use flexible production lines comprising multi-skilled cutting and sewing units. The machinist usually works either on a production line in a larger company, where each machinist specializes in one or two operations using a range of industrial machinery, or in a unit where they individually assemble whole garments. Most machinists receive in-house training in machine operating to achieve the required accuracy, quality, speed and proficiency.

Other employment opportunities for machinists include working independently from home, as an outworker manufacturing small production runs, or working as an alterations machinist for a boutique, department store, bridalwear company or an independent design unit.

Typical Skills Required

===

✖ *Excellent knowledge of manufacturing techniques*
✖ *Accurate construction skills*
✖ *Quality workmanship and ability to work with a wide range of fabrics*
✖ *Good attention to detail*
✖ *Ability to work to a deadline with speed, accuracy and proficiency*
✖ *Knowledge and experience of a range of industrial sewing machines*

===

Fabric Technologist

A fabric technologist works closely with the design team/product developers, buyers and suppliers, and is responsible for all issues related to fabric from quality checks to sourcing and price negotiations. It is their responsibility to ensure that the fabrics meet the requirements of the customer, working with suppliers' quality systems and developing new fabric ideas suitable for a season's collection. A thorough knowledge of fabric types, construction, dyeing and finishing is required. A fabric technologist must ensure the fabric is fit for purpose and that the fabrics pass all tests required for the product. Fabric, weave and fibre defects, colour conformity and finish are all tested.

A fabric technologist must have excellent communication skills and be able to liaise with a wide range of people. Opportunities often arise for travel both nationally and internationally to source fabrics from mills and suppliers, and to check the production quality.

Entry level into the industry is as an assistant fabric technologist, with progression to fabric technologist, who both report to a senior fabric technologist. Usually a formal textile technology qualification is required.

Typical Skills Required

===

✖ *Complete understanding of fabric performance and finishes*
✖ *Good administration skills*
✖ *Excellent technical knowledge*
✖ *Strong communication skills*

===

Garment Technologist

A garment technologist is involved in the product development, monitoring the production process and ensuring that fitting and quality standards are set and maintained. The garment technologist works alongside the design team, liaising with the designers, pattern cutters, production team, managers, factories and suppliers, and is responsible for all the technical, sizing and finishing details and quality control. They will check product, size, style, material and colour conformity, checking for defects such as oil stains, unsecured stitches, thread ends, incorrect hem width and seam allowances and irregular stitch size. Substandard products equal lost sales and dissatisfied customers and clients.

QUALITY CONTROL

Defective samples	Critical	Major	Minor
Defect from style: Vadar			
Wrong sewing effect		02	
Serious unclear thread end		01	
Visible white stitch of back side		05	
Slight visible white stitch of back side			07
Oil stain		01	
Hem wavy		01	
Unsecured stitch		02	
Thread end			06
Defect from style: Ortatio			
Colour yarn			01
Wavy seam (puckering)		01	
Defect from Style: Pamela			
Zip hard to run		01	
Hem width size (relaxed) too small (short 4cm)		01	
Defect from style: Rotty			
Not found any serious defect except few thread end			
Total defects:		15	14
Maximum allowed:		10	14

Requested AQL	☐ Within AQL	Found	☐ beyond AQL	
Major defective maximum allowed: **10**	☐ Within AQL	Found **15**	☐ beyond AQL	
Minor defective maximum allowed: **14**	☐ Within AQL	Found **14**	☐ beyond AQL	

To be a successful garment technologist you must have sufficient experience to assist with the development of garments from sample through to production, first checking samples in style, size and conformity to the design specifications. All technical adjustments and alterations required are noted, ready to change on the final sample range. Entry into the industry is usually at a junior level – assistant garment technologist; however, there are good opportunities for progression to garment technologist, senior garment technologist and product manager.

Typical Skills Required

===

- ✘ *Excellent understanding of garment construction, fabrics and finishings*
- ✘ *Knowledge and understanding of manufacturing techniques*
- ✘ *Good communication skills*
- ✘ *Good time management*
- ✘ *Ability to multi-task and work under pressure*

===

Right: *Cleaning and restoring a decorative bow, Consorzio Tela di Penelope, Prato, Italy*

Far right: *Cleaning and restoring a tapestry, Consorzio Tela di Penelope, Prato, Italy*

Costume/Textile Conservationist & Restorer

Costume/textile conservation and restoration is very specialist work, which can be painstaking. It involves analyzing the composition and construction technique of a fabric in order to reconstruct and preserve an artefact. It may involve working with minute, delicate fragments of fabric, as well as cleaning, restoring and repairing fabrics, counting threads in fabric weave and working with the warp and weft of a fabric to reconstruct part of a tapestry, textile or part of a garment. Recording and extracting information on the history of an item is important to the work of a fabric restorer.

Costume and textile conservationists usually work in museums, galleries and conservation centres in the areas of textiles, archaeological textiles, and costume/fashion research. They also work with associated professional bodies and individual clients. To be successful working in the field of fabric restoration and conservation you should be interested in history and in the history of art and design. Formal study in restoration and conservation is usually required.

Typical Skills Required

===

- ✘ *Manual dexterity*
- ✘ *Knowledge, appreciation and understanding of the history of fashion and textiles, and art and design*
- ✘ *Excellent attention to detail*
- ✘ *Patience and accuracy*

===

Chapter 3: Business and Management Opportunities

*B*usiness and management are vital to the success of the fashion and textile industry and represent excellent career opportunities. To work in this sector of the industry you must be business-minded, financially astute, a creative thinker and organized; you also need to be methodical in your approach to work. There is a multitude of career options and this chapter discusses the many opportunities available.

The retail industry is very competitive and is one of the fastest growing areas, with a range of different types of retail set-ups, from the large multinational department stores to high street chains, independent boutiques, mail order businesses and online retailers.

Multinational Department Stores

The multinational department stores trade in different places under the same name, and have the same organization and management structure in each store. Department stores sell a wide range of products, from fashion merchandise to cosmetics, furniture, soft furnishings and electrical items. Many department stores offer concession outlets – a store positioned within the department store, but trading under its own name.

High Street Chains

A high street chain is a group of stores working within the same management structure, usually positioned in shopping centres and shopping villages.

Independent Boutiques

Independent boutiques or stores are individually owned with all aspects of the business being the sole responsibility of the owner(s). This includes responsibility for the purchasing, ordering, merchandising and pricing of stock, as well as budgeting and accounting and customer care.

Mail Order

Purchasing goods or services by mail order is a convenient method of shopping, which can be done from a catalogue or brochure, and the items are then delivered directly to your door. Mail order businesses include large high street retailers who also operate mail order services to their customers and companies who operate solely by mail order.

Internet Retailing

Internet retailing and shopping online has seen significant increase in recent years due to growth in customer websites and with the development of many online-only retailers. Many large multinational department stores, high street

Buyer and merchandiser liaising over a new season's range

chains and smaller independent boutiques offer online retailing to their customers. Other retailers trade solely through online retailing to a niche market clientele.

Where to start

If you are interested in a career in the business and retail sector, whether as an assistant store manager, merchandiser, visual merchandiser or buyer, it is advisable to gain as much experience as possible working as a sales assistant in a variety of retail outlets, which will give you an understanding of organizational structures. Shop-floor experience will give your job applications more credibility.

Having a relevant qualification in business or retail management will give you a huge advantage when applying for a position in this sector of the industry. Undergraduate retail degrees offer programmes of study relating to retail operations and the retail environment, international retailing, retail law, buying, finance, consumer behaviour, store management, merchandising and store design; and often offer a placement in industry, providing an insight into this very fast-moving, competitive sector. On completion of their studies many graduates will enter a company in a trainee managerial position. Alternatively many retail outlets offer their own training programme, encouraging staff to develop their skills through hands-on business and retail experience.

Buyer

A buyer must have a good understanding of design, the retail industry and an understanding of forthcoming trends. Buyers usually work in buying teams and work closely with management and merchandisers, who assist in developing a marketable and profitable product range that will sell. The responsibilities of the buyer include planning a collection, buying merchandise within a budget for a specific target market, working with suppliers and keeping abreast of trends.

Fashion buyers attending 'The Source' at Bread and Butter trade fair, Barcelona, Spain

To be successful, a buyer must have an excellent understanding of their target market – who the customers are; their age group, lifestyle, income range and consumption trends. They must have knowledge of what is happening season to season, what will sell and, importantly, who their competitors are.

Buyers need to be confident decision-makers: creating and selecting ranges, monitoring sales, planning and negotiating prices with suppliers and monitoring competitors. Many buyers initially study fashion or business studies and, while studying, gain retail experience through work placements and part-time employment.

Promotional prospects tend to be excellent. Most buyers start their careers as assistant trainee buyers, are promoted to assistant buyers and then, after one or two years' experience, move into buying positions and then into managerial positions.

Travel opportunities are also excellent and include attending trade shows, exhibitions and fashion shows and visiting suppliers.

Typical Skills Required

==

- ✖ *Knowledge of market trends in order to develop an exciting fashion range appropriate to the target market*
- ✖ *Financial acumen with good negotiation skills*
- ✖ *Commercially minded*
- ✖ *Confident, with excellent communication skills*
- ✖ *Ability to work under pressure*

==

Buyer's Administration Assistant

To work as a buyer's administration assistant it is very useful to have retail experience and preferably some administration and office experience. A buyer's administration assistant works as part of a buying team, assisting with general office filing, the administration of orders, dealing with samples, and gathering and inputting data including data of sales and stock. The work includes assisting the buyer with product development, working with suppliers, negotiating and dealing with manufacturing issues.

Knowledge and understanding of competitors is all-important, with competitor shopping being part of the job. Careful studies and analysis of competitor products, price range and stock provide important input to the buying process. Many buyers' administration assistants complete formal training through study on fashion and business courses or retail training programmes; however, experience in retail sales is essential.

Typical Skills Required

==

- ✖ *Strong administration skills*
- ✖ *Computer literate: word processors, spreadsheets, databases*
- ✖ *Enthusiastic and highly motivated*
- ✖ *Financially astute with good negotiation skills*
- ✖ *Commercially minded*
- ✖ *Excellent time-management skills*

==

Merchandiser

The role of the merchandiser is to work closely in liaison with the buyer in developing a marketable and profitable product range that will sell, meeting the sales targets and the financial forecasts of the company. Financial strategic planning and financial reviews are vital to the success of the business and it is the responsibility of the merchandiser to develop sales forecasts and to monitor stock flow, maximizing stock availability, analyzing sales, and marking down goods where necessary to achieve the set sales targets. For a retail business to be successful it is crucial that stock keeps moving, increasing product turnover, and that sales targets are met in line with the product plan.

In retail business rents and rates are usually high and space is at a premium, therefore space must be optimized to maximum efficiency, through careful planning within the store.

Entry into a career in merchandising can be through a company training programme, starting work as a retail sales assistant then gradually moving into a supervisory role, a managerial position and then into the position of a merchandiser. Other routes into a career in merchandising include studying for a formal qualification in fashion management or business studies.

Typical Skills Required

==

- ✖ *Commercially astute with excellent numerical and analytical skills*
- ✖ *Understanding of consumer trends*
- ✖ *Good team skills*
- ✖ *Strong organizational skills*
- ✖ *Computer literate: word processors, spreadsheets, databases*
- ✖ *Ability to communicate at all levels*

==

Merchandising Allocator

The role of the merchandiser allocator involves liaising with buyers, merchandisers and suppliers and monitoring stock flow, with responsibility for maximizing stock availability. To maximize sales it is important that the allocator ensures the flow of the right stock at the right time, replenishing stock when required.

An allocator must have good commercial knowledge of the retail market. At entry level it is useful to have retail and office administration experience. Often positions are advertised which request that candidates have at least one year's shop-floor experience. The work is fast-paced and can be pressurized. Frequently, quick decisions have to be made, dealing with the allocation and re-allocation of stock, managing stock inventories and regulating profit margins.

Many allocators are recruited from a business or economics background, with formal training to degree level. Prospects for promotion are very good, as merchandisers, senior merchandisers and buyers.

Typical Skills Required

==

✖ *Commercially minded*
✖ *Numerate*
✖ *Computer literate: word processors, spreadsheets, databases*
✖ *Strong administration skills*
✖ *Excellent organizational skills*

==

Visual merchandising, in-store display

Visual Merchandiser

The role of the visual merchandiser is to create and produce window and in-store displays, promoting retail brands, introducing a new trend to inspire the customer and attract them into the store. In recent years there have been exciting developments in visual merchandising with the design of new modular systems including innovative flexible display systems and freestanding units, providing scope for more innovative approaches to the art of display.

To be successful in visual merchandising you must have knowledge of seasonal trends and the in-store merchandise. You must have an innovative approach to design, supported by strong practical skills, and be able to source props and accessories to make displays when necessary, working within a budget. You must also have knowledge of retail promotion, ergonomics and store planning.

Larger stores usually employ a team of in-house visual merchandisers led by a visual merchandising manager, who liaises with the store management team to make decisions about the choice and schedules of window and interior displays. Other stores may be advised by their Head Office what is to be displayed, how and when. Alternatively, some companies employ visual merchandisers to travel from store to store working on their visual displays to give a corporate identity to the brand. Some of the smaller stores rely on retail assistants to keep all displays up to date, and many owners of independent retail outlets do their own visual merchandising. Other opportunities for employment include working on a freelance basis or working on exhibition and trade fair displays.

Typical Skills Required

==

✖ *Excellent visual and spatial awareness*
✖ *Strong creative and practical skills*
✖ *Awareness of current trends*
✖ *Ability to work under pressure*
✖ *Ability to work within a budget*

==

Window display celebrating Oscar de la Renta's 35th anniversary at Bergdorf Goodman in New York

Retail Manager

The role of a retail manager is to ensure that the day-to-day operational management of a department or store runs smoothly and efficiently, working with both staff and customers, and also ensuring that the store reaches its sales targets. Other responsibilities include: organizing staff rotas, holiday leave and staff wages; recruiting, training and motivating staff. A retail manager must have excellent communication and motivational skills, working closely alongside the sales team to achieve set sales targets and also offering excellent customer service.

The retail industry has a high staff turnover due to many employers working part-time and it's the manager's responsibility to ensure stability within the retail team through strong leadership skills, motivating them to meet company targets and then reporting figures back to Head Office.

Many retail managers train from the shop floor, starting off as retail assistants. Alternatively, some positions request formal qualifications in retail management.

Typical Skills Required

==

- ✖ *Motivational selling skills*
- ✖ *Ability to train and manage a sales team*
- ✖ *Excellent communication skills*
- ✖ *Excellent customer service*
- ✖ *Numerate and commercially minded with the ability to achieve sales targets*
- ✖ *Financially astute with good negotiation skills*

==

Retail Assistant

Retail assistants work in a variety of outlets from department stores to independent retail outlets and market stalls. Usually they work as part of a sales team supervised by a retail manager and an assistant retail manager. Depending on the size of the outlet the retail assistant is usually responsible for the general presentation and maintenance of the store, sales transactions and the operation of cash tills, returns, customer service and stocktaking. A retail assistant must be well presented, approachable and be able to offer excellent customer service. They should have knowledge of the product range and be able to advise customers on choices of merchandise, and must also have excellent selling skills to achieve targets.

In the retail industry there is a high staff turnover and there are many job opportunities available for positions as retail assistants. Formal qualifications are not necessary, as retail training is usually offered through the company. With a good work record there are many opportunities for progression from retail assistant to assistant retail manager or junior merchandiser. A basic salary is usually paid with additional incentives on top, which usually include a uniform allowance and also discounts on merchandise within the store.

Typical Skills Required

==

- ✖ *Excellent selling skills and customer service*
- ✖ *Good knowledge of merchandise*
- ✖ *Approachable; ability to work within a team*
- ✖ *Numerate*
- ✖ *Strong communication skills*

==

Agatha's window display attracts customers by showcasing a vibrant, individual look

Agatha: Independent Retailer

Agatha is an independent UK high street boutique, opened in 1996 by Carl and Roberta Jacklin, specializing in womenswear designer labels and accessories. Both Carl and Roberta have spent many years working in fashion retail, with Carl also working as an independent retail consultant.

An Interview with Carl Jacklin

What retail experience did you have before becoming an independent retailer?
None, I am an engineer by trade and Roberta was a hairdresser. In 1987 I was made redundant from my job as an engineer and decided to use my redundancy money to open a menswear fashion store. After ten years' trading we went into partnership and had four menswear shops. After successful trading we decided to pull out of the partnership and in 1996 opened Agatha's, specializing in womenswear.

Who is a typical Agatha's customer?
Aspirational and professional.

What garment ranges do you stock?
We stock something for most occasions from jeans to ballgowns; quality classics that are fashionable and international designer labels. Big names approach us automatically to stock their collections. The majority of brands are sourced through London showrooms and agencies.

How do you keep up to date with forthcoming trends?
We read lots of fashion magazines and historically we know what we are looking for, for our customer base. We are always striving for something different, but not so different that we frighten our customers away.

What exhibitions and trade fairs do you attend?
London Fashion Week, Pure, Bread and Butter, Barcelona and CDP in Copenhagen.

An ultra-feminine contemporary boutique interior presenting their latest merchandise gives a clear message to Agatha's customers

What is the most challenging part of your job?
Buying; if the buying's not right then you've got problems.

What training did you have in buying?
We are both self-trained. We have always liked clothes and fashion. The criteria we use when we are buying are: would we pay £150 for this dress, this coat? I feel we have a natural ability in buying but we are also confident in knowing our customers and what they want, and from this our customer base has grown.

What is a typical working day?
Work starts around 8 am when I start checking the accounts, making sure all cheques issued are going through; this is then followed by a meeting with the Manageress, Annabel, to discuss jobs for the day; otherwise each day is very different.

What does it take to succeed as an independent retailer?
Knowing your customer base, providing good customer service – this is number one for Agatha's – and of course knowing the market that you are operating in.

Have you made many mistakes along the way?
Yes, buying jeans that turned out to be a very poor fit!

What is the key to Agatha's success?
Agatha's success lies in its ethos of high-quality customer service.

Have you any future plans for Agatha's?
Absolutely, to expand on a franchise basis.

What words of advice would you give to someone who wants to become an independent retailer?
Thorough research, location and an understanding of the marketplace that you want to operate in; stick to budgets and set yourself targets, and keep to them.

Independent Retailer

Many people dream of having their own shop, selling the latest garment ranges and specialist brands. To be self-employed, working as an independent retailer, you must have a good business mind, be multi-skilled and have an entrepreneurial approach to your work, supported by knowledge of the workings of the retail industry. If you are considering starting your own retail outlet it is advisable to gain as much retail experience as possible before opening your own retail outlet.

To be successful, you need to consider all aspects of your business from the location of your shop to the general overheads and the employment of staff. Other areas of the business to consider include: understanding the customer base and the type of merchandise to be sold, price and buying of merchandise, advertising and promotion of the business, and the general day-to-day running of the business. This involves the tracking of sales, re-ordering and dealing with the legal and financial implications of running a business. (See also Chapter 11 – Starting in Business.)

Typical Skills Required

===

- ✖ *Knowledge of market trends*
- ✖ *Entrepreneurial skills*
- ✖ *Excellent managerial skills*
- ✖ *Strong communication skills*
- ✖ *Ability to multi-task*
- ✖ *Financially astute with good negotiation skills*

===

Personal Shopper

When they go shopping many people are daunted and confused by the choice of products, labels and outlets. Other people just do not have the time to spend hours looking for just the right outfit and employ a personal shopper to do retail research on their behalf. To be successful as a personal shopper you must have excellent product knowledge and know what's new, and be able to guide your client through the shopping process, offering an exclusive personal service.

Personal shoppers advise clients on the latest fashion trends, updating their wardrobes and selecting items to suit their requirements. This may involve shopping for the client or taking the client shopping. Some personal shoppers are employed by a retail outlet, department store or shopping centre and work for the various concessions based there. A personal shopper based in a department store will have a small consultation room with fitting area. Many personal shoppers work on a freelance basis, offering an image consultancy service to clients, updating their image and introducing them to new seasonal trends. Many personal shoppers/image consultants are trained designers or have worked in the fashion retail/fashion styling industry.

Typical Skills Required

==

✖ *Knowledge of the latest trends and merchandise*
✖ *Ability to develop good relationships with clients, department managers, concessions managers and sales assistants*
✖ *Excellent understanding of style, silhouette, colour, fabrics and texture*
✖ *Understanding of figure types*
✖ *Understanding of colour*

==

Fashion and Textile Recruitment Agent/Consultant

Fashion and textile recruitment agencies work with both industry clients and candidates, searching for applicants to fill job vacancies from entry level junior positions to senior executive positions. They recruit for all areas in buying and merchandising, retail management, design, technical, manufacturing and wholesale sales and marketing. Many recruitment agencies focus on selected industry sectors. Agencies deal with permanent full-time, part-time and freelance positions.

The work of an agency involves all aspects of the recruitment process from screening and assessing possible candidates on their suitability for a job to interviewing candidates. This saves the clients time and money, and also in some instances the agency will offer careers advice and guidance.

Formal qualifications are not always necessary to work as an agency recruitment consultant; however, it is useful to have a relevant industrial background supported by strong administration and interpersonal skills.

Typical Skills Required

==

✖ *Excellent communication skills*
✖ *Strong interpersonal skills*
✖ *Good administration and organizational skills*
✖ *Strong interest in all areas of the industry*

==

Chapter 4: Media Opportunities

*T*here are many opportunities in media and
communications related to the fashion and textile industries,
from fashion editor, journalist and writer through to PR,
event planner, photographer, stylist and model booker.
Many students train in fashion design, but opt for a career
in the media industry, or complete work placements in the
fashion industry before entering the media. Other students
study courses in journalism, media or communications, or
a multi-disciplinary media programme that might include
radio journalism, multi-camera production, photography,
new media and script writing. Rather than complete a
course in fashion or media, many people choose to start
their career working in a junior position within a company
that offers on-the-job training, and then work their way up
through the ranks.

Working in Journalism

The world of journalism is very tough, hard work, but also exciting at times, depending on the publication and the team dynamics. There are myriad fashion-related jobs within journalism: fashion director, editor, features writer, researcher, stylist and editorial assistant, to name a few. Each magazine or newspaper works in a very different way and no two jobs or positions will be the same. Usually at the front of any publication the names of all the editorial team are listed, identifying their full job title, which acts as a useful contact list if you want to get in touch with a specific person directly about a possible work placement or job.

Due to the growth in internet and dotcom related businesses there are growing job opportunities to work as researchers, online journalists, writers and copywriters. Many of these sites are subscription-based, and are potentially financially lucrative to the entrepreneur.

'Dreams': fashion photography
by Eugenio Recuenco

Cinzia Brandi: Contributing Fashion and Lifestyle Editor, Elle Italia

Cinzia Brandi has worked for 20 years in the fashion media industry, for many international magazines including: *Glamour* (Russia), *Arena* (UK) *Gear* (US), *Anna* (Italy), *Lo Donna* (Italy), *Amica* (Italy) and *Grazia* (Italy).

Cinzia studied courses in film making and production at New York University, USA, and professional journalism courses in Rome and Milan. She completed a PhD in Foreign Literature and Languages at the Universitá La Sapienza in Rome, Italy. She is fluent in Italian, her mother tongue, and also in English, French and Spanish.

An Interview with Cinzia Brandi

What are your main roles and responsibilities?
When I lived in Italy I was employed at *Elle* magazine. I then moved to New York, where I am now based, and I am employed on a freelance basis. I've been with Italian *Elle* for 14 years and I cover the news and New York events. I started work as a fashion stylist and lately my role has evolved in a more journalistic way, which I really enjoy.

How did you get into this line of work?
I love photography and I've always been involved in fashion. My boyfriend wanted to become a photographer and I considered that being a stylist would be complementary to his job. It rapidly evolved into something very interesting and it's practically what I've been doing all my life.

How do you decide on a fashion story?
As a fashion editor you need to be up to date with trends and attend the fashion shows in New York, Milan, London and Paris twice per year to see the designer collections. However, with the availability of websites, it is possible to see the shows in the same day, so there is much less travelling involved.

I first discuss a story with the Fashion Director or the Editor-in-Chief and we plan each issue and the looks we want to create. We book the photographer, the location, the model, the hairstylist and make-up artist. Usually it takes two to three weeks to prepare for a shoot. It's important to be precise and diligent in order to establish a good relationship with the showrooms or PR offices.

What makes a successful fashion editor?
It depends on what you consider success. If it is your career profile within a magazine, then I would say patience to wait for promotion. Sooner or later there will be an opportunity to advance your career.

Personally, I would say the ability to develop a personal style, which you need to keep up to date, due to fashion being so transitory. Also, I think success is the ability to create a cinematic story and give a personal interpretation to a look.

How important are communication skills to the success of your career?

In this business excellent communication skills are definitely a necessity. My career has not been an individual achievement – each story is the result of teamwork. The crew usually consists of eight to ten people, with the editor working like a director in the movies. The editor needs to convey his or her vision to the team in order to obtain what he or she wants.

What is your biggest career achievement to date?

At the beginning of my career I worked within the magazine's team, but for the past ten years I've been freelancing and I think that's been my best achievement. I work for several magazines, but I'm always Cinzia Brandi first. Working freelance has been challenging at times. I still love fashion shoots and styling, but now I also enjoy writing.

What advice would you give to a student wanting to work as a fashion editor?

You must really want it. It is not an easy path. I would recommend working alongside somebody extremely good, which is the best way to learn. You must also be very diplomatic, corporate and very politically correct. There are often office politics to contend with. The most important thing is to be lucky to work within a team where everybody works well together. If you find that group, stick with it.

Fashion Editor

A fashion editor works on magazines, journals and newspapers within an editorial team, consisting of the Editor-in-Chief, who manages the team, and also works with assistant editors, picture researchers, fashion stylists, fashion photographers, fashion writers and contributing editors. To be successful, a fashion editor must be aware of trend directions: silhouette, styling, detailing and accessories. What's essential for the season? What's new? What's happening on the high street? They must be aware of new fashion stories promoting a trend, the season's looks, what's happening on the catwalk and on the high street. They will make editorial decisions on the topic of each edition of a magazine or journal, reflecting the interests of the publication's readers.

The work can be very glamorous: attending fashion shows, openings of new stores, previews to exhibitions and trade events, gallery openings and parties. These offer many networking opportunities and are a fantastic opportunity to make new and retain existing contacts.

A fashion editor must be able to manage and oversee the ideas and work of fashion journalists, freelance contributors, feature writers, stylists and fashion photographers. They must be able to research, write and edit effective and innovative copy appropriate to their target market.

Typical Skills Required

==

- ✖ *Understanding of target market*
- ✖ *Strong directional ideas and an awareness and understanding of trends*
- ✖ *Excellent communication skills – verbal and written*
- ✖ *Research skills*
- ✖ *Networking skills and book of contacts*
- ✖ *Ability to write excellent copy*
- ✖ *Ability to work to tight deadlines*
- ✖ *Flexible approach to working hours*

==

Fashion Journalist

Fashion journalism is a challenging, fast-paced profession, which includes reporting on the latest seasonal trends, catwalk shows and the latest collections, what's new, general fashion news and interviewing designers. In recent years opportunities in journalism have grown due to the increase in new national and international titles being published, along with the development of opportunities in online journalism.

A career in fashion journalism involves researching, writing, analysing and reporting on interesting stories with news value. Languages and shorthand are both useful skills that enhance your reporting ability.

There are many different routes to a career in fashion journalism, from in-house training – working for a publisher and working your way up the ladder – to receiving training through formal study. There are many types of training courses on offer, which provide grounding in reporting, interviewing, writing and editing, knowledge on how to cover a story and networking to develop useful contacts in the industry. Many publishing houses offer work experience, providing opportunities to gain practical experience. There are many opportunities to work freelance as a result of publications always needing new stories. If you are to succeed in this industry it is important to have a fantastic book of contacts and the confidence to approach commissioning editors of appropriate publications with proposals for new ideas.

Typical Skills Required

===

✖ *Ability to research, write and edit excellent copy*
✖ *Awareness and understanding of forthcoming trends*
✖ *Ability to spot a newsworthy story*
✖ *Creating strong contacts through networking*
✖ *Research skills*
✖ *Excellent time management skills, with the ability to meet deadlines*

===

Feature Writer

Feature writers are usually employed on a freelance basis, working for several publications and producing articles for magazines and journals or the internet. Feature writing involves generating new ideas and writing articles of topical interest in the house style of the publication. A feature article is often longer than a news item and covers a topic of interest to the reader.

When writing freelance, it is usual to submit a query letter to the editor of the paper, journal or magazine with an attached article proposal summarizing potential articles that you are interested in submitting, which could include subjects such as beauty, lifestyle, fashion, accessories and events. Remember that journals and magazines usually work at least six months ahead of publication, so consider the seasonal element. For example, if you are interested in writing an article about the forthcoming autumn/winter trends for a women's magazine you would need to submit the article six to nine months ahead of publication, depending on the publication.

If you are interested in writing, do your research, finding out which magazine, journal or website is most suited to your work. It is very easy to work for an international publication via the internet, so do not limit yourself to local or national publishers. Most publishers produce author guidelines that outline the topics the magazine covers, article length and format of submissions, as well as image information, payment details and to whom the submission should be sent. Always make sure you send any proposals to a named editor.

Tony Glenville, Fashion Journalist

Tony Glenville is a UK-based freelance journalist whose work has appeared in a wide range of international publications, including: the *Independent*, *Textile View*, *Harper's Bazaar* and French *Vogue*. In 1996 he joined Condé Nast publications and became European Editor at Large for *Vogue* Australia and Fashion Director for Asia-Pacific, working with *Vogue* in Taiwan and Korea. He continues to work in journalism, acting as a consultant and also writing for various publications, which include *Urban Junkies*, *Design Direction*, *ABM* and *Zurich*; he is also a contributing Editor for *Harper's Bazaar*, Australia.

Interview with Tony Glenville

How did you first get involved in journalism?

I wrote a great deal for all the fashion consultancy companies, working from the mid-1970s onwards. Then I worked in Paris and started to write small pieces for *Drapers Record* and *Fashion Weekly*. Later I started to write seriously about catwalk for magazines in Australia and then finally joined the *Independent* writing anything and everything.

What qualifications does a fashion journalist require?

I believe there are a few key attributes which the great fashion journalists such as Cathy Horyn, Suzie Menkes or Sarah Mower possess. It is vital to develop the ability to contextualize and reference, when writing about fashion, anything from current music trends to historical references. The ability to encapsulate a complete fashion review/mood/item in a few hundred words is also required, and, above all, the knack of not personalizing but being objective about what one writes about. The journalist is paid for their professional opinion, not their personal viewpoint. Finally – speed. It is no good waiting for the muse to descend if the news desk is waiting or the magazine lacks a piece due to a late delivery by another writer. Just sit down and write.

How did you get your first commission?

In the first, early instances, through the fashion editors of *Drapers* and *Fashion Weekly*. Later, when I really started writing, it was Marion Hume who passed my name to an Australian publication called *Fashion Quarterly* and I covered international catwalk for them.

What has been your most enjoyable commission to date?

Interviewing designers has been wonderful: Azzedine Alaïa, Thierry Mugler and Emanuel Ungaro, amongst others. Any job which involves sitting watching catwalk and then reviewing it has been enjoyable! Especially haute couture. Writing, at present, for *Luxure* magazine is a joy, both because of the types of commissions and the superb quality of the publication in the visual sense.

What are the main skills required by a journalist?

Write to word count, write to deadline, write in a manner appropriate to publication: for example, if you are writing for the *Mirror* and the *Times* you cannot use the same 'voice'. Writing for a trade publication or for a glossy is very different. It is about communicating, through the written word, a visual image.

*Portrait of Tony Glenville,
fashion journalist*

What are the biggest challenges a journalist faces?

Interviews are always a test. Getting on with writing regardless of how 'not in the mood' you feel is also important. Pitching ideas to editors – that is finding endless reasons for people to employ you and feature your work, since a lot of writing is freelance and not always directly commissioned.

In journalism, what is a typical deadline that you work to?

This is a very great variable. Newsdesk stuff is as the show finishes and might still be read over the phone to a copy-taker if tip-top speed is needed. Glossy magazines can give you a few weeks, or it might even be a lovely long deadline. Big, well-researched pieces take time and most editors know this, so for an in-depth piece you will generally get a fair amount of time.

How important are contacts to a fashion journalist?

The simple truth is your contacts make your career. The more people you know and get on with the better. You need to know everyone from the designers through to the event manager. It is always about being able to call or email someone, knowing who to contact and what type of response you will get.

What advice would you give to someone interested in a career in fashion journalism?

Know your fashion history, because designers work within a surprisingly strong formula of pieces and looks. Develop a good telephone manner and, even more important, develop patience, both to wait and to keep asking until you get what you need. Don't throw tantrums, shout, argue or get on the wrong side of people: it will do your career absolutely no good whatsoever! Cultivate charm and good manners, say thank you for help, smile, and be well turned out so if you are interviewing someone you don't look like a bag lady or the cleaner.

Lose your shyness – it is vital you learn how to work a room and chat and introduce yourself to people.

Read good writing, fashion and general journalism, both past and present and develop your own 'voice'. Above all, enjoy what you do and be interested in the people you work with. As a writer and observer, if you don't like people and don't enjoy communicating both through conversation and writing you have chosen the wrong profession.

There are many excellent books that have been published guiding you through the stages of writing for publication, outlining the dos and don'ts for achieving success, providing sample letters of approach and containing information regarding contracts and what to expect.

Typical Skills Required

==

* ✖ *Highly motivated with the ability to meet deadlines*
* ✖ *Excellent writing and communication skills*
* ✖ *Strong research skills*
* ✖ *Good creative ideas*
* ✖ *Sound administration skills*

==

Fashion Marketing Manager

Fashion marketing offers creative and practical solutions in the promotion and marketing of a product or service through publicity and brand development. Marketing involves identifying a target market, and thinking of strategies to develop a brand or service through brand management and positioning, advertising and promotion, development of brand literature, designing websites, leaflets and brochures and the organization of promotional and launch events.

There are many opportunities in the area of fashion marketing, from junior marketing assistant/marketing graduate, to marketing co-ordinator, marketing manager and marketing executive. In a large company with a marketing or communications department, the role of marketing manager involves the responsibility for supporting the marketing and communications team, ensuring that market trends, competitor intelligence and customer data are all readily available to present to the company's senior management team, which provides direction and research for developing business plans. In a smaller company, many of these functions come together in one role.

If you are interested in a career in fashion marketing it is advisable to study an international accredited programme. To be successful in fashion marketing you need to have strong communication and business skills, and understand the branding of a company, product or service. You need to be able to meet goals, work to deadlines and be able to work within a budget, as well as understand any legal restrictions and implications.

Typical Skills Required

==

✘ *Creativity, resourcefulness and forward thinking*
✘ *Imaginative writing skills*
✘ *Strong networking skills*
✘ *Ability to meet goals within budget, with excellent commercial acumen*
✘ *Excellent communication skills – written, verbal and visual*
✘ *Ability to listen to, discuss and understand the client's requirements*

==

Public Relations Officer

Public relations (PR) is a very important factor in the business success of a company; it involves helping to raise the company's profile and improve its reputation. To be successful working in PR you need to have an understanding of the role of marketing and promotion, and be able to work with a range of companies. This may involve developing innovative strategies and solutions, and writing press releases and editorials. You may be involved in planning and organizing promotional events or dealing with a crisis situation, which may entail a company restructure.

Many companies and businesses have their own in-house PR department, promoting the company through the publication of regular newsletters, issuing press releases providing updates on current news and events and dealing with press queries. Other positions are agency-based, where promotional activities are overseen by PR/marketing teams who work closely with the client. To be successful they must have a good knowledge of their company, their customers, trade, products and services.

Typical Skills Required

==

✘ *Creativity, resourcefulness and forward thinking*
✘ *Imaginative writing skills*
✘ *Strong networking skills*
✘ *Ability to meet goals within budget*
✘ *Excellent communication skills – written, verbal and visual*
✘ *Ability to listen to, discuss and understand the client's requirements*

==

Christina Faulhaber:
Public and Media Relations

Christine Faulhaber established Faulhaber Public Relations Inc. in 2001, and is now a recognized leader in public and media relations working in the fashion, lifestyle, design and retail sectors. Christine and her team work with a broad client base offering services that include media relations, promotional campaigns, sponsor liaison, event planning, business development, branding, press launches and celebrity affiliations.

An Interview with Christine Faulhaber

What is the concept behind Faulhaber Public Relations Inc?
Faulhaber PR connects fashion and lifestyle brands to unexpected places. Our intimacy with a business means we're always looking for new and creative ways to build the brand and the business. We build a brand, package it up and get it out there to a company's existing clients and new ones.

What is the key to the success of Faulhaber Public Relations Inc?
Faulhaber PR is a highly interactive and intimate agency. We work with our clients every step of they way and ensure that every task we do is done with the highest degree of detail. Professionalism, accuracy and timely communication are key and Faulhaber PR's success is based on this simple concept.

What is the key to your own personal career success?
Honesty, drive, passion and hard work.

You know many people who work in fashion, beauty, media, music, film and retail – how important is industry networking to your success?
Industry networking is extremely important, especially in public relations, primarily because these are the people that are helping you get the results you need for your client. Editorial spreads, television appearances and newspaper hits featuring our clients happen because we pitch to those people that create the magazines, produce the shows, and write the articles. Knowing who these people are is critical in making your pitches turn into a reality.

Also, relationship building is key to success. People move around a lot and you never know where they might end up. A junior fashion stylist today could be the editor of *Style* next year. Be kind and people remember.

Which clients have you represented and in what capacity?
Our clients range from top denim brands to boutique-size retailers to major trade shows. Our extensive client roster includes Fidelity Denim, Project Runway Canada, Interior Design Show, Explore Design, Para Paints, Starbucks, Brave Beltworks, Over the Rainbow and Finishing Touches.

How did you develop your client base?
All referral. We decline more than we take on – and those we take we have a strong interest in.

Christina Faulhaber,
founder of Faulhaber Public
Relations Inc.

What media coverage has Faulhaber PR secured?

We have secured hits in various media outlets: print, television, radio and online. Some of our successful hits have been in *Fashion* magazine, the *Globe and Mail*, *Flare* magazine, Breakfast Television, *Elle* Canada, e-talk, *National Post* and the *Toronto Star*.

What is your greatest career challenge to date?

Human Resources Management. People are hard to find, hard to train and harder to keep.

What is a typical day in your working life?

The interesting thing about this job is that there is no typical working day. Every day I am presented with different jobs, tasks and challenges. Days include: client calls, off-site meetings, store visits, photo shoots, runway shows, vendor meetings, staff meetings, in-office paperwork, new client calls...

What has been your most enjoyable commission?

The people I have met in the industry have been one of the highlights of my working experience. I have had the opportunity to meet some of Canada's most talented designers, writers, producers, and reporters – each having a unique style/taste and an immense passion for what they do.

I also love seeing a client grow.

What is the most challenging part of your job?

As the principal of Faulhaber PR, I have to oversee the operations of the entire company. Faulhaber PR is a fast-paced agency with a big clientele base. I am constantly on the move acting in various roles throughout the day. Being able to multi-task, prioritize and meet tight deadlines is fun, but always challenging.

What advice would you give to someone who wants to develop a career in public relations?

I cannot emphasize how important networking is. Making yourself known to the industry professionals and developing relationships is key to advancing in your career and becoming successful. Getting your hands dirty and immersing yourself in the PR environment can give you an idea of what areas of PR you are most interested in. Internship and volunteer opportunities are also great ways to jump-start your career and experience the PR industry first-hand. So get out there, and put yourself on the map!

Special skills are also of great interest to anyone hiring a new associate. An expert in graphic design? Speak a second language? Travelled the globe? All these things add value and set you apart from the competition.

Events Planner/Trade Show Organizer

Many people are natural organizers and enjoy co-ordinating events. The role of events planner involves the management and organization of trade shows, charity fundraisers, trade and corporate events and fashion shows. An events planner needs to be a creative thinker with an organized and analytical mind and must be able to consider every possible detail in the planning of an event.

Trade shows, exhibitions and fashion shows are all marketing tools for the exhibitors, so are very important to their success. If you are interested in a career in events planning there are many large national and international companies who organize various events and are often keen to offer work placement opportunities, which usually involve answering the phone, making tea and coffee and helping wherever necessary, but will give you a fantastic insight into the roles and responsibilities within an events organizing company.

Typical Skills Required

==

- ✘ *Strong organizational skills*
- ✘ *Excellent promotional skills*
- ✘ *Decision-making skills*
- ✘ *Good networking skills and contacts list*
- ✘ *Ability to work to a budget*
- ✘ *Attention to detail*

==

Fashion Show Producer

A fashion show is a fantastic venue for designers to present their seasonal collections to journalists, buyers, retailers and customers. A fashion show involves a huge amount of organization, and the input of a wide range of people, including the fashion show producer, the lighting and sound manager and technician, the choreographer, backstage manager, make-up artists, hair stylists and dressers.

JOANNE MCKENNA
Venetian Vintage

Anticlockwise from top:

Presenting a collection
to the industry: buyers,
manufacturers, designers and
the media; collection by
Joanne McKenna

Fashion show rehearsals
require careful choreography
of models

Exhibition organizers at Bread
& Butter, Barcelona

Planning a fashion show – considerations

Element	Things to consider
Venue	Location, size and suitability
Time and date of the event	Dress rehearsals - choreography Times of show(s)
The catwalk	Location, positioning, length, width and height Set-building, the catwalk
Plan of the venue	Seating of the audience - type and number of seats and positioning Positioning of the media, VIPs and camera/video crew
Backstage and front of house	Communication between backstage and front of house - walkie talkies
Dressing rooms	Location and proximity to catwalk Number of dressing rooms, size Garment rails - how many? Mirrors
Lighting and sound manager	Positioning of the sound system Music licence
Collections	Collections - how many sets are being shown and the sequence of sets
Accessories	Belts, bags, footwear, hosiery
Music	Music licence Music system Music selection Employment of sound manager
Models	Number of models required, size and height of models Number of sets for each model
Dressers	Number of dressers required
Styling	What is the look that is required? Number of hair stylists and make-up artists required
Advertising of the event	Hoardings, newspapers, journals, broadcasting
Promotion of the event	Catalogues, brochures, signage, PR
Invitations	VIP list, guest list Design and production
Tickets	Design, size, turnaround time of printing and production costs Number required Mailing or via the internet Online booking Reserving seats
Brochures	Design, printing costs, turnaround time for printing and producing Number required
Goody bags	Cost and contents
Video/photography/internet	Design and production Copyright, cost
Health and safety	Risk assessments
Security	Venue, exhibitors, visitors, products
Insurance	Exhibitors, visitors, models and organizers Collections

*Behind the scenes: models,
dressers and dress rails
backstage at a fashion show*

Parking	Availability, location, cost
Transport	Parking and unloading
	Cost
	Insurance
Cost	Total cost and funding
Sponsorship	Number of sponsors
	Types of sponsorship

Typical Skills Required

- ✖ *Fantastic organizational skills*
- ✖ *Decision-making skills*
- ✖ *Good networking skills and contacts list*
- ✖ *Ability to work to a budget*
- ✖ *Multilingual*
- ✖ *Attention to detail*

Fashion Stylist

The work of a fashion stylist involves creating strong fashion images and looks to promote trends in newspapers and magazines and on television, in film and the music industry, and advertising and promotional materials such as fashion collections, exhibitions and trade events. The work includes researching and sourcing clothes, accessories and make-up to create a particular look or image. A fashion stylist's role within a company may also include booking photographers, models, hairdressers and make-up artists, preparing photographic shoots, booking photographic studios and sourcing locations.

To be a successful fashion stylist it is important to be aware of developing trends and fashion stories and have knowledge of colour and fabrics, and also to build up excellent contacts including editors, photographers, hair and make-up artists, models and agents. You must have a good working knowledge of the industry, excellent creative skills and an awareness of trends with a strong vision for generating new ideas. You must have strong communication skills and be able to work with a client, understanding their concept and in return communicating your ideas clearly. This is often done through a mood board, explaining the concept of the look or plans for a campaign through visual images.

In recent years fashion styling has become a popular career choice, favoured by many fashion students, and there is much competition in this field. One of the best ways to gain experience in styling is to complete a work placement working alongside a stylist or an assistant stylist or working backstage at a fashion show. A work placement in styling may involve contacting designers or retailers for the loan of garments, collecting and returning clothes, pressing them, sorting them out and compiling accessory cupboards, answering the phone, organizing refreshments and providing general assistance to the production team and models.

Many fashion stylists are self employed, so to be successful, in addition to excellent creative flair, you will need first-rate communication and networking skills to develop and expand your links within the industry and strong administration skills to manage the day-to-day business of working for yourself.

Typical Skills Required

===

✘ *Awareness and understanding of fashion trends*
✘ *Strong vision and ability to create exciting images*
✘ *Ability to prepare for photo shoots, including sourcing clothes, accessories and make-up*
✘ *Good networking skills and a fantastic book of contacts*
✘ *Ability to work within budget*
✘ *Excellent communication skills*

===

Make-up Artist

Make-up artists are usually employed on a freelance basis and work in the specialist fields of fashion photography, catwalk, theatre, television, film, music videos and advertising, creating looks through make-up and hairstyling that are appropriate for the image required. Make-up artists work with art directors, producers, fashion stylists, editors and designers to produce a required look. Work is highly competitive and to be successful you will need a thorough understanding of skin, hair and beauty products, and detailed knowledge of types of make-up and application.

Make-up artists usually study courses in make-up and beauty therapy, gaining the necessary skills and experience to collate a portfolio of examples to present to clients. Many make-up artists register with a specialist recruitment agency.

Typical Skills Required

===

✘ *Knowledge of skincare and new make-up products*
✘ *Awareness of trends and fashion stories*
✘ *Excellent knowledge and understanding of colour, shape, form and texture with good attention to detail*
✘ *Excellent networking skills, with a good book of contacts*

===

*Strong fashion image designed
and created by Alicia Lawhon*

Alicia Lawhon:
Costume Designer/Stylist

Award-winning designer and stylist Alicia Lawhon's career has been very varied
She started her fashion career working as an assistant buyer for Ron Herman/
Fred Segal Melrose, managing employees at the Melrose store in California,
and, as Head Merchandiser, creating looks for each forthcoming season
promoting trends in theme, garment silhouettes, colour and texture.

In 1996 she started designing and producing individual customized clothing for
celebrities, which were often used in music videos and commercial shoots. He
success enabled her to establish her own labels: Alicia Lawhon, AL
Construction and Wabi Sabi. Through her companies she sold quarterly
collections with an emphasis on handcrafted detailing, which were bought by
Barney's, New York, Collette in Paris and Ron Herman, among other fashion
retailers worldwide.

With this experience and an extensive network of industrial contacts, she
started working as a fashion stylist and today is widely recognized for her
wardrobe consultations and personal shopping, working closely with individual
clients. She has a celebrity clientele that has included Christina Aguilera,
Jennifer Aniston, Cher, Courtney Cox, Linda Evangelista, Angelina Jolie,
Courtney Love, Elle McPherson, Alanis Morrisette, Vanessa Paradis, Gwen
Stefani and Liv Tyler.

Her work has regularly been featured through the editorial coverage, ad
campaigns and commercials in many international magazines, including:
Blackbook, Cosmopolitan, Dazed & Confused, Elle, Esquire, The Face, French
Vogue, Nylon, Time Out, Vanity Fair, Visionnaire, W Magazine and *Women's
Wear Daily.* Her name is synonymous with success, achieving personal
recognition from the industry through the presentation of many prestigious
awards including Women's Ad Campaign of the Year 2007 awarded by SIMA
(Surf Industry Manufacturing Association) for Billabong, and Fresh Face Award

*Alicia Lawhon in
her studio*

An Interview with Alicia Lawhon

What advice would you give to an aspiring costume designer/stylist?
Learn how to construct. Then deconstruct. Study nature. Study people. Always
show up first, and leave last. Say yes to everything, with a smile, and bring a
good attitude.

What makes a successful fashion stylist?
Imagination and people skills.

Describe your work.
It is a combination of designing, shopping, and communicating. It feels like we
are all working on the same canvas. The client, photographer/director, talent/
producer, prop stylist and lighting assistant are all involved. Our visions of the
finished product should be similar. We all bring our strong points to the table to
create a beautiful result.

Who are your style icons?
Joan Ashby (who was married to Hal Ashby, the director) – a platinum bob and
fire in her lips and nails. She was my introduction to earthy elegance. I also love
Edith Head. She had a spectacular career and provided my favourite quote:
'What can I do for you today?' Other favourites include: Sophia Loren, Nick
Cave, Marcello Mastroianni and Steve McQueen.

What is the key to your success?
I love what I do.

**How do you keep up to date on trends, industrial developments and new
technologies?**
I love to read. I also have a nice network of friends in the fashion industry.
Magazines and the internet are always good sources for information. I
subscribe to: BLOOM, Dailycandy, Italian *Vogue* and style.com. I love picture
books, but I will read and flip though anything, from catalogues to newspapers
and tabloid magazines. I am interested in every kind of image.

What is your greatest achievement to date?
Working with great musicians, actors, directors, and photographers. I also enjoy my
private clients; the transformation once they are educated is very satisfying. I would
say that the greatest achievement is supporting creativity, and getting paid for it.

Cristy Guy: Fashion Stylist and Make-up Artist

Cristy Guy, a fashion stylist based in the US Midwest, started her career in fashion design, studying to degree level at the Fashion Institute for Design and Merchandising in Los Angeles, CA. After a successful career in fashion design Cristy moved into styling, working as a fashion stylist and make-up artist for individual clients. Her work has appeared in commercials, corporate ads, television and film, publications and the music industry, where she styled bands for live performances. She has also worked with professional athletes and sports personalities.

Cristy's work has appeared in many publications: *Hallmark* magazine, *Diane*, *GQ* and *Twist*. Her clients have included: Sam Sarpong, Keith Jackson, Krista Klaus and Jim Belushi.

An Interview with Cristy Guy

You started your career as a fashion designer: was it easy moving from fashion design into fashion styling?
Actually, it came as a feeling of relief. I like designing and am glad I always have that option to create a piece if I'm just not finding what I'm looking for, but I love pulling outfits together. In design, I learned how to distinguish between the different markets and customers. This has been a great asset in styling for different clients as well as individual personalities.

How would you describe your work?
My work is sexy, comfortable and cool. I love to mix pieces which usually shouldn't go together. For example, athletic inspired boots with a vintage 1970s evening gown. You will always find a punch of colour or an element of 'metal or roughness' in my work. My style is like mixing J. Lo with Gwen Stefani and sprinkling in a little Fergie.

Who was your first client?
Hallmark Inc. was my first official client.

What is the concept behind your company?
I'm in this business because I absolutely love it. It is wonderful to be able to make a living doing what I love. Therefore, I am always readjusting, growing, learning and changing. The more I 'fill the well' with great information and images the better ideas I have to offer my clients. By listening to my gut, the better decisions I make for the business. The happier I am, the happier my clients will be. I am able to provide them with great ideas, wardrobe choices, concepts and superstar service.

What is the key to your success?
The key to my success is using the talents I was blessed with: creativity, passion, persistence and drive. These characteristics keep me moving, keep the expression of ideas flowing and in turn keep my clients happy.

Above: *Gold make-up by Cristy Guy*

Right: *Image created and styled by Cristy Guy*

How do you keep up to date with developing and changing trends?

I visit a few key websites regularly, keep notes about my dreams, subscribe to magazines, constantly gather items of interest – tear sheets, fabric swatches, books of matches – watch people, attend movies, watch music videos and awards shows and keep an eye on celebrities.

What is your greatest career challenge to-date?

One of my biggest challenges has been collecting the work that I have done. Another is trying to slip a vacation in for myself once a year.

What advice would you give to an aspiring fashion stylist?

One of the most important things to do starting out is to test and/or assist with the best possible photographers and stylists. Make sure you have a good credit card. It doesn't hurt to have a little savings in the bank for your down time. Don't gossip about people... you never know who knows who and you never know where your next job could come from!

'Caperucita Roja'
for Vogue España;
photograph by Eugenio
Recuenco

Fashion Photographer

Working as a photographer in the fashion industry is a very competitive career, which is difficult to get into. It is important to understand the competition and be prepared to gain as much experience as possible, developing a list of clients and gaining a reputation for the quality of your work.

The opportunities within this field of work range from working for magazines, newspapers, trend books, catalogues and advertising to editorial and promotional work or, alternatively, being a catwalk photographer. Most photographers work to commission on a freelance basis, and have an agent to organize contracts. The development of a portfolio of work is essential. This should be updated regularly to demonstrate your skills, abilities and assignments completed, identifying the clients for whom you have worked.

Most successful photographers start working as assistants to established photographers. This could involve setting up lights, cameras, equipment, backdrops and settings, and generally supporting the photographer, whose role includes scheduling, directing and developing sets, using props, lighting and taking pictures including working on post-production: developing films or organizing digital shots and editing the images to the client's requirements.

Work may be studio-based or on location. Some fashion photographers have their own studio; others hire a studio space for the length of a shoot. A good fashion photographer understands and can interpret the photographic commission or brief. They must be able to work under pressure to meet the required deadlines for publication and have the ability to work with models, stylists, art directors and editors, achieving the look required to produce original and innovative photographs.

Typical Skills Required

===

✖ *Good visual and fashion awareness*
✖ *Technical understanding of photographic effects that can be achieved to give the best results*
✖ *Ability to interpret the client's needs*
✖ *Understanding and knowledge of image manipulation software*

===

Model

Many people see the world of modelling as very exciting and glamorous, which can be true if you are a successful fashion model working for magazines such as *Vogue* or *Elle* and travelling around the world. However, behind every job there is a great amount of hard work involved, and the type of modelling assignments vary greatly and require different types of models, depending on the kind of work.

✖ Catwalk or runway models need to be confident, with good deportment and have presence on the catwalk to promote designer collections. They need to have a unique look, be photogenic and carry clothes well.

✖ Promotional models usually work at trade fairs and exhibitions promoting products, which vary from cars to household and lifestyle products.

✖ Commercial models are used to advertise goods and can be seen in advertisements in newspapers, billboards and television commercials.

✖ Editorial models appear in magazines, journals, retail publications and fashion brochures, and need to be tall and photogenic. This is very competitive work.

✖ Plus-type models are required for fashion, photographic, catwalk and editorial work.

✖ Life models are usually employed by art institutes and life drawing groups who want to draw the body. This type of work requires men and women of all shapes and sizes. The model needs to be very patient and be comfortable posing nude, as required, and must have the capacity to hold a pose for periods of time, often in very unnatural positions, while artists are drawing, painting and sculpting.

Eugenio Recuenco:
Fashion Photographer

Eugenio Recuenco is one of Spain's most recognized fashion photographers, renowned for his strong fantasy and pictorial images and for his creative approach to photography and recognizable style.

An Interview with Eugenio Recuenco

When did you first become interested in photography?
I took my first photo at the age of 13; at this time cameras weren't as accessible as they are now and it was during a school trip that I first became interested in photography, when my father loaned me his old Kodak Retinet.

What training did you have?
I studied at the Fine Arts University, Spain, and there I was taught to see with another perspective. I have never been worried about my talent, in fact, I don't believe in it. I live with eyes wide open, sometimes I don't understand fully what I see, but I think that comes in time with experience.

What were your first steps to becoming a professional fashion photographer?
After completing my studies I started working for many international magazines, which included *Madame Figaro*, *Wad*, *Spoon*, *Planet*, *Vanity Fair*, *Stern*, *Zink*, Spanish *Vogue*, *View*, and *Vanidad*.

I have also worked on many international campaigns: Boucheron, Baby Phat, Diesel, Rammstein, Mágnum, Nina Ricci, Festina, Custo, Carrera y Carrera, Caramelo, Codorniu, Mango Adorably and Loewe.

Do you also exhibit your work?
Three years ago I entered a photographic competition and was awarded the Photography's National Reward ABC. I realized then that it was not only my mother who liked and appreciated my photographs. After that I was contacted to exhibit my work at 'After the mirror' at the Museum of Contemporary Art Reina Sofía in Madrid. Other exhibitions have followed including: BAC (Barcelona Arte Contemporáneo) in the CCCB of Barcelona; Circuit 8 (Art and Fashion) in Barcelona; 'La Santa' (Space of Experimentation and Contemporary Creation); FEM (Art Edition Madrid's Festival).

In 2005 I was awarded a Gold Lion in Cannes for my PlayStation photographs and I have also won the award for the Best Art Project at FEM IV.

Other work has included the 2007 Lavazza calendar, adverts for Nina Ricci and Loewe, and I participated in PhotoEspaña, in the Naarden Fotofestival in Holland. I have also exhibited my work in the Parisian gallery Bertin-Toublanc in the Photography Festival of Miami.

How would you describe your photographic style?
Many people ask me about my 'recent obsession' with fairy tales. I have never been particularly interested in them, until one day I discovered that many fairy stories are more interesting than many things that purport to be fantastic today.

There are references throughout fairy tales that inspire me; I enjoy distorting them
and projecting my own vision on them, as I do with film or painting.

I enjoy creating characters with a story behind them. I'm not interested in
women or men in a posture, but in characters captured during a moment of
their lives.

What is your dream project?
Nowadays I'm very interested in videos and film making and I've been working
on videos like 'Para Nada', 'Silk' or 'Essence' – you can see them on my
website, www.eugeniorecuenco.com – and I am now trying to develop my
work in the world of video and film making.

Modelling Agencies

There are many agencies worldwide advertising their businesses on the internet. Models are usually required by agencies from the age of 14–22 years old, and to be a fashion model you should be between 168 cm (5 ft 7in) and 180 cm (6 ft) in height. If you are under 18 years old you will require parental consent to appear on the books of an agent.

You should thoroughly research any modelling agency you plan to approach, finding out which models they represent and who their clients are and where they are based. If you are interested in a career in modelling it is important that you register with a reputable agency that will organize modelling assignments and manage all the business aspects for you. Most modelling agencies now request details via email, supported by images – including full length and portrait images – to support the application. If the agency is interested in seeing you they will then contact you. If a model scout approaches you, check their credentials by contacting the agency they represent.

Modelling Portfolio

When approaching an agency initially a few snapshots showing a full length image, a portrait and a profile shot should be sufficient. Agencies are experienced enough to be able to spot any possible potential. Don't pay to have an expensive portfolio of photographs produced. If they legitimately want you on their books they will produce the photographs and a composite card individual to you, giving your details: name and height; chest, waist and hip measurements; as well as hair length and eye colouring, supported by images demonstrating your versatility as a model.

The modelling world is a tough and competitive world and you have to be realistic – do you really have those unique qualities, attitude, stamina and potential to be successful?

Typical Requirements

===

* ✖ *At least 168 cm (5 ft 7 in) tall*
* ✖ *Excellent hair, skin and figure*
* ✖ *Poise, posture and presence*
* ✖ *Confidence*

===

Model Booker

Model bookers work within modelling agencies and represent a selection of allocated models. This involves building up a model's profile and assisting in building their portfolio; making sure they get the right kinds of jobs; assisting them in organizing their work and casting schedules; negotiating their fees. The work is fast-paced and can be stressful. A good knowledge of the industry is a must. Model bookers need patience for coping with working to tight schedules and organizing the models' travel, security and itinerary of events.

Typical Skills Required

==

✖ *Excellent organizational and administration skills*
✖ *Confidence*
✖ *Strong negotiating skills*
✖ *Ability to multi-task*
✖ *Patience*

==

Model Scout

A model scout represents a modelling agency and it's their job to discover the next new face and to recruit new models. They must have a good understanding of what's happening in the fashion industry, and what the next new 'look' is. They will attend events, visit clubs, and scour the high street for what potentially is the next big look. A model scout must be confident, outgoing and friendly and be able to work independently handing out modelling agency business cards to anyone who has the potential to be a model. Model scouts will often take photographs of potential models, which are then taken back to the agency and reviewed by the agents to decide on the person's suitability to work on modelling assignments within the agency.

Typical Skills Required

==

✖ *Ability to spot the next new face of modelling*
✖ *Understanding of trends*
✖ *Confident, outgoing and friendly*
✖ *Ability to recognize potential model talent*

==

High-profile campaign shots featuring some of View Management's male models

View Management: Modelling Agency

View Management modelling agency in Barcelona, Spain was established in 2004 by Tom Buxeder, and represents both male and female models for runway, campaigns and commercials. View Management has many international clients around the world with models working for high fashion brands which include Armani, Hugo Boss, Dolce & Gabbana, Tom Ford, Etro and Trussardi.

An Interview with View Management

What is your career history?

As a matter of fact, I myself took my first steps in the fashion world as a model. During this time I learned about the fashion industry, its wants and its needs. I continue to profit from this experience, because I just know how the models have to perform, what hard work it is and what they are capable of doing.

After modelling I worked as a booker in Madrid for several years, which allowed me even deeper insights into the world of fashion and trends. During this time I met many people from different brands and companies, and made my most important contacts for the future on both sides. I knew all the models on the markets worldwide and I had the client contacts on the other side.

How important is networking to your agency in finding new clients?

Knowledge of the market is, as in any other business, essential for running a business. I grew up in this world and was fortunate enough to meet many great people with whom I work wonderfully well. I am friends with many of them and together we actively try to enhance working conditions for models and work out new ways to give potential new faces better opportunities.

How do you find new models?

New faces play a very important role in our daily work. I have my own unique way of selecting potential models. The Spanish press once called it 'the eye'. Some I looked very hard for, and others walked by me on the street. Several of these discoveries are some of the best in the world today.

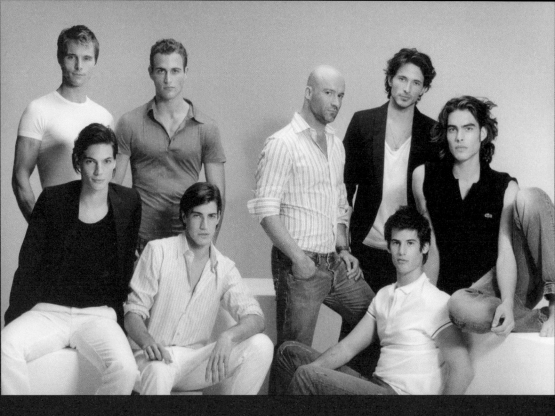

Group shot of male models, showing the range of looks catered for by the agency.

Do you help new models in creating their photographic portfolios?

Definitely: a model's book is, so to say, a model's sales proposal. It is the first – sometimes even the only – thing that clients will see of a model in order to make their decision.

What advice would you give to someone who is interested in modelling as a career?

If you want to work as a model, you have to be 100 per cent convinced. Modelling will influence your life very much. You will experience high physical and mental stress, and you have to be very responsible for yourself. Furthermore you need to be reliable, loyal and trustworthy towards clients and your agency.

To get started working as a model you first have to be self confident and realistic about yourself. Look for agencies that might be interested in your type of person and do not hesitate to send the pictures right away.

Despite these requirements, the stress and long working hours, working as a model is a wonderful thing to do and for me the best way to earn a living there is.

Chapter 5: Alternative Career Options

*Y*ou may have trained in fashion and textiles but, having come to the end of your studies, realize that a career in the fashion and textile industry is not for you; or maybe you want a change of career. So what are the alternative options? This chapter discusses opportunities that are available outside the fashion and textile industry which utilize similar skills.

Teacher Training

Due to the continuous demand for teachers and lecturers, many graduates choose to work in the education sector – teaching within a school, college or university environment. There are many opportunities available at all educational levels.

Most jobs in education will require some form of teacher training qualification. A teaching qualification may be your sole course of study or an additional postgraduate course, 'topping up' your previous qualifications. Courses vary from certificates in education to postgraduate certificates of study or courses at language academies, for example ESOL courses – teaching English to speakers of other languages. There are many excellent education websites that help you identify which qualification you need. Always check that a qualification is professionally and internationally recognized if you are interested in teaching in another country.

Typical Skills Required

==

✖ *Excellent communication skills*
✖ *Strong administration and organizational skills*
✖ *Ability to provide support, guidance and pastoral care to students*
✖ *Confidence in a classroom situation*
✖ *Proficiency in chosen specialist subject*

==

Graffiti workshop, producing a mural using graffiti imagery, held by Kamal Dollah at Outram Secondary School

Maria Manning:
University Senior Lecturer

Maria Manning studied fashion at the University of Derby, UK, and graduated in 1983 from Central St Martins College of Art, London, with an MA in Fashion. Following graduation Maria left the UK to work as a womenswear designer for the Italian fashion house Missoni. During this time Maria's work for Missoni was presented on the catwalk at the Milan Collections twice annually, and sold throughout Europe, America and Japan. Maria has also worked for Tom Scott, Orde of Jedburgh, Peter Barran and many other international designers, and her work has been exhibited in a range of trade and cultural exhibitions.

Since returning to the UK and successfully establishing herself as a designer, Maria continued to combine consultancy and freelance work with teaching fashion design and related subjects in further and higher education. She is now employed full-time as a Senior Lecturer in Fashion Studies at the University of Lincoln.

An Interview with Maria Manning

What advice would you give to someone who is interested in a career as a lecturer in higher education?

I think it is valuable to have several years' experience working within the industry and I would also recommend having a teaching qualification, as not only do you need subject knowledge, but also life experience: you need people skills and the ability to communicate, be caring and see individual students in a holistic way, making sure the students are absorbing the information, because everyone learns in a different way.

What is a typical day for a full-time lecturer in higher education?

Every day is different; an average day is likely to encompass writing and answering emails, teaching classes, giving lectures, group and individual tutorials and offering care and support to students, and attending meetings with colleagues...

What subjects do you teach?

My main teaching subjects are: fashion design, fashion illustration and the business of fashion on the BA (Hons) Fashion Studies programme. I am also a tutor on the BA (Hons) Fashion Studies programme, assisting students with their academic studies, and I mentor students on the MA Design Studies programme.

Other subjects taught within higher education fashion programmes include: tailoring, technical drawing, knitwear design, footwear design, millinery, fashion marketing, fashion communication and promotion, fashion buying, merchandising, fashion styling and photography, and fashion journalism etc.

What sort of commitment do you require to be a successful lecturer in higher education?

100 per cent commitment and interest in fashion, education and development of the course you are involved in.

Maria Manning, Senior Lecturer in Fashion, University of Lincoln, UK, advising a student on the development of a toile

How do you keep up to date with trends, industrial developments and new technologies?

I think you need to stay in touch with people in the industry – that is why it is so useful to have worked within the industry. You need to attend trade fairs, shows, exhibitions and other fashion-related events; reading newspapers, the fashion press and journals, especially the fashion journal *Drapers*, which is essential.

What opportunities are there to develop your own work within an institution?

Institutes encourage this. However, there are difficulties in balancing your own work commitments with other demands on your time in the fashion departments.

University Lecturer

Lecturing may be at undergraduate or postgraduate level within a university environment. The level of work is interesting and provides you with opportunities to keep abreast of industrial developments by attending conferences, meetings and seminars, with the opportunity to continue to develop your own professional work.

Lecturers are usually involved in the planning, design and development of teaching materials, the implementation of assessments and marking work, developing innovative teaching and learning methods, curriculum development, supervising students' work and research activities and developing collaborative links with industry, commercial, educational and other external organizations. The university sector encourages academics and subject specialists to continue their own personal development, working as practitioners and carrying out research, consultancy and collaborative projects.

Typical Skills Required

===

✖ *Keeping up to date with emerging fashion trends and developments in industry and education*
✖ *Subject-specific skills: design – womenswear, menswear, childrenswear, knitwear; pattern cutting; manufacturing; business; illustration and CAD*
✖ *Project writing*
✖ *Excellent communication skills*
✖ *Strong administration and organizational skills*
✖ *Research skills*
✖ *Ability to provide support, guidance and pastoral care to students*

===

Research Assistant

Research assistants are required in the media, forecasting, television, theatre, conservation centres and museums, and also by the academic sector, working within a research department. They are appointed to work alongside academics and research co-ordinators, assisting them in their work. The work involves supporting research, working on funded projects, assisting with the development of publications, indexing, proofreading copy and conducting interviews. Usually part of the job involves establishing focus groups, sourcing opportunities for research funding to financially support research projects nationally and internationally and assisting in the administration of bids. The position usually entails collecting and analyzing data, compiling databases and dealing with general administration related to research being undertaken.

Many research assistants in the academic sector will also work on their own independent or collaborative research project within the institution.

Many research assistant positions are advertised through academic websites and are usually on open or fixed term contracts. Most institutions require an undergraduate and postgraduate degree in the relevant subject specialism.

Typical Skills Required

==

✘ *Understanding of research methodology*
✘ *Excellent organizational skills*
✘ *Strong administrative and communication skills*
✘ *Highly motivated with the ability to work independently*
✘ *Ability to source grants and funding*

==

Fashion/Textile Technician: University/College Sector

Tricia Clark, Fashion Technician, University of Lincoln, UK, working with an undergraduate fashion student

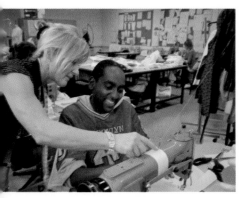

The principal role of a fashion/textile technician is to provide technical expertise and support in the teaching of fashion- and textile-related subject areas, with overall responsibility for managing workshops and studios. This usually includes preparing samples for demonstrations and providing technical assistance with machine handling and product development. This could include knowledge of sewing, knitting and linking machines, steam- and heat-transfer presses and weaving equipment, depending on subject specialist areas within the programme. Technicians are usually responsible for the care and maintenance of equipment and machinery, monitoring repair needs and undertaking general ordering and stock control. Safety in the workshop is all-important, and health and safety checks are usually administered by the technician.

Most technicians have received formal training through study on a fashion and technical production course and also have working knowledge of the industry.

Typical Skills Required

==

✘ *Understanding of machinery and equipment*
✘ *Strong organizational skills*
✘ *Highly motivated, with the ability to work independently*
✘ *Excellent practical skills in a specialist area*

==

Art and Design/Textile Teacher

Many graduates study to degree level in a specialist areas of design and then decide to enter the teaching profession, returning to their studies to complete a teacher training course. Teaching positions are available both full- and part-time, with opportunities and openings for supply teaching (when short-term cover is required for an absent teacher).

An art or textile teacher must have excellent knowledge and practical expertise in a broad range of art media. Teaching is a profession that requires dedication and patience but can be very rewarding. A career in teaching requires a good classroom practitioner, who is confident, enthusiastic, motivating and has strong management, communication and interpersonal skills.

Teaching responsibilities include lesson planning, delivering lessons, planning, organizing and assessing homework activities, classroom management, keeping student records, assessing work, preparing pupils for examinations and exam invigilation. Besides teaching their subject most teachers are involved in the general day-to-day activities within the school, such as involvement with parents evenings, organizing educational visits and assisting with or running extra-curricular activities including lunchtime and after-school art groups.

Typical Skills Required

===

* ✖ *Creative design skills*
* ✖ *Proficiency in a wide range of media*
* ✖ *Project writing*
* ✖ *Excellent communication skills*
* ✖ *Strong administration and organizational skills*
* ✖ *Ability to provide support, guidance and pastoral care to pupils*

===

Art Therapist

Art therapists usually work in the healthcare sector within specialist facilities in hospitals, medical units, community centres, education, detention centres, secure units or in private practices. The job usually involves working with the medical profession – psychologists, counsellors, social services and community support groups – and working with people of varying ages and backgrounds who may have psychological or sociological problems or physical difficulties. Art therapists usually work on a one-to-one basis or with very small groups of people. They offer support and encourage creativity, communication and freedom of expression through experimentation with art and design.

There are various pathways into a career in art therapy. Art therapists are usually graduates who have trained specifically in art therapy or who have studied in art and design and then developed their skills and learning by gaining a professional qualification and then become registered practitioners in art therapy through postgraduate study. Art therapy programmes include the study of human development, psychotherapy and therapeutic practices and techniques, and are supported by placements in educational, health and community care settings. Studio practice and creative workshops help to encourage the students to explore their own creativity and express themselves and their emotions through, for example, painting, sculpture, textiles, montage, collage, ceramics, print making and writing. Art therapy is a vocation that requires patience, understanding and creativity.

Typical Skills Required

==

✖ *Patience and sensitivity*
✖ *An excellent listener and observer*
✖ *Warm, friendly personality with a mature attitude*
✖ *Creative artist/designer*
✖ *Understanding of ethical procedures and standards and the regulatory framework required*

==

Community Artist

Community artists are usually trained artists or designers who choose to work on collaborative art projects with community groups. The work involves promoting the arts through community art schemes, contributing to the local community and providing opportunities for groups such as schools, youth clubs, the prison sector and arts organizations to work alongside an artist. The work could include school-based projects or running workshops with charity groups, for example.

Community artists usually have a wide knowledge of art skills crossing many disciplines. One week a community artist may be involved in a textile project with a community group, another time it may be a group mural in a town centre or an environmental or cultural project. There are many opportunities within this field of work. You must be flexible in your approach and be prepared to work in various locations.

Many community artists work freelance or part-time and are also practising artists or designers in their own right, exhibiting their own work and organizing workshops in their own studios.

Research grants, award schemes, sponsorship and funding are often available for community projects. Many professional artists and designers write and submit funding bids to arts councils for arts projects.

Lois Blackburn:
Community Artist/Illustrator

Lois Blackburn is a self-employed artist and textile designer who has a broad range of experience working in schools and colleges, delivering programmes in general textiles, embroidery, illustration, drawing, design, business skills and computer design. She has worked as an artist in residence in schools, libraries, education facilities and hospitals, and also worked as a community artist and a freelance illustrator.

An Interview with Lois Blackburn

How did you first become involved in community arts?
When I left college I was lucky enough to be employed as an 'artist in residence' in an adult education centre in Kent, UK. It was the first of many artist in residencies that gave me practical experience of working in the community.

Did you require any formal qualifications?
I left Manchester Polytechnic in 1991 with a first-class (Hons) degree in embroidery. I was employed to do those first arts projects because the employer liked my work and my project proposals. As your career develops, your experience certainly pays off, and I would recommend looking for placements and training schemes to give yourself a head start. I undertook various free training programmes in business, to assist me in setting up my own business.

Do you work on a freelance basis?
I'm a self-employed artist and illustrator and co-director and lead artist of the arts and health organization 'arthur+martha' CIC.

What projects have you been involved in?
I have facilitated numerous art workshops, working with all ages and abilities in a range of settings, such as primary school children, children at risk, older people in care, adults, family groups and holocaust survivors.

I have many years' experience within the arts and health field. In 2006 I worked with a colleague, experimental writer Philip Davenport, in setting up the community interest company 'arthur+martha'. We use innovative, contemporary, challenging art and writing techniques to work in collaboration with diverse communities.

What have been difficult projects for you?
Community arts projects often come with a steep learning curve. A recent one was working with young people in risk of exclusion from school. Their needs were complex and challenging, but in the end, with careful planning, most of our sessions stimulated great amounts of creativity and a good deal of fun too.

I often work with vulnerable and frail people, who suffer from depression, as well as multi-faceted physical health conditions. The work is incredibly rewarding, but some aspects are very emotive, especially as they reach the end of their lives.

Participant Hilda Hewitt and lead writer Philip Davenport, photographed during an arthur+martha workshop session

What is your dream project?
My dream project is one with a fantastic budget, supportive staff and venues, with guest artists stimulating and bringing new ideas and methods of working. The project would be of significant length to allow development of relationships and of the artwork. The project would be in easy commuting distance, with a good light and airy workspace, working with a fantastic group of older people and sharing the resulting work with the wider public at the end of the project.

What is the most enjoyable aspect of working as a community artist?
Working with people who challenge and question, stimulate, surprise, delight and make me laugh everyday. Being able to choose what the workshop content and theme is going to be… rather than sticking to a set curriculum.

Have you been involved in grant applications for specific projects?
I have worked on successful grant applications for arthur+martha, since it was formed in 2004. Next year we will be working with a professional fundraiser, as the process takes up so much time and energy.

Alongside your work as a community artist, do you also work as a solo artist exhibiting your own work?
Since graduating, I have exhibited my work all over the country. My illustration work has been used in a wide variety of media commissions: newspapers, magazines, greetings cards, wrapping paper, children's books, children's toys and promotional materials. Clients include: the *Times, MOJO, Yours, The Big Issue, The Spectator,* Manchester City Council, Lip International and Ling Design.

I have also worked on a range of different public art commissions in textiles, ceramics and mosaic.

What advice would you give to someone who wants to become involved in community arts programmes?
Get out there and get experience, apply for artist in residencies, write and introduce yourself to your local art officers and community groups. Do placements or volunteer on existing projects. Be prepared to work with lots of different client groups; you never know who you are going to gel with. You may be formally trained in one discipline, but you probably have transferable skills to work in others; try them if the options come up. Don't give up, it can be a really hard slog getting your work and yourself out there, but incredibly rewarding. Look out for courses in business or arts training. Get yourself a good mailing list, and use it. Create a website and update it regularly. Talk to others in the field, it can be isolating working on your own; share your experiences, whether with a web network group or people in the flesh. Most of all, try to have fun and always remember why you wanted to do it in the first place…

Pupils working on a group project in the Graffiti Workshop held by Kamal Dollah at Outram Secondary School

Typical Skills Required

==

✖ *A wide variety of creative skills that can be transferred and adapted to a variety of projects, encouraging and promoting an interest in the arts*
✖ *Excellent communication skills*
✖ *Patience*
✖ *Ability to work with people from all walks of life*
✖ *Sensitivity to working in a variety of situations, meeting peoples' needs*
✖ *Good organizational skills*
✖ *Ability to write funding proposals*
✖ *Ability to manage and work within a given budget*

==

Artist in Residence

Many schools and colleges, as well as other institutions, employ artists in residence. Every artist in residence experience will differ due to the terms and the length of the contract, which could range from a few weeks to a summer residency or annual residency, depending on the type of project commissioned. The job may require the artist to work alongside a school teacher or college tutor offering additional expertise in a specialist area and providing an interchange of ideas, or the artist may work in a hospital unit, art gallery, museum, youth centre or studio within the organization, offering people access to observe the work being produced with an agreement to have an open studio once or several times a month.

Residencies are often advertised in art and design magazines. Interested artists are usually requested to apply through a formal application process, including submission of a CV, completion of a project proposal, provision of examples of their work and an outline of the final outcome of the residency, which may be the commission of a piece of work, an exhibition or a project carried out with art and design students or the general public. Funding is usually available for residencies from a varied range of sources such as government schemes, council grants and association funding from specialist associations.

In return for the use of studio space, with access to facilities and additional use of equipment, the artist will share their skills through a range of workshops.

Typical Skills Required

==

✖ *Good communication and interpersonal skills*
✖ *Excellent creative skills in a specialist field*
✖ *Ability to work with a diverse group of people*
✖ *Ability to manage a workspace*
✖ *A wide variety of creative skills that can be transferred and adapted to a variety of projects, encouraging and promoting an interest in the arts*

==

Archivist

The term 'archivist' is very broad and involves the restoration, preservation and conservation of artefacts, and may involve working with clothing, textiles, general artefacts, books, papers, prints and videos, depending upon the nature of employment. Opportunities for employment usually involve working for local government, museums, national archives, associations and businesses, and may also involve working alongside editors, authors, publishing houses, the media industry, researchers and the general public.

The work includes identification of artefacts and individual objects; looking after, maintaining, handling, storing and packing items of historical value; managing and maintaining records; cataloguing and dealing with enquiries and researching for forthcoming exhibitions. Archivists may specialize in a particular area, for example costume and textile conservation or working in a museum environment.

Jobs are usually advertised through national newspapers or conservation societies. However, if you are interested in a career as an archivist it is useful to gain some experience working in a voluntary capacity at the local records offices, in a library or museum. It is also useful to join a professional body of archivists, such as The Society of Archivists, UK, which also provides a training scheme for archivists and conservators. Many archivists study a first degree in a specialist area and then choose to study further courses specializing in

The role of the archivist includes identifying, recording, maintaining and cataloguing artefacts such as this 1940s knitted lace doily and knitting pins

conservation and restoration, focusing on the theoretical knowledge and practical skills required for a career as an archivist.

Typical Skills Required

==

✖ *An organized and logical approach to your work*
✖ *Good communication and interpersonal skills*
✖ *An understanding of the ethical and theoretical implications of working in the areas of conservation and restoration*

==

Picture Researcher

A picture researcher (or picture buyer) sources, selects, edits and supplies visual material to the publishing and media industries. Finding the perfect image to support a magazine or journal article can be difficult and time consuming, so many companies employ picture researchers on a freelance basis or in a permanent position. A picture researcher must be able to understand the context of the material they are working with and will work very closely with the editorial team on a magazine or journal, with the editor and authors within a publishing house or a director on a film or television production.

Networking contacts are very important in the sourcing of images, which can be found through internet searches, picture libraries or direct contact with photographers, artists and designers. An image must be compatible to the text and must also be of the correct quality, resolution and format. To be successful working as a picture researcher you must have an excellent knowledge of information technology to complete internet research and supply images in the right format.

To get into this line of work it is useful to have skills in photography, with the ability to create and manipulate imagery and produce digital files. It is useful to complete a work placement in a publishing house or a picture library in order to appreciate and understand the processes of research and image selection.

Typical Skills Required

==

- ✖ *Editing, selecting, sourcing and supplying images*
- ✖ *Setting and managing budgets*
- ✖ *Negotiating reproduction fees*
- ✖ *Art direction and commissioning photographers*
- ✖ *Ability to liaise with editors and authors*
- ✖ *Computer-literate*
- ✖ *Good photographic knowledge*
- ✖ *A good comprehension of languages helps, enabling you to make international contacts*

==

Gap Year: Working Abroad

Many students opt to take a gap year, acting as a break from their education between school, college and university, or as a career break. There are many exciting opportunities out there, from taking a year out of your studies to travel with friends, to working on specific projects learning new skills and gaining experience. Some positions are voluntary, however many of the positions are salaried.

Many see a gap year as a once-in-a-lifetime opportunity for adventure, which can be challenging and life-enriching. It can also be a time to reflect on your future aspirations, your career or your life. You may make new friends and contacts globally, improve your language skills and broaden your general life experience.

The disadvantages of taking a gap year include the cost of travel and the impact of taking time out of your formal education, as well as the difficulties you may find in returning to the commitment of studying or work, and the safety aspects of travelling either alone or in a group.

Careful research and planning will help you think about all eventualities. If travelling is involved, find out what visas, work permits, travel insurance and vaccinations you may require. Consider your travel destination – the mode of transport, how long you intend to stay for and where you will be staying.

Annalaura Palma: Freelance Picture Editor and Picture Researcher

Annalaura Palma studied photography at the Istituto di Fotografia e Comunicazione Integrata in Rome. On successfully completing her degree studies Annalaura started working as a freelance picture editor/researcher, working on a wide range of publications on fashion, art and contemporary architecture.

She has gained an excellent reputation working for a wide range of companies which include: *Colours* magazine, Fabrica-Benetton, Treviso; The British Film Institute, London; The Illustrated London News Picture Library, London; *Internazionale* – a weekly current affairs magazine, Rome; La Terza Publishing, Rome; The *Sportsman*, London; *The New Yorker*, New York and the Istituto di Fotografia e Comunicazione Integrata, Rome and FotoGrafia – International Photography Festival, Rome.

An Interview with Annalaura Palma

How did you first become interested in this line of work?
While I was training as a photographer, I realized that I was as interested in seeing and editing photos as in taking photos. In addition I was always fascinated by how images work in the world: being a picture editor/researcher gives me the chance to explore the potential of pictures in our daily lives.

Did you have any formal training?
I studied photography and history of art which I am sure helped me to develop a good eye, which is essential if you want to succeed in this career. However, to do this job the most important thing is to have a true passion for pictures.

What is a typical number of publications that you work on at any one time?
The number of publications varies: a book could take six months but in the meantime you can work on other projects, depending on how good you are at being organized! For example, in the last six months I have been working on five different projects, but sometimes I have only had a couple of publications to work on and more time for myself!

How closely do you work with the author of a book and the editorial team?
I tend to work very closely with the editorial team and authors as I need to understand what the spirit of the publication is and its target audience before I start researching, commissioning and editing the images. Most of the time authors and journalists give you an idea of what they have in mind but it is for the picture researcher to translate this into pictures and the right images.

How important is the internet to your work?
The internet is essential for researching images. Most picture agencies and libraries have their pictures available online, which makes the work easier and faster but also, and most importantly, it is a great help to research images from outside the big agencies (for instance independent photographers, illustrators, artists, institutions, galleries, museums and commercial companies).

Annalaura Palma – Freelance Picture Editor/Researcher

What makes a successful picture researcher?

A good eye, a passion for researching the best image all the time even if the final image will only be tiny when it's published, or if the publication isn't great. You should be curious about your work and want to understand more about your project. Good communication skills are essential to create a good relationship with authors and editors and to understand exactly what they need.

Is there anything about your work as a picture researcher that has surprised you?

As a freelancer I work across different projects with different subjects and I am always surprised by how many things you can learn through this work, and how many interesting contacts you can make.

What advice would you give someone who was interested in a career as a picture researcher?

The best way to learn is to start working; invest your time in work experience instead of attending a course. The more experience you have the more your confidence will grow and you will feel in control of your project. I'd strongly recommend trying different environments: magazines, books, agencies, and start with something you like very much. For example, if you studied fashion try to gain work experience on a fashion magazine, where your academic knowledge will be very useful. Picture research work can be very exciting and creative but it's important to remember that you are responsible for everything concerning the images. A vital part of your work will involve negotiating the fees, clearing copyrights and licensing images so you must be organized and thorough as well as creative.

Chapter 6: Career Action Planning

*E*ntry into the fashion and textile industry is extremely competitive, with many highly qualified graduates leaving universities and colleges each year. Determination is essential to be successful in this rapidly changing industry. Your first position should allow you to put into practise all the skills you have learnt at university or college. During your working career it is then usual to change positions several times, gaining new experience and giving you a greater understanding of how different companies work.

Before you begin job hunting, whether you are looking for your first position within the industry or seeking the next step up in your career, it is important to consider what you want from your career, to research potential careers and then, having chosen a path, to analyze your skills against those required for potential jobs. This process is called the 'career action plan'.

This chapter looks at three stages in this process before examining how to pull all your research together in support of a job application by writing a curriculum vitae (CV), filling in an application form, and composing a covering letter.

CAREER CHOICE

Consider:
What you want from a job or career and where you want to work

Different options – discuss them with a careers officer, course tutor or industry practitioner

RESEARCH CAREER

Research:
What the career involves and the qualifications required. You may need to think about undertaking further full-time education, short courses, completing work placements, or an in-house training scheme within a company

Career guides and job specifications

ANALYZE SKILLS REQUIRED

Analyze:
What skills are required for the position and level of entry

Your own skills, and see how well they match those needed

Choosing a Career

When looking at your future career it is helpful to spend some time considering what you want from a career, where you want to work and your expectations of a position. Use the following list of questions to evaluate yourself:

- ✖ What type of career do I want?
- ✖ What are my short-term goals?
- ✖ What are my long-term ambitions?
- ✖ How achievable and/or ambitious are my goals?
- ✖ Do I intend to continue my studies in the future?
- ✖ What choices do I have?
- ✖ What do I have to offer?
- ✖ Will I have to retrain or upgrade my skills?
- ✖ Do I need to gain further experience?
- ✖ What type of work am I interested in?
- ✖ What kind of company would I like to work for?
- ✖ What size of company do I want to work for?
- ✖ Do I want to work for myself?
- ✖ Where do I want to work?
- ✖ Do I want to work in this country or an international market?
- ✖ What salary would be appropriate?
- ✖ Do I have strong administration skills?
- ✖ Do I have good keyboard skills?
- ✖ Do I have strong managerial and supervisory skills?
- ✖ Do I have good manual dexterity?
- ✖ Do I enjoy a challenge?
- ✖ Am I able to cope well under pressure?
- ✖ Do I enjoy implementing new ideas?
- ✖ Do I have a clean driving licence?

Reflect on your answers and see if there are any patterns to your responses. What is important to you? Consider which your strongest skills are. Do they meet your career aspirations? Analyze your career options by weighing up your answers. This exercise will help you to fully understand the opportunities available and will help you to manage your job search and career action plan.

Researching a Career

There are many ways to research a career. Visiting a careers centre and talking to an adviser is a good starting point. They will have a variety of guides available and may also know people working within the industry to whom you can talk; developing a network of contacts is a vital part of developing your career. Undertaking work placements is another way of extending your network while also allowing you to research a job and gain experience in the workplace (see Chapter 7, page 145). This type of research can also be undertaken on a gap year (see page 119).

There are many trade publications, directories and organizations who will also have useful background material about different jobs and careers, a selection of which are listed in the Resources Directory at the end of this book (see pages 240–249). It is also useful to look at jobs that are advertised – send off for the job specification and study the roles and responsibilities of a particular position.

Of course, as a result of your research, you may find that you need additional qualifications. If you have previously studied to undergraduate degree level, there are now many opportunities available to study internationally at postgraduate level on a subject-specific programme of study: MA, MPhil or PhD. Studying abroad gives you the opportunity to experience living and working in a different economic and cultural climate, expanding your professional qualifications beyond undergraduate level. However, always check that a qualification is internationally recognized before embarking on a course of study.

Analyzing Your Skills

Career action planning involves analyzing and identifying your skills and abilities, which is an important process in successfully finding employment. Having identified a career path, it is useful to analyze your skills against those required for a job in terms of your level of ability and the level of experience you have to offer. This chart outlines the process of analyzing skills, showing you how to identify your level of ability and evaluate supporting qualifications and evidence.

Skills Analysis Chart

Skill identified	Level of ability	Qualifications/evidence
Example: Accurate pattern cutting	Confident in flat pattern cutting, modelling on the stand and pattern grading	Degree in Fashion Studies with units in technical production
Example: Good working knowledge of computer programs	Microsoft Word PowerPoint Microsoft Excel Proficient use of Adobe Photoshop and Illustrator	Short courses in computer literacy (identify) Short courses in CAD (identify)
Example: Adept at fabric and trim sourcing	Good book of industrial contacts Knowledge of industry	Work experience (identify) Regular attendance at national and international trade fairs Sourced fabrics and trims for a denim womenswear collection
Example: Strong administration skills	Keyboard skills Computer-literate	Administration position working as an office junior over a given time period (identify)
Example: Creative design skills	Good supporting technical knowledge Understanding of trends	Successful completion of a degree in fashion design (identify) Completion of a denim womenswear collection for design through to production (identify) An up-to-date portfolio of design work Regular attendance at trend forecasting seminars (identify)

Now fill in the following chart (extending it as necessary) identifying your own skills, the level of your ability and your qualifications or other supporting evidence. This will help you appreciate your strengths and will assist you in writing your CV and filling in application forms and personal statements. Many people undersell their abilities, taking for granted their strengths and their experience and what they can offer a company. It will also help you to identify where you need to improve, enabling you to work out a strategy to achieve the job of your dreams or to take the next step on the career ladder.

SKILL IDENTIFIED	LEVEL OF ABILITY	QUALIFICATIONS/EVIDENCE

The following list of self-promotional words may also help you to identify your skills and abilities. Look at the list and select words that describe you and your skills. These are good words to use on your CV, application forms, covering letters and personal statements.

Self-Promotional Words

Able	Efficient	Persistent
Ability to mix at all	Encouraging	Personable
levels	Energetic	Persuasive
Accommodating	Enterprising	Poised
Accomplished	Enthusiastic	Positive
Accurate	Entrepreneur	Practical
Adaptable	Experienced	Principled
Adroit	Expert	Productive
Adventurous	Flexible	Professional
Alert	Focused	Proficient
Ambitious	Friendly	Punctual
Analytical	Generous	Purposeful
Appreciative	Good team leader	Quick-thinking
Approachable	Good time-keeper	Rational
Articulate	Hardworking	Reliable
Artistic	Highly motivated	Resilient
Assertive	Honest	Resourceful
Astute	Imaginative	Responsible
Bilingual	Independent	Robust
Bright	Informed	Self-assured
Calm	Innovative	Self-confident
Capable	Intelligent	Self-motivated
Capacity to thrive	Inventive	Sensitive
under pressure	Investigative	Spirited
Caring	Knowledgeable	Sociable
Collaborative	Lively	Strong researcher
Committed	Logical thinker	Successful
Communicator	Loyal	Supportive
Competent	Mature	Team worker
Confident	Methodical	Technical
Conscientious	Motivated	Tenacious
Consistent	Multilingual	Thorough
Controlled	Negotiator	Thoughtful
Co-operative	Networker	Trained
Creative	Objective	Trilingual
Decisive	Open-minded	Trustworthy
Dedicated	Organized	Unique
Dependable	Original	Versatile
Determined	Outgoing	Vigorous
Diligent	Outstanding	Visually imaginative
Diplomatic	Patient	Willing
Dynamic	People-oriented	
Educated	Perceptive	
Effective	Performer	

Your CV

Your CV is an important promotional document that provides a brief professional history. This is your first opportunity to make a good impression and is the first step to gaining that job. A CV can be used when responding to job vacancies, applying for sponsorship, approaching a company requesting a work placement or cold-canvassing a company, enquiring into suitable vacancies for full- or part-time work. It is not required when applying for a position using a company application form (unless requested), as it would duplicate most of the information on the form. When sending out a CV, always include a covering letter to support your application. (See page 134.)

Writing a CV

When writing a CV, consider the type of employment you are seeking and think about the type of skills that are required for the position. A CV should be word processed in a clear typeface (such as Arial or Tahoma) and printed in black ink on plain, good-quality white or cream paper (or saved as a PDF file). It should be grammatically correct (run a spell check and ask someone else to read it), the layout should be easy to read and it should be one or two pages in length.

Information to Include

==

✖ *Personal details: name, address including postcode, phone/fax number, mobile, email address, date of birth and nationality. When including an email address, always use one that projects a professional image.*

✖ *Personal profile/statement: a brief statement identifying your personal attributes, for example:*
'A highly motivated fashion graduate with experience in designing for both the menswear and womenswear markets. Enthusiastic, dedicated and hardworking with an outgoing personality and the ability to communicate at all levels.'

'A fashion graduate with strong technical skills in pattern drafting, pattern grading and garment construction. Knowledge of both flat pattern cutting and modelling on the stand with the ability to develop garments from fit sample through to production. Hardworking, reliable and highly motivated, with the ability to meet deadlines and work under pressure.'

'A highly creative illustrator with an excellent understanding of trends, colour and computer applications. Good understanding of the use and application of a range of media techniques, with the ability to work to tight deadlines.'

'A creative knitwear designer with five years' experience developing knitwear ranges for the high street with a good working knowledge of both cut and sew and fully fashioning processes. Enthusiastic and outgoing personality who enjoys working using own initiative and also enjoys working as part of a team.'

✖ *Education history: in this section, list the schools, colleges and/or universities you have attended, in chronological order with the most recent first. Highlight any awards and qualifications achieved. For example:*
'BA (Hons) Fashion Studies, University of the South Pacific 2008–2011
Subjects studied: Fashion design, pattern cutting and grading, garment construction, fashion forecasting, knitwear design and illustration techniques.'

✖ *Employment history: state employment experience and track record, identifying work responsibilities, summarizing specific duties and what the role entailed. List positions in chronological order with the most recent first. For example:*
'Garment Technologist – Childrenswear, Jeanie Clothing, USA 2006–2008
Development of childrenswear department with the responsibilities for fit, grading and quality control through the garment development process and production.'

✖ *Work experience: identify previous relevant experience, briefly noting roles and responsibilities completed during the placement. For example:*
'The Fashion and Textile Design Group, New York, USA 2005–2006
Areas of responsibility included working in the editorial department, assisting the Fashion Editor, reading and checking copy, preparing and pressing garments for fashion shoots, phoning companies and organizing refreshments.'

✖ *Other skills/additional information: in this section list any further skills. For example:*
Good working knowledge of software packages (specify, for example: Microsoft Word, Adobe Photoshop, Adobe Illustrator, Lectra, Gerber).
Strong illustration and presentation skills using a range of media
Clean driving licence.

✖ *Activities and interests: adding interests and hobbies to your CV is optional but provides the employer with further information as to what sort of person you are.*

✖ *References: it is usual to include the details of two referees, including names and contact details, but it's also quite acceptable to write 'References available on request'. Always ask your intended referee if they'd be happy to be contacted in this capacity.*

✖ *Don't include salary requirements; this can be discussed later on, if you are offered the position.*

It is important to keep your CV up to date, changing it as you develop new skills, attend short courses and gain more experience; as a result, your CV will improve over time. Always ensure that all the information on your CV is relevant to the position you are applying for, highlighting the skills that match the post you want. Treat each job application individually and respond to the job description. Learn to analyze job adverts and descriptions by reading the information carefully and identifying what the company is looking for in an employee. Break down the job description and consider carefully how your skills and abilities fulfil their requirements. If you are seeking a position in design it is a good idea to attach an A4 sheet of your most relevant work, providing examples of your design work for the interviewer's reference.

Make sure all information included on your CV is accurate, truthful and correct. Making up additional qualifications and experiences is very dangerous and can easily backfire. If your employer checks your references, qualifications and employment details and finds them to be incorrect, this could lead to you being fired or even prosecuted.

Professional CV services will write and print a CV for a fee. However, this does tend to be an expensive option and there are free government sources that offer useful assistance. Alternatively there are excellent publications and computer programs that offer guidance in completing a CV and producing well-written letters of application.

Major CV Errors

==

✘ *Poor spelling and punctuation*
✘ *Underselling your skills*
✘ *Poor layout making the CV difficult and time-consuming to read*
✘ *Use of gimmicks*

==

Example CVs

The Europass CV

The European CV was launched in 2002 and has been replaced by the Europass CV, an initiative of the European Commission developed to provide greater understanding and recognition of education, qualifications and training throughout Europe. The National Europass Centre has been established to provide information relating to the Europass documents. Some companies may request that you submit a Europass CV; this is a standard CV identifying education, training qualifications, work experience, language ability and other skills and abilities. Blank templates for the CV are available in thirteen different languages supported by instructions and completed examples for reference from the Europass website.

CV

Sarah Lau	Green Gables, 19 St Mary's Green, York, YO3 4NX UK
	Tel: (00000 000000) Email: sarahlau@email.co.uk
Date of Birth	27/09/70
Nationality	British

Personal Statement

Experienced and creative designer with innovative pattern cutting skills in both woven and knit fabrics. Commercially aware of the retail market. Good practical administration skills and able to present informative reports and complete professional presentations understanding the importance of marketing and promotion.

Education and Qualifications

1992–1993	Postgraduate Certificate in Art Education	University of Southfields, UK
1992–1993	Art Teachers Diploma in Education	University of Southfields, UK
1989–1991	BA (Hons) Fashion and Textiles	University of Leicester, UK
	(Fashion design, pattern cutting, manufacture, illustration, fashion forecasting, knitwear design and the business of fashion)	
1987–1988	Foundation in Art and Design, Cumbria College of Art & Design	

Employment

2008–2010	Established Company – Design Line Ltd
	Produced short-run fully fashioned knitwear ranges for independents – teen market
2007–2008	Knitwear Designer/Sampler – freelance; Olan Knits, Anna Tryntja
	Produced concept boards for exhibitions, promoting new yarn ranges, pattern writing and sampling for new ranges
2004–2006	Fashion Illustrator – freelance; Knit Styling – Trends Forecasting Agency
	Illustrated and produced design ideas for knitwear prediction packages
1999–2004	Designer and Range Builder – part-time, The House of Colour
	Development of new collections and sample ranges promoting new yarns, working closely with design team and buyers
1997–1999	Junior Knitwear Designer – Maden Ltd, London, UK
	Collating mood boards and sample boards, assisting in the development of design and sample ranges, drawing up specs

Achievements/Awards

Bilingual: English and Cantonese
Computer-literate: Word, Adobe Photoshop, Adobe Illustrator

Membership/Association

Textile Institute

Interests and Activities

Flying, dancing, skiing, reading, interior design

Referees   Available on request

Online CVs

Due to the boom in online recruitment and the use of cyberspace to advertise jobs, online or electronic CVs have become a popular marketing tool to promote and showcase skills and talents on the internet 24 hours a day, and can be changed and updated instantly and easily accessed from anywhere in the world. An online CV can be very useful if you are travelling or having a gap year, making it an efficient way to promote yourself and add to the marketability of your work.

When designing an online CV it is important to use a simple format (PDF) to make the CV quick to download and access, whether you are using the latest technology or an old computer. The content should include a brief careers statement, details of your skills, qualifications, education and contact details. Remember never to disclose your personal details such as home address,

---

CV

Lisa Jane Johnson

New York, USA
Email: ljj1978@email.com

Career Profile A highly motivated and experienced garment technologist with 10 years' industrial experience, who enjoys working in a challenging environment and thrives under pressure.

Career History

2004–present   Production Technologist, Mardens Ltd. New York
Experienced working with the design team and pattern room to manage production, producing technical specs, liaising with international factories. Worked closely with buyers to achieve quality-led products.

2000–2004   Assistant Product Technologist – Denli Junior Group, New York
Experience of working with both jersey and woven fabrics. Production of technical flats, assisting with pattern room production, assessing samples, components and implementing revisions.

1999–2000   Assistant Product Technologist – Mardens Ltd. New York
Experience of working with woven fabrics, producing design flats and assessing samples.

Education and Qualifications

1996–1999   Bachelor of Science in Production Management, Fashion Institute of Technology, New York, USA
Factory Processes; Product Analysis; Materials Management; Production and Manufacturing; Processes, Cost Accounting, Global Sourcing

1995–1996   Patternmaking Certificate Programme, Fashion Institute of Technology, USA
Developing patterns, pattern making techniques, industrial techniques, grading, pattern layout, construction techniques

Employability Skills

Five years' womenswear design experience
Knowledge of computer programs: Microsoft Word, Photoshop
Good knowledge of flat pattern cutting and modelling on the stand
Strong fabric and trim sourcing
Bilingual – Italian, English

Achievements/Awards

1999   Presented garments in University Fashion Show, Milan

1998   Student Mentor and Year Representative, Nova Accademia Di Belle Arti Milan

Additional Information

Clean driving licence

Interests   Travel, Music, Swimming, Tennis, Skating

References   Available on request

telephone/mobile number and date of birth, which could be stolen and used by someone else. It is important to protect yourself from potential identity theft.

Keep this type of CV to one page, making sure the layout is simple and easy to read, inserting key words and identifying the type of employment you are looking for and the skills you have to offer. Often employers will type in key words to search for new recruits on CV-hosting websites. Include a website link if you have one, as this offers substance, adding further opportunity to promote your skills, work and employment prospects. Your website could include visuals to support your online CV.

Covering Letter

Always write a covering letter to accompany a company application form or a CV; it should reiterate the main points in your CV. The covering letter should be targeted at a specific person in a company if possible. (This may involve contacting the company by phone and making a few discreet enquiries.) Keep the covering letter short, never exceeding one page in length, with two to four paragraphs that are focused and to the point. The letter should identify the job title and reference number in the first paragraph, followed by a brief statement identifying your background skills, why you are applying for the position and what you are able to offer the company. Read the job description carefully and select one or two key areas that utilize your skills and experiences and include this information in the letter. The aim of the covering letter is to convince the recruiter that you are a possible candidate to consider for the position, and then this should lead onto the CV.

Always proofread all covering letters and CVs, reading through them several times; carefully checking and re-checking your spelling, punctuation and grammar. Many recruiters will dismiss an application if they find any error in a covering letter, application form or CV.

Important Points to Remember

==

✖ *If you know the person's name write to them specifically, for example:*
   Dear Mr Jones... (This letter should conclude: Yours sincerely...)
✖ *If you do not know the person's name (if you're writing to Personnel, for example):*
   Dear Sir/Madam... (This letter should conclude: Yours faithfully...)
✖ *Write clearly and formally. Include all punctuation – commas, full stops, capital letters – where and when required.*
✖ *Always put your address in full including the correct postcode.*
✖ *Use good quality white or cream paper and envelopes.*

==

Example Letter of Application

Your address
Including postcode

Date

Name and position of addressee
Department
Address of company
Including postcode

Dear Ms Lindsay

Re: Assistant Designer

I wish to apply for the position of Assistant Designer, as advertised in *(name of journal and publication date)*. I am in my final year of study on the BA (Hons) Fashion Studies programme at the University of Northfields and will graduate in June. My degree classification is expected to be a 2.1.

(In this paragraph it is important to identify any relevant information relating to your course or your previous experience that demonstrates you have the skills that are identified in the job description.)

I am available to attend an interview at your convenience and this would provide me with the opportunity to present my portfolio, which is available for viewing, demonstrating both my design and technical skills. If you require any further information regarding my application please do not hesitate to contact me.

Thank you for taking the time to consider this application. I look forward to hearing from you in the near future.

Yours sincerely

(Signature)

Jayne Smith (Print name)

Cold-Canvassing

Many jobs in the fashion and textile industry are never advertised formally and can be found only by word of mouth. If you are interested in working for a particular company it is worth contacting the company directly in writing (enclosing your CV), or alternatively by email or telephone, to offer your skills and experience. This speculative approach to job hunting is called cold-canvassing, marketing your knowledge and skills directly.

Advertising company vacancies can be an expensive and long drawn-out business that takes time. Occasionally, due to someone suddenly leaving a company, a restructure, illness or a company being generally short-staffed, a position becomes available that needs to be filled as a matter of urgency and you may just be the right person, in the right place, at the right time. Cold-canvassing is definitely worth trying.

Cold-Canvassing by Email

It's now common practice to cold-canvas by email. Do remember, though, that it is important to give a very professional image even when using this more informal medium. When emailing never use 'text language' and always run your letter through spell check and make any amendments where necessary.

Completing an Application Form

When you are completing an application form, follow the instructions carefully. It is advisable to photocopy the form first and complete a rough draft before attempting the final version. Read the whole form thoroughly and the job specification carefully. Often, employers will ask you to offer evidence of your suitability, which gives you the opportunity to promote your skills and personal qualities.

When sending off an application form, complete a short covering letter to introduce yourself and to support your application (see page 134). Always photocopy your completed application form to refer to if you are called to an interview.

Example of a Speculative Approach Letter

Your address
Including postcode

Date

Name and position of addressee
Department
Address of company
Including postcode

Dear Mr Gabbons

I am at present studying in my final year on the BA (Hons) Fashion Studies course at the University of Eastfields, UK. I am writing to enquire if you have any vacancies in your company. I enclose my CV for your reference, supported by examples of my work.

I am a person who is… (Include information about your skills and how they could benefit the company you are approaching – refer to the list on page 127.)

I have excellent references and an up to date portfolio of my design work is available for viewing. I would be delighted to discuss any possible current or future vacancies with you at your convenience. In case you do not have any suitable openings at the moment, I would be grateful if you would keep my CV on file and notify me of any future openings, which would enable me to use my knowledge and skills.

Thank you for your consideration. I look forward to hearing from you in the near future.

Yours sincerely

(Signature)

Jayne Smith

Example of a Standard Application Form

STANDARD APPLICATION FORM *Please complete in BLACK ink or typescript*

Post title for which you are applying............................... Post Ref No ....
Title (Mr/Mrs/Miss/Ms/Dr/Prof).............................. Surname ....
Forename(s)...............................
Address...............................
....
.... Post code...............................
County .... Tel. day...............................
Email............................... Tel. evening...............................
Fax no............................... Tel. mobile...............................
Date of birth............................... Marital status...............................
Nat. Ins. number............................... Are you a licensed car owner? Yes/No...............................
Are you registered disabled?...............................
(If yes, please give details)...............................

Employment History – *please state exact dates where possible*

Current or most recent work experience (including voluntary work experience)

Name and address of employer...............................
....
Job title and brief description of position...............................
Start date............................... Date of leaving...............................
Full time or Part time............................... Salary/grade...............................
Notice required...............................

Previous work experience – *please continue on a separate sheet if necessary*

Date from	Date to	Employer's name and address	Job title	Full or part time	Salary / grade	Reason for leaving

Education

Date from	Date to	Name of institution	Level of study	Date	Subject	Grade

Further or Higher Education

Date from	Date to	Name of institution	Qualifications obtained	Grade

Training

Name of institution or correspondence college	Title and nature of course

Membership of professional bodies

Name of institution	Membership details

Any further information in support of your application (*Please attach further sheets if necessary.*)

References

Please provide the name, addresses and telephone numbers of two persons to whom professional references can be made, one of whom should normally be your present or last employer.

Note: references are usually taken up immediately, in respect of candidates selected for interview. Please place an 'x' in the relevant box if you do not wish us to contact your referee prior to interview.

Personal Statements

Most application forms request a personal statement (sometimes called 'further information'). This can be broken down into three main areas: introduction, main section and summary.

The introduction should include a brief statement identifying the position you are applying for, where and when you saw the position advertised and why you want to apply for the position.

The main body of the text should outline your past experiences and the knowledge and skills you can bring to the job and the company, identifying the roles and responsibilities that the employment position entails. It is important to gear your personal statement to the job you are applying for, stating what attracted you to the position, exactly what you are capable of doing and, most importantly, offering evidence of your suitability.

The summary should reiterate your reason for applying for the position of employment and state your interest in applying for the job.

Always check through your work carefully and get someone to proof read the statement and check that it meets the criteria of the job specification.

Example of a Personal Statement

I would like to apply for the position of Trainee Graduate Retail/Fashion Recruitment Officer, as advertised in *(journal and date)*.

I recently graduated from the Xxxxxx in France after successfully completing the BBA Degree in Design and Management, with the award of a 2.1 classification. On the programme I studied units including: fashion design, business studies for fashion, professional practice, fashion studies, brand marketing and production, product development and selection. I also completed a Graduate Training Programme consisting of one-to-one training and structured group training sessions to support my career development, enabling me to offer the company a good understanding of the complex nature of the industry. This should help me to make an impact within the company by being involved in all aspects of recruitment including: cold-calling new and existing clients to develop new job opportunities, managing existing client relationships and developing new business. I am confident in meeting new clients for one-to-one business meetings organized to discuss opportunities to sell their services and I feel able to give presentations to new clients selling the company's services.

I have good working knowledge of computer programs such as Microsoft Office, which will assist me in the day-to-day organization of databases, as well as planning and giving presentations.

During my degree studies I completed a three-week internship with Graduate Fashion Ltd, London, UK. My work placement provided me with the opportunity to work within the recruitment sector, assisting the Graduate Recruitment Officer with general running of the office, advertising vacancies online, registering a range of professional candidates for temporary, contract and permanent work and preparing and arranging interviews for candidates with clients.

Through my graduate studies and work experience I consider that I would be able to work productively within the company meeting the challenges of working in this exciting industry working independently using my own initiative and also contributing well in team situations. I have a strong work ethic, being conscientious, punctual and able to work under pressure to meet deadlines.

I would be delighted to be considered for the position of Trainee Graduate Retail Recruitment Officer and I am available to attend an interview with you at your convenience.

If you require any further information to support my application, please do not hesitate to contact me.

Lori Sinclair

(Date)

Chapter 7: Job Hunting

Y*ou need to take job hunting seriously if you are to be successful. It helps to know where to start looking, which organizations can help you, and who to contact. You have to use your initiative to stay ahead. This chapter discusses how to manage your job search, where jobs are advertised and what employment opportunities are available, and the importance of completing work experience and developing good networking skills to build business contacts.*

Managing Your Job Search

How many times have you heard people say 'searching for a job is a full-time job in itself'? This is due to the time it takes to research a vacancy and company, to send away for the job description, to complete the application form or apply online and to attend the interview (or interviews).

Most people apply for many jobs before achieving any real success. Some people are lucky and are appointed for the first job they apply for, while others apply for dozens of jobs before achieving any real success. It helps if you are highly organized so that you don't lose track of which companies you have contacted, who the contact person was and when and how you contacted them.

It is useful to write down all the details of your contacts, listing the company name and address, the name of the person you have contacted, their position within the company and when you contacted them (see the form on page 142). Keep a copy of the letter or email you sent for reference, details of any correspondence, how you followed up on your initial contact and details of the outcome. Recording all the details and keeping a copy of any correspondence with a company will help you to keep track of your job applications. It may also help you to see patterns, showing what you are doing right or wrong.

Pure, London, UK: fashion and textile trade fairs are important events for fashion buyers, designers and manufacturers, providing an update on industry developments and excellent networking opportunities

Managing Your Job Search

Company contacted	Name of contact	Contact details	Date	Follow up	Outcome
Belladonna Knitwear	Marie Therèse	Tel. no. Email address	10/02/2010	Contacted by phone and followed up with covering letter and CV. Sent 12/02/2010.	

Don't limit your search too early on; it is useful to keep an open mind and research different kinds of job. When looking for employment, whether it is your first job or a career move, it is important not to give up; persevere and use your time as productively as possible, gaining more experience through the completion of additional work placements and further training, thus adding vital experience to your CV and making you a marketable candidate for employment.

The Importance of Organization

One graduate's experience highlights how essential it is to be methodical in your approach to job hunting: after graduating with an Honours degree in Fashion Studies, specializing in knitwear design, Harriet applied for over 100 jobs – some advertised, others through word-of-mouth or by cold-canvassing companies. Because of the volume of her applications, she soon lost track of which jobs she had applied for and whom she had written to. Whenever the phone rang and it was a potential employer asking her to attend an interview she was forever scrabbling through masses of paper looking for a copy of the relevant correspondence, and consequently seemed unprepared and flustered. Despite attending several interviews she received no job offers.

Harriet knew that she needed to focus on developing her organizational and management skills, and took a course in interviewing skills. With a more realistic, organized and professional approach to her job hunting mission, just seven applications and seven interviews later she was appointed as an assistant designer, and within nine months was promoted to the position of designer. Addressing her approach to job hunting has ensured that, 15 years later, Harriet has never applied for a job without being offered the position, and now heads up a design team as Design Director. Being well organized pays off.

How and Where to Look for Vacancies

It is essential to have an active approach, to be forward thinking and to be one of the first to hear when vacancies and new opportunities arise. There are many places where you can look for vacancies, but here are some of the main sources.

✖ **Local and national newspapers:** keep abreast of what is happening in the industry through your local and national newspapers. Jobs are also advertised. Many newspapers now publish online editions.

✖ **Trade journals and specialist magazines:** keep up to date with what is happening in your specialist field. If you see that a company is expanding, contact them by sending an introductory letter and a copy of your CV. There may be new openings.

✖ **Local radio and television stations:** media internet directories provide live links to many local radio and television stations. Some radio and television channels advertise jobs on their news bulletins.

✖ **Professional associations and societies:** many international organizations provide sources of information, including industry updates, calendars of events (trade fairs, exhibitions and conferences), details of their newsletters and specialist publications, careers information, employment opportunities and vacancies.

✖ **Directories:** fashion and textile industry directories are published annually, listing details of companies and their specialist trade and providing an excellent source of information. (See Resources, page 240.)

- ✖ **Internet:** the internet offers an invaluable research tool for finding quick references or more detailed information. Use search engines as well as specialist websites and online directories to find companies, agencies, associations or just details of a particular designer label that you are interested in. Search trade associations and job websites for details of employment opportunities.

- ✖ **Company websites:** if you are interested in working for a particular company, check out their website – often vacancies will be listed. Company websites are frequently an excellent source of information when you are researching for an interview.

- ✖ **Recruitment agencies:** specialist fashion and textile recruitment agencies operate nationally and internationally. Research the agencies and find out who their clients are and then select one or two to register with. Always check with the agency what their recruitment policies are. You should not be charged a fee for registering (it is usually the client who is charged the fee on a position being filled). You can also find recruitment agencies online.

- ✖ **Local business centres:** local business centres offer varied services from short courses for starting up in business and training courses to support existing businesses, to conference facilities, managed office space and business units for rent. They also offer networking opportunities.

- ✖ **Careers centres:** these provide advice and guidance on writing CVs, job applications and interview techniques and may also advise on vacancies within the sector. Many centres offer training programmes to enhance your skills, as well as practical advice on the funding available for starting up a business venture.

- ✖ **Job centres:** they provide advice and guidance on training, and also advertise local and national job and business opportunities and provide assistance with the completion of application forms.

- ✖ **Recruitment events and fairs:** go to graduate recruitment fairs for careers information, networking opportunities, advice and guidance on the job market, the chance to meet company representatives and attend seminars.

- ✖ **Cold-canvassing:** if you are interested in working for a specific company it is worth contacting them directly by phone and discussing the possibility of any job opportunities. Find out the name of the person you need to speak to and if they are unavailable, send them a covering letter introducing yourself, supported by a current CV (see page 129). After a couple of weeks follow your letter up with a phone call.

- ✖ **Graduate training schemes:** these schemes offer in-house training and are a popular route into employment. Many recruit specifically into the areas of advertising, promotion, marketing, retail management, merchandising and buying. Many of the larger retail outlets offer training programmes but competition is fierce. Always look carefully at the closing date for applications – you are usually required to apply at least ten months before you complete your studies. You can usually find out about these schemes on specific companies' websites.

✗ **Head-hunting agencies:** head-hunters work to find the right candidate for a position on behalf of a company. Possible candidates are approached and vetted by the head-hunting agency.

Work Experience

Completing work experience provides you with the perfect opportunity for meeting new people and extending your list of contacts. Many job offers also result from the completion of successful work placements.

Work placements are often the first introduction people have to the world of work. They provide valuable experience and the opportunity to sample various career paths. A work placement can be stimulating, informative and helpful for career development, expanding your subject knowledge. Try to complete as many work placements or internships as you can – they will give you additional experience to support your qualifications, which could make all the difference to your search for a job.

Make the most of any work experience placement or internship, taking the opportunity to gain experience in as many areas of a company as possible, and taking on as much responsibility as you are able to deal with.

Why Should You Do a Work Placement?

===

✗ *To explore career paths that are of interest to you*
✗ *To gain first-hand experience of the industry you are interested in*
✗ *To give you a head-start in the job market*
✗ *To boost your confidence and motivation*
✗ *To provide an opportunity to network within the industry*
✗ *To secure a reference on successful completion of the work placement*
✗ *Possibility of sponsorship of future projects you are involved in*

===

What Do You Want to Achieve?

Think carefully about the length of time you are able to commit to a work placement. Many companies want an intern for a minimum of three months, while others are happy to offer a week's placement. Consider what you want to achieve from a placement. Do you want to shadow someone or participate in the day-to-day business of the company or would you rather spend time working in a team situation in one department, observing the team's daily routines, job responsibilities and duties?

If you are interested in completing a work placement or internship with a company find the address and details of the company, then consider the following:

✗ Where is their head office? It is important to understand the workings of the company – where their head office is located in relation to the rest of the company, for example, and the relationship between sites – what happens where.

✖ Who is the person to contact to discuss the organization of a work placement? Is it the head designer or human resources? (Ring up and discuss this with the receptionist, who should be able to advise you.)

✖ Ask to speak to the relevant person, and make a note of all the details and information you discuss.

✖ Send a copy of your CV (see page 129) to the relevant person, as an email attachment or with a short covering letter, introducing yourself and stating your experience, and requesting a work placement.

✖ If you are unsuccessful in finding a work placement with the first company you approach, keep trying.

Some Thoughts about Work Experience

'I've always been interested in buying, so when the opportunity arose to complete a work experience placement as a buyer for Oscar and Alison's in Skegness – a designer store – I jumped at the chance to work alongside fashion houses such as D&G, Hugo Boss and Ted Baker. My job involved spending three weeks in London helping the owner to choose the next season's stock.

'I got so much from the work experience: I felt I gained a good understanding of the world of fashion buying. I realized it may be fun and exciting, but also it's very hard work with long hours. After getting on so well in my work experience, I have had the privilege to carry on working with Oscar and Alison's over the last two years, choosing their autumn/winter and spring/summer collections.'
Gemma Clews

'Just looking for a work placement opens your eyes to how many career opportunities there are available in the fashion industry.'
Sophie Miller

'Makes you see what you can do in the fashion industry and helps you to realize what you can go into when you finish your studies.'
Cindy Yuan

'I really enjoyed my time spent during my work experience. It was exciting to see how the fashion industry works and to be part of it. This experience has made me a lot more confident about getting a job after graduating.'
Laura Smith

'My work placement helped me to better understand the textile industry and gave me confidence when applying for jobs.'
Paul Mason

'Through my university work experience in costume I've learned how to deal with clients, keeping to tight deadlines, and how to solve problems in garments without losing that creative edge! It has helped me to open my eyes to our constantly moving industry. From completing it I've achieved a fantastic fashion role.'
Stacey Richards

Networking

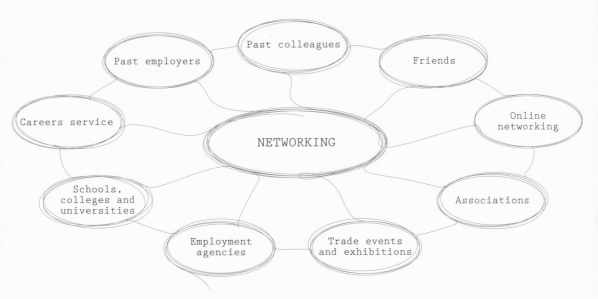

Networking is the process of developing new contacts (and maintaining existing ones). It is essential to make contacts within the industry, to enable you to share work-related information, to learn and develop new skills, to give and receive support and to develop future work opportunities.

There are many networking opportunities in the fashion industry, for example through attendance at business meetings, conferences, exhibitions and trade fairs where you can network with attendees, organizers and speakers.

In recent years many online networking sites have been developed to improve contact opportunities between professionals in similar industries and provide information relating to forthcoming business and social events. Many online networking sites are funded through membership subscriptions, but can be a useful networking tool, providing contact with people with similar aspirations.

Finally, always carry a business card with you, providing your contact details, to present a professional image. And always thank anyone who has helped you – you may need his or her help again. Do not take anyone for granted – from the Director to the office junior who may one day be your manager.

The Fashion Calendar

Research into the fashion calendar in order to attend trade shows and international events will help with your networking, allowing you to meet designers and agents and make many useful industrial contacts. Excellent fashion calendars are published in many of the fashion trade journals, listing national and international fashion and textile exhibitions, trade fairs, catwalk shows and events. Or you can search one of the online fashion websites that lists details of many of the major international fashion and textile trade fairs.

Exhibitions and Trade Fairs

International fashion and textile exhibitions and trade fairs present new collections of designs seasonally and offer excellent networking opportunities. Many exhibitions and trade fairs specialize in specific areas of the market such as ready-to-wear, womenswear, menswear, childrenswear, bridalwear, accessories or fabrics. These also showcase trend presentations, highlighting the seasonal key looks, and inspirational catwalk shows. Trade events provide an excellent opportunity for designers who are producing and presenting their first collection to reach a wide audience, enabling them to promote their products and services, make potential sales and attract media interest. However, you don't have to be an exhibitor to attend. You can also attend as a visitor and gain a greater understanding of how the industry works and keep up to date with the latest developments.

If you are considering attending a trade event, always check what the entry requirements are. Many trade events have very strict trade-only entry and request proof of identity; however with a little bit of initiative this can often be overcome. For many exhibitions and trade fairs visitors are requested to pre-register prior to the event. This can usually be done online with discounts offered on the entry fee. It also avoids great delays in having to queue to purchase tickets on the day of the event. Free floor plans are usually available, identifying which companies are exhibiting and where they are located. Catalogues are generally available to purchase, giving full contact details of all exhibitors and a brief summary of their trade. The details here give a very brief outline of the types of trade events held throughout the world, including events specializing in bridal/eveningwear, footwear and accessories. (See Resources, pages 245-246 for more details.)

Pure, London – Trade fair exhibiting young, creative design and directional fashion

UK

London Fashion Week is a creative venue for designers presenting new collections to an audience of press and buyers from the UK and around the world. This bi-annual event includes New Generation, the sponsorship scheme for new designers, and Fashion Forward, which supports designers in the next stage of their development.

Pure is the UK's largest fashion event for the womenswear market, showcasing everything from contemporary brands, popular high fashion and casual wear to new young designers' work, accessory collections and footwear. Detailed trend presentations provide an update on the season's trends, forthcoming predictions and catwalk shows.

Londonedge and Londoncentral are quite unique trade events aimed at the alternative youth and urban clubwear market, specializing in fashion, footwear and accessories. Londonedge was launched in 2000, catering for an alternative market, while Londoncentral was launched a few years later and specializes in the clubwear market, showing items such as hoodies, combats, surfwear, hippy and skate gear.

Sourcing fabrics at Première Vision, Paris

France

Première Vision (PV) has an international reputation for being one of the leading fabric shows. It is held twice a year in Paris with spin-off events in New York, Shanghai and Moscow. In addition to the exhibition, there are supporting fashion and trend forecasts, audiovisual presentations and fashion seminars.

Indigo is held in Paris, sharing the exhibition centre – Parc d' Expositions, Paris-Nord Villepinte – with Première Vision exhibitors. The trade fair specializes in textile designs created for all product sectors: menswear, womenswear, childrenswear, lingerie, swimwear, sportswear, and accessories. Trend offices and bookstands offer trend information and fashion and textile journals.

Tissu Premier in Lille specializes in fabrics and accessories for womenswear, childrenswear and casual wear. Prediction and market conferences offer interpretations of forthcoming trend information.

Germany

CPD is the international trade fair held at the Düsseldorf Exhibition Centre in Germany. The fair specializes in womenswear and accessories, from modern classics to casual wear. The programme of exhibitors includes established and new name designers, plus-size and maternity wear labels and a fashion gallery featuring 'high-end' designer collections. Fashion and designer shows and seminars run throughout the event, providing updates on forthcoming trends, fabrics and colour stories and analyzing global sourcing. The fashion trade events HMD Düsseldorf (menswear), Body Look and Global Fashion are held simultaneously alongside CPD.

Techtextil – International Trade Fair for Technical Textiles and Nonwovens – is a trade fair promoting new developments from research through to production presenting technology, machinery and accessories, fibres and yarns, wovens and knitted fabrics, coated textiles, and innovative apparel textiles. The Techtextil exhibition has a programme of symposia and competitions for innovation in the development of textiles.

Body Look is the international trade event in Düsseldorf that specializes in lingerie, nightwear, body and beachwear, leisure wear and hosiery, and is held at the same time as CPD and HMD Düsseldorf.

Italy

Milan Fashion Week is an exciting showcase for international designers to present their collections on the catwalk to buyers, fashion representatives, the press and celebrities. Extensive international daily press coverage records the shows, highlighting the new trends and looks for the forthcoming season.

Intertex **Milano** is an international textile trade show in Italy held in line with Milan Fabrics Week. Exhibitors mainly include fabric manufacturers showing wovens, knitted fabrics, lace and embroideries for womenswear, menswear and childrenswear. Fashion accessories, yarns and clothing and also shown.

Pitti Immagine Filati, Florence is one of the oldest and largest international trade fairs for showcasing yarns for the knitting industry. This event also features Fashion at Work, an area dedicated to trend information, knitting machinery and accessories.

Pitti Bimbo, Florence: presenting GRANT autumn/winter childrenswear collection

Spain

Bread and Butter is Spain's premier trade show for cutting edge fashion, and is internationally recognized for its street and urban wear. Exhibiting collections include: womenswear, menswear and unisex collections, fashion active wear and sportswear. Trend seminars and catwalk shows highlight forthcoming themes, colours and styling directions.

TextilModa, Madrid is one of Spain's most important trade fairs, organized by the IFEMA for the textile sector and aimed at an international market for clothing manufacturers, designers, buyers, wholesalers, textile retailers and agents. Products range from fabrics to garment trims. Trend forums provide updates on the latest styles, colours and textures within all sectors.

Portugal

Modtissimo is a Portuguese trade show occurring twice a year, exhibiting fabrics and accessories for clothing and presenting Portuguese garment manufacturers and Portuguese tanneries. Catwalk shows run throughout the event and the new gallery, Textiles for Tomorrow, showcases the work of new young designers.

Australia

Exhibiting at Bread and Butter trade fair, Barcelona

Bread and Butter – signage advertising the cutting edge sports and streetwear labels

Rosemount Australian Fashion Week (RAFW) is managed and produced by the media company IBM and is one of Australia's and the Asia–Pacific region's premier events. Collections presented include: individual, ready-to-wear, New Generation, lingerie and swimwear ranges.

Fashion Exposed is a business event aimed at importers and exporters of garments, which is aimed at the womenswear, menswear and childrenswear markets, including active wear, urban wear, lingerie, footwear, accessories and furnishings. Features of Fashion Exposed include the International Designer

Showcase, presenting the latest talent, and the satellite shows that are presented throughout the event, providing the opportunity to view forthcoming trends.

China

China International Fashion Trade Fair (IFFAIR) presents a wide range of products from the following categories within the fashion, garment and textile industries: menswear, womenswear, professional wear, childrenswear, accessories, garment machinery, fabrics and textile and fashion news.

Hong Kong Fashion Week presents a wide selection of products ranging from mass market to high fashion, designer collections, bridalwear, eveningwear, childrenswear and accessories. Catwalk shows and seminars are held throughout the week with seminars providing buyers and exhibitors with information on forthcoming predictions and developments within the fashion industry, and providing analysis of market trends.

Interstoff Asia is held in Hong Kong. Products exhibited include functional and novelty fabrics, fibres and yarns, textile designs, fashion garments and accessories. Fashion design and styling services are on offer together with trend forecast information and publications.

India

Texworld is an international trade fair for apparel fabrics and accessories for buying-houses, department stores, designers, distributors, garment manufacturers, importers, retailers and wholesalers. This trade event showcases a huge array of fabrics and accessories and has a supporting programme of fashion shows, seminars and trend presentations.

USA

The International Fashion Fabric Exhibition in New York is the largest textile event in North America and provides a resource for sourcing woven and knitted fabrics, leathers and suedes and trims. The event provides updates on new design technology through a series of seminars. Fashion publications and trend services are also on offer.

New York Fashion Week is held twice a year and provides a showcase for international fashion designers to present their latest collections to buyers, the fashion press, fashion insiders and celebrities. Collections are reviewed with the publication of runway reports and video footage promoting the latest designs and detailing trends for the forthcoming season.

South America

Couromoda – the international shoes, sports goods and leather goods fair – is held in the city of São Paulo and presents the latest fashion collections in: bags, travel luggage, sports goods, footwear and technology for the footwear industry, and fashion accessories. Fashion shows feature throughout the event, promoting future fashion trends.

Fenatec international textile trade fair is targeted at designers, manufacturers, wholesalers, stylists, large retail chains and industry professionals. It promotes fabrics, threads and trimmings, sewing supplies and accessories, dyeing and processing accessories and technical publications.

Perumoda is an international Peruvian fashion industry trade event with companies exhibiting from USA, European Union, Latin America and Asia, showing fashion, footwear, accessories and jewellery, and presenting an area of machinery and equipment, trims and machine accessories. A programme of seminars and fashion shows support the event with a special catwalk and competition features, focusing on young designer collections.

Canada

Ontario Fashion Exhibitors (OFE) is Canada's premier fashion event and is held twice a year to cover the autumn/winter and the spring/summer seasons, exhibiting collections of ready-to-wear fashion, knitwear and accessories.

This list of events is not exhaustive. Further information is listed in Resources, see page 245.

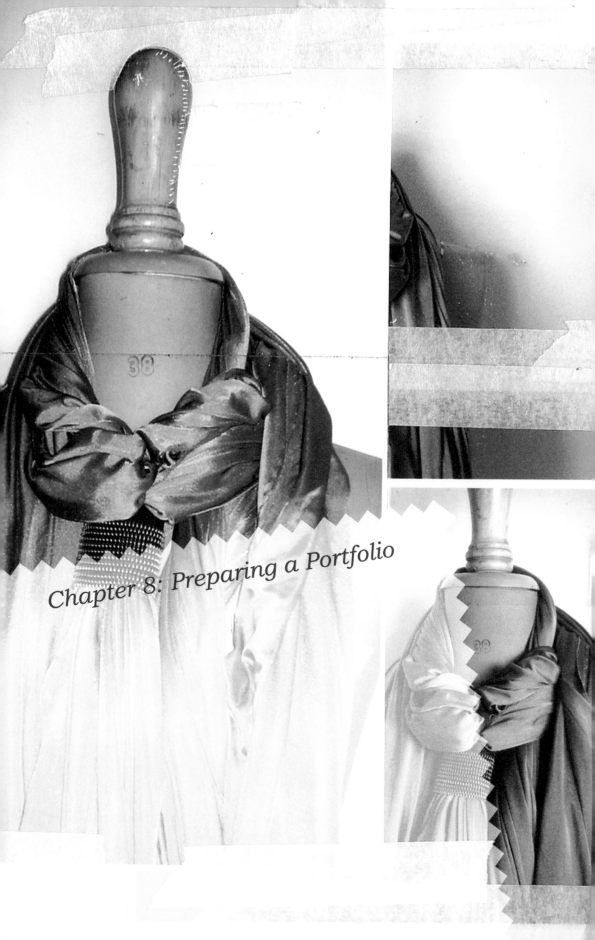

Chapter 8: Preparing a Portfolio

*T*raditionally, portfolios are used by designers to present a range of design work, for marketing their skills when going for interviews, to negotiate a promotion within a company or to show their work to an agent or client. For most designers, a portfolio is the first opportunity to make a good impression.

Your Portfolio

Presentation portfolios come in a range of sizes from A1 to A4 and are usually made out of plastic or leather with zip fastenings and ring mechanisms for use with detachable plastic display wallets. Work can be inserted and displayed on both sides of the plastic wallets, which are usually ultra-light with reinforced holes for added strength, giving a professional look to the content of your portfolio and providing excellent protection for your work. Most designers tend to use A3 or A4 portfolios, but this depends on the type of work being presented.

When assembling a portfolio it is advisable to include 20 to 25 pages of work, depending on the position you are applying for. Research into the company will enable you to focus your portfolio, making it relevant to the position you are interested in. Always put your best work into the portfolio – never include substandard work just to fill it up. It may be necessary to complete new work to fill gaps in weaker areas.

Right: Double-page portfolio spread of illustrative work presenting a range of ideas for contemporary separates inspired by active wear. Designs and illustrations by Alice Binns

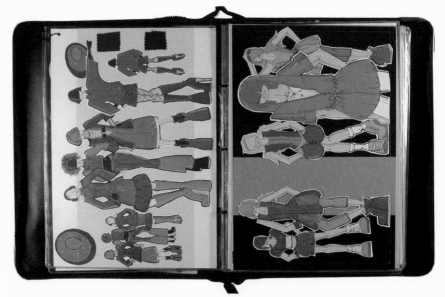

Left: Preparing for interview: portfolio and design work by David Steinhorst

WOMEN'S KNITWEAR DESIGNER

This position will involve being responsible for the design of high-fashion directional knitwear that reflects key seasonal trends for fashion-conscious young women with an eye for trend. Responsibilities will include the design of all knitwear from fine-gauge through to chunky knits, including crochet and hand knits.

Your responsibilities will include attending initial brainstorming/trend meetings with the design team and liaising with the sales team to analyze past-season sales and identify bestsellers.

Contract: Full time

Plan the sequence of projects carefully, editing the contents and removing any dated pieces of work. Try to keep all your work flowing in the same direction, either landscape or portrait. Be prepared to talk through your portfolio, discussing the project content, if required. However, your work should be able to stand alone without lengthy explanations.

Depending on the position you are applying for, the content of your portfolio could include: storyboards/mood boards, design developments, examples of range-building with supporting fabric ranges, schematics, cost sheets, lay plans, fashion illustrations, photographs of your work, examples of CAD work and any fashion editorials.

For example if you were applying for the position in the advertisement shown on the left, you should include a variety of knitwear ranges in your portfolio, demonstrating your knowledge of techniques, stitch structure, patterning and your ability to use colour and texture. You could support this by the inclusion of hand- and machine-knitted samples as appropriate. Further work could include mood boards demonstrating inspirational thematic ideas, design developments and also forecasting boards.

Specific Portfolio Requirements

If you are applying for a position as a fashion designer in a company, it is advisable to show design developments demonstrating your thought process, range-building and specification drawings, supported by additional technical work to demonstrate your understanding of the full process from design through the production stages. You'll also need to demonstrate an eye for shapes, silhouettes, embellishments, details and CAD skills.

If you are applying for a textiles position, your portfolio could include examples of storyboards/mood boards depicting your ideas; print, weave or knit designs; examples of design ranges including alternative fabric colourways; illustrations of the utilization of the fabrics; and samples of CAD work using Illustrator and Photoshop.

If you are presenting your work to a recruitment agency, plan to show a wide variety of work demonstrating your full breadth of skills, enabling the agency to understand your potential and giving a comprehensive overview of your abilities. Build variety into your portfolio, selecting the best examples of your work that will also demonstrate a range of skills. If you include photography in your portfolio, make sure the quality is excellent.

Digital/Electronic Portfolios

As an alternative to the traditional presentation portfolio, many designers are now presenting examples of their work in the form of digital, or electronic, portfolios (sometimes called 'e-portfolios'). A digital portfolio is a set of digital pages, or screens, which can be produced as a simple slideshow or as a creative digital presentation.

Many designers work in multimedia formats and find creating a digital portfolio a convenient method of presenting examples of their work to wider audiences. It is easy and economical to email a digital portfolio to a client, a potential employer or an agent, for competition entry and for gallery and exhibition submissions. Many artists and designers from all disciplines are now displaying their work in the form of digital portfolios or online galleries on the web, which is perfect for marketing their work to an international audience.

Producing a digital portfolio requires careful planning and organization of your work. Consider the order of the slides, and the use of text in the form of titles, subtitles and key words to explain the background to a project. Include a CV providing your contact details and outlining your abilities and experience (see page 157). You can find help in producing a digital portfolio in the form of software or short courses.

If you are attending an interview and presenting a traditional portfolio of work, it is also worth leaving the interviewers with a copy of your work in digital format (on a CD-ROM) for their reference.

Online Portfolios/Galleries

There are now many portfolio/gallery websites providing services to showcase and advertise your work for you, allowing the general public to browse your portfolio at leisure. If you are considering using one of these sites it is a good idea to browse several. Assess the other designers' work, the general design of the site, its accessibility and the information that is provided to support each designer's work – this usually includes a brief biography listing recent clients, awards and qualifications achieved. The site will usually include a 'guestbook', inviting visitors to your site to make comments relating to your work, and also, most importantly, a link to your own website. These sites often have varying service rates from 'basic portfolio' to 'advanced portfolio' (which usually permits you to include more images). Check out and compare costs, terms and payment details before committing yourself to a particular site. Occasionally they will have free trial periods of which you can take advantage.

Planning the Contents of Your Portfolio

To produce a successful portfolio it is important to plan the contents carefully and include a range of work that represents your full skills. It is a good idea to tailor it to each position you apply for, adding extra work that relates directly to the company. The research you undertake for this will also give you greater insight in preparation for the interview.

Consider the order of work carefully, and place your strongest work at the front. Maintain a logical order throughout, making it easy to talk through during an interview. Use the chart below as a checklist.

	CONTENTS	Date to be completed	Completed
	EXAMPLE: Mood board - Capsule collection		
	Design development sheet Capsule collection		
1			
2			
3			
4			
5			
6			
7			
8			
9			
10			
11			
12			
13			
14			
15			
16			
17			
18			
19			
20			
21			
22			
23			
24			
25			

Portfolio Checklist

===

Check the following points to make sure that your portfolio is working for you:

✖ *Edit your work so you include only your very best examples.*
✖ *Check that the content of your portfolio is targeted to your intended audience.*
✖ *Check that you have sufficient breadth of work in your portfolio, demonstrating your full range of skills.*
✖ *Check that all projects are self-explanatory.*
✖ *Check that your portfolio has sufficient information supporting each project and explaining the background to the project: What was the brief? Who was the client?*
✖ *Make sure all pieces are secured, using glue or spray mount that doesn't distort the work.*
✖ *Always put your best work at the front of the portfolio – first impressions are vital.*
✖ *Whether you present your work in a traditional portfolio case or as a digital portfolio, always make sure you label it clearly with your name and address.*
✖ *Keep your portfolio simple and make sure that it is kept up to date by regularly reviewing it and adding new projects.*
✖ *Remember it is important to include a copyright notice for each piece (including the word 'copyright' or the copyright symbol, ©). This provides you with protection against your work being used without your permission.*

===

Portfolio Elements

Every designer's portfolio will vary in content depending on their specialist area of study; however, this summary provides advice and guidance on each element of the portfolio.

Sketchbook

Presenting a sketchbook at interview is only necessary if you are applying for your first position as an assistant designer, and should be an inspirational book of your preliminary ideas. You may find a sketchbook too bulky to carry with you to an interview, so it is totally acceptable to photocopy several pages to present in your portfolio. The selected pages should demonstrate your ability to research, develop and record your preliminary ideas, showing where the initial idea came from and its development, demonstrating your ability to analyze an idea, for example through theme, colour and texture.

Mood Board

In a portfolio for a design position it is useful to include one or two mood boards that demonstrate your initial ideas and how you pulled a theme together. A mood board (also known as a concept board or storyboard) is a collation of ideas and selected images that should be visually stimulating, focused around a chosen theme. It is used to communicate and summarize your ideas and inspiration.

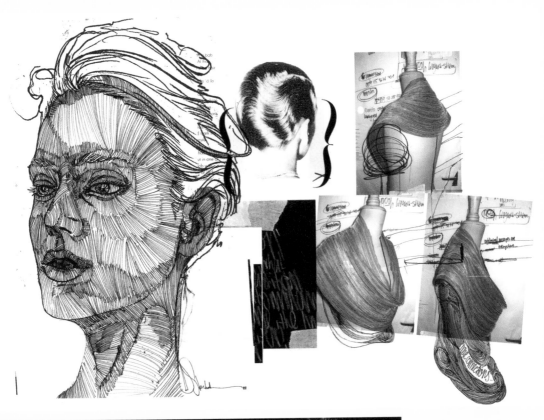

Above: *Sketchbook pages by David Steinhorst documenting and developing design ideas*

Left: *Sketchbook exploring the theme 'Old Rose' and developing initial ideas through the use of visual imagery, colour and texture*

Opposite top: *'Poetics of Nature', an inspirational mood board collating ideas and forecasting theme and colour palette for the forthcoming season by Laura Pledger*

Opposite right: *Example of a mood board exploring themes and initial design ideas through drawing, fabric exploration and collage techniques by Keighley Hines*

The size of the mood board you include in your portfolio depends on its finished use. If you are completing a range of moods boards for a company you will be advised to complete the work to a given size within a commissioned brief and this usually tends to be A2, A1 or A0. If you are producing a mood board as part of your studies, the project brief may advise you on the size of board required, otherwise the most popular size is A3 or A2, depending on the size of your portfolio.

Customer Profile Board

When designing a collection, whether it is a range of garments, accessories, footwear or fabrics, it is important to know and understand your customer – who they are, their age range, gender, lifestyle, geographic location, spending habits and income. If you are applying for a design position, it is useful to include an example customer profile board in your portfolio. This shows that you have a good understanding of your target market. Present the information visually, supported with relevant text.

Design Development

When applying for a design position, always include several ranges of design development sketches from your best collections, whether fashion collections or collections of woven, knitted or printed fabrics. The work presented should demonstrate your ability to work through the design process, exploring initial design ideas and analyzing the design thoroughly, through line, form, proportion, colour, texture and style.

If you are including a series of design development ideas for a garment range, always include front and back views of garments with attention to detail, supported by fabric and yarn samples. If you are including developments for a range of fabric samples, whether print, knit or woven, always include ideas for alternative colourways, supported by yarn or fabric samples where appropriate.

Range-building

It is useful to include examples of garment/textile ranges in your portfolio, demonstrating your ability to work through the design development process and concluding with cohesive ranges of samples or garments that work together. It is useful to include a range designed particularly for the specific market of the company interviewing you, demonstrating your knowledge of their target market and the relevance of your work.

If you are designing a collection of garments, the collection may consist of six outfits comprising a co-ordinating range of separates, for example:

Outfit 1 – Coat + dress

Outfit 2 – Jacket + trousers + shirt

Outfit 3 – Cardigan + blouse + skirt

Outfit 4 – Jumper + trousers

Outfit 5 – Jacket + trousers + t-shirt

Outfit 6 – Coat + shirt + skirt

Top: Design development sketches and photographic recordings exploring ideas for necklines and draping details by David Steinhorst

Above: Design development exploring a range of ideas for pockets and intricate detailing through a series of sketches analyzing the potential of the garment by Alice Binns

Left to right:

'Because Tailored Men Wear It Better.' Design ideas for menswear range presented with inspirational source material and fabric ideas, by Daniel Clark

'Highlander.' An illustration board presenting a range of ideas for a casual tailored menswear capsule collection using a combination of wool tartans with contrasting denim fabrics, by Daniel Clark

The range would be designed for the same season and theme, producing a collection of garments that can be worn in many permutations to create a wearable, flexible range of co-ordinating separates.

When presenting a range of textiles in your portfolio, the range may demonstrate various contrasting and complementary colourways within the collection, designed using specialist equipment or CAD software. The sample range could include exploration of scale of pattern, various textile processes and surface treatments that have been applied to the range, demonstrating your knowledge and use of domestic and specialist industrial machines and finishing equipment.

For a position as a knitwear designer, one range presented may include a cut and sew collection of knitted fabrics for a menswear or womenswear diffusion range. By contrast you may also choose to include sample ideas using the latest CAD technology system for a junior range of fully fashioned knitted garments, supported by a range of samples in variety of yarns and weights and produced on various gauge machines.

Illustrations

Fashion illustrations are used to illustrate garment designs for a variety of areas, which include: advertising and editorial in newspapers, magazines, fashion journals, fashion forecasting and prediction packages; promotional work for exhibitions and trade fairs; packaging; or for a fashion house.

Above: Illustration boards presenting designs for fashion active wear, including sample fabric swatches, by Alice Binns

Right: Illustration board presenting design ideas for a contemporary footwear range, by Parveen Chana

Far right: Design development board illustrating a range of ideas for contemporary footwear design, by Mike Brown, De Montfort University

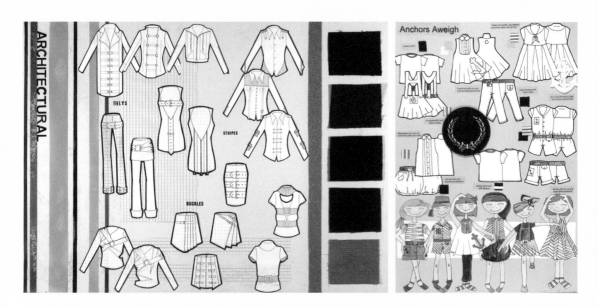

Left to right:

Schematics by Sarah Handy, analyzing the garment range inspired by the theme 'Architectural', showing front and back views and including a fabric sample range

Schematics and illustrations by Sarah O'Hara. Childrenswear range for spring/summer with illustrations indicating front and back views of garments, supported by fabric samples

Including fashion illustrations in your portfolio is useful for reflecting the feel of a collection and they should be sympathetic in style. If you are applying for a design position, work in a forecasting company or freelance work with a journal, it is useful to include fashion illustrations in your portfolio. This work should demonstrate a good use of media techniques, such as marker pens, collage, montage and Adobe Photoshop and Illustrator.

Working Drawings

If you are applying for a design or technical position, for example assistant designer or garment technologist, it is useful to include several examples of working drawings/production drawings, or 'technical flats' as they are also known, which demonstrate your knowledge of garment analysis. Working drawings are precise diagrammatic drawings that are produced to scale, and are drawn by hand or by using graphics software. They should communicate the design fully, identifying all the features of the garment, and provide an accurate record of the garment for a pattern cutter to refer to when drafting the pattern.

Cost Sheets

Once you have designed a garment it is important to cost out the idea, translating the design into a finished product. A completed cost sheet should contain all the garments specifics, including the cost of each individual component of the garment and the exact amount of fabric used, including linings, interfacings, trims and threads. Cost sheets also identify the calculation of labour and the production time, which can be generated by hand or computer. If you are applying for a design or technical position it is very useful to include a sample cost sheet.

Textile Samples

Presenting woven or knitted samples can add bulk to your portfolio, often distorting other pieces of work and the portfolio itself. If you are a knit-, print- or weave designer it is useful to present samples using a sample card header,

Above and right: *An evocative, retro feel was created for these photographs, to match the mood of the exquisite Caroline Mitchell hats*

noting the details of the sample on the back of each header. If you are presenting a range of samples at an interview, carry the samples in a small hold-all to give a professional image.

As a textile designer, companies may request that you complete a small project relevant to their brand to provide them with greater understanding of your abilities and your knowledge of their ranges and competitors.

Using Photography in Portfolios

If you choose to include photographs in your portfolio, it is essential that they are clear, well-focused images that reflect the quality of the work presented. If you are including photographs of a garment range, consider your choice of model, accessories and the overall styling of the image. All photographs should reflect the mood and the essence of a collection. Photographs can be taken on location or styled for a studio shot. Whatever the situation, discuss the image you need with the photographer, the different poses required, the look you want to create and the lighting necessary to achieve that result.

Constructed textiles – fabric manipulation, exploring the techniques of layering and stitching for garment design

Photographing Knitted/Woven Textiles

Close-up photography is a useful medium to record your work and also to explore intricate design detail in greater depth. Digital cameras are excellent for close-up photography, focusing and zooming in on detail to magnify and emphasize the stitch structure, fabric construction or garment details. The photographs can then be transferred to the computer and manipulated using software to crop the photograph, produce more accurate colour or even change the colour and texture.

'Lace' design by Lene Toni Kjeld. Transitional wallpaper design produced using traditional rotary printing methods

From top:

Sample board of machine-knitted swatches exploring the theme 'Dark Ages', incorporating weaving and tuck stitch techniques, designed and produced by Siobhan Noon

Close-up detail of space-dyed and lurex machine-knitted sample produced using a slip-stitch technique, creating a reversible fabric

Transitional wall decoration 'Wave Leaf' design by Lene Toni Kjeld

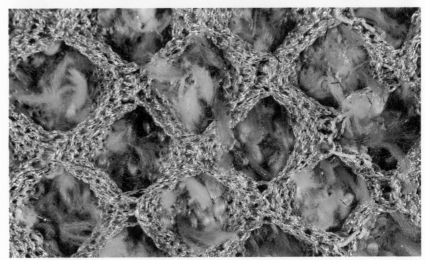

Chapter 9: The Recruitment Process

*O*nce you have sent off your application for a position of employment, you have entered the recruitment process. Academic qualifications, past experience, CVs, application forms, letters of application, interviews and aptitude tests all form part of this process.

Understanding the Recruitment Process

Over the page is a diagram identifying a typical recruitment process from the consideration of the application to the offer of employment. This process will vary depending on the position and the company.

The Interview

Interviews are an important part of the process of selecting an appropriate person for a job. An interview provides the employer with the opportunity to gain an understanding of the candidate's skills and experience, assessing how they would fit into the organization and whether their skills meet the required responsibilities of the position.

After the initial contact through the submission of a completed application form or the submission of a CV, the employer will then shortlist candidates and will usually request that they attend an interview. There are several different types: screening interviews, telephone interviews, one-on-one interviews, group interviews and panel interviews.

Screening Interviews
The aim of a screening interview is to check the applicant's qualifications and experience, making sure they meet the minimum requirements for the position advertised. Sometimes these types of interviews are completed online. The applicant is usually requested to verify their qualifications and experience and to complete a series of questions.

Telephone Interviews
A telephone interview is often set for a pre-arranged time, enabling you to prepare any notes you may want to ask the interviewer. Occasionally telephone interviews are automated and you are asked to respond to questions through the keypad.

APPLICATION FORM RECEIVED

Once the company has received your application they should send you written confirmation of receipt of your work. However, so many companies are bombarded with applications on a day-to-day basis that many do not have the resources to respond, unless you have been shortlisted.

SHORTLIST

Shortlisting is the process of assessing all application forms received against the job description and requirements. If you are successfully shortlisted as a potential candidate for the position advertised, you will enter the interview process.

TELEPHONE INTERVIEW

Companies sometimes use telephone interviews to screen applicants, as one of the first steps in the shortlisting process.

APTITUDE/PSYCHOMETRIC TEST

Aptitude or psychometric tests are frequently used by companies to gauge a candidate's intellectual potential and capacity to cope with different situations.

ONE-ON-ONE INTERVIEW

The interview may take the form of a one-on-one meeting between interviewer and interviewee.

PANEL INTERVIEW

An interview panel usually consists of between three and four interviewers; however this will depend on the level of the position. For senior positions there may be more.

SECOND INTERVIEW

If you are successful in your initial interview you may be called back for a second interview, particularly for more senior positions.

SELECTION PROCESS

Once the interviews have been completed the interviewer or panel will assess your results and make their recommendations. References will be taken up for consideration.

OFFER OF EMPLOYMENT

After the selection committee has assessed the results of the interview and reviewed the references, the recommendation will be formalized and, if successful, an offer of employment is made.

Always make sure you are in a quiet environment when being interviewed. When responding to questions, remember to be professional in your answers, speaking in a clear voice, giving precise responses. Often these interviews will be recorded for the interview panel to review at a later date.

When being interviewed by telephone, always be prepared, have a copy of your CV to refer to and keep a pen and paper handy to make notes. Recruitment agencies and some employers initially screen candidates by telephone, rather than waste time and money on travelling expenses.

Face-to-Face Interviews

The aim of a face-to-face interview is for you to meet the potential employer and the employer to meet you. The employer has the chance to find out if you are suitable for the position. Visiting a company gives you the opportunity to meet other employees, view the working environment and to have a tour of the company, giving you better knowledge of the company's business and a greater understanding of your possible role and responsibilities. It also provides a forum for you to ask questions relating to the position.

Group Interviews

A group interview involves several people being interviewed at the same time, which is economical in terms of time and staffing but is also useful in observing how candidates react to each other. A group interview may take the form of a question-and-answer session or a group discussion or other activity between the candidates. The interviewers may lead the discussion or activity or may sit back and observe your communication skills. During a group interview it is important to listen carefully to other candidates responses and try to add further information if you can, providing a more complete answer or a different perspective to the original response. Never interrupt the interviewer or a fellow interviewee. Group interviews are an excellent means of ascertaining leadership qualities, communication skills, the candidates' knowledge and understanding of the topic being discussed and their level of confidence.

Panel Interviews

An interview panel usually consists of a manager, a senior member of staff and a representative from the personnel or human resources (HR) department, who oversees the administration of the interview and answers any queries regarding entitlements. HR personnel are often the first point of contact in the recruitment process, and offer advice to staff on the terms and conditions of employment, such as rates of pay, expenses, taxation, holiday and other entitlements, sickness benefit pay and pensions.

Don't be overly concerned about facing a panel of interviewers, as each panel member is usually there to ask a different type of question. However, it is important to remember, when answering any question, to speak directly to the person who asked the question, but also to maintain eye contact with the rest of the panel.

First Interview

Once you have been invited for an interview, always contact the company and confirm that you will be able to attend on the date and at the time requested. In preparation for the interview, do your homework. Research the company as much as you can, using the internet, trade journals and company newsletters. Find out as much information as possible regarding the type of business and the organizational structure, the history of the company and its products and services. Other useful information includes details relating to opportunities for promotion along with the company's financial statistics. Some of this information may be available on the company website or in its Annual Report. Alternatively, research the company through newspapers, trade publications and business indexes, which are available in most public libraries.

On the day of your interview, always make sure you arrive in good time, giving you sufficient opportunity to compose your thoughts. If you are late due to unforeseen circumstances always ring the company and explain the situation immediately, to avoid any embarrassment later. Always take extra copies of your CV, enabling you to distribute them as necessary during the interview, while you refer to it during the interview questions. After any interview it is useful to reflect and to make some notes – recording questions you were asked and your responses, the names of people you met and notes on the structure of the company.

Questions You May be Asked

Listed here is a range of sample questions that may be asked during an interview. The questions have been divided into categories: company questions, general employment questions, subject-specific questions, aspirational questions, personal questions and open-ended questions, with an example given for each category. Read through the sample questions and practise giving a full response of your own.

Company Questions
- ✖ What do you know about the company?
- ✖ What do you know about the structure of the company?
- ✖ What do you know about the position you have applied for?
- ✖ What do you think the most important issues facing this company are at the moment?
- ✖ What do you think you will be able to contribute to the company?
- ✖ If we offer you the position, what can you bring to the organization?
- ✖ Why do you want this job?
- ✖ Why have you applied for this position?
- ✖ What appeals to you about the position on offer?

✖ What additional training will you need to do the job?

✖ Why should we offer you the position?

✖ Why should we appoint you rather than another candidate?

✖ There are a lot of applicants for the position – what makes you special?

✖ What are the attributes you think you need for the job you have applied for?

✖ If you were offered this position, how do you think you would spend the first two weeks with the company?

Example Question: What do you know about the company?

===

✖ *Example answer: I understand the company was established in 1996 and has grown substantially over the last few years. You produce both clothing and accessories for the luxury brand market sector, with your latest collections including ranges of outerwear and tailoring, as well as dresses, shirts, knitwear, trousers and jersey items, which are sold in stores and franchises globally, and during the last year this has expanded to included concessions in the UK.*

✖ *Advice: In preparation for the interview, research the size of the company, the company's history, the structure and roles within the company, the company's mission statement, products/services, recent developments, growth and who their customers/clients and competitors are.*

✖ *Thorough knowledge of the company is required to answer this question adequately. Interviewers want to know that you are serious about working for their company and that you don't see the position as just a stopgap between other jobs. Look at the company's own website as a direct source of information. Many companies produce annual reports identifying their accounts, goals and aspirations. Look through current and back issues of trade magazines.*

===

General Employment Questions

✖ What have you been doing to keep your knowledge and training up to date since graduating?

✖ How would you describe your career progress to date?

✖ What are your short-term/long-term goals?

✖ How well do you respond to deadlines?

✖ What makes a good employer?

✖ Give an example of a work situation that was problematic.

✖ How would you deal with a difficult manager or customer?

✖ What would you do if you had a problem you could not deal with?

✖ How did you prepare for this interview?

✖ Would you be able to use your previous experience in this job?

✖ If offered the job, when would you be able to start?

✖ What sort of salary are you looking for?

Example Question: Would you be able to use your previous experience in this job?

==

✖ *Example Answer: My previous experience working in the design team as an assistant designer gave me a good understanding of the design process. I was given responsibility for my own line in designing childrenswear for ages 9-12. This position involved using CAD to draw up the design ranges. I am now seeking a position within a larger company that will challenge my abilities and use my skills more fully. I also want to have the opportunity to extend my knowledge and work, producing more extensive design ranges.*

✖ *Advice: This question gives you the opportunity to explain your skills in greater detail and suggest how the company could use your skills to their advantage.*

==

Subject-specific Questions

✖ Have you completed any work placements within the fashion industry?
✖ What are the most important attributes you consider a designer/visual merchandiser must have?
✖ What experience do you have of managing patternmaking deadlines between design and production?
✖ What experience do you have of fabric and trim sourcing?
✖ Who or what inspires your design work?
✖ What do you think of this season's catwalk collections?
✖ What do you think of next season's fashion forecasts?
✖ What trade events have you attended during the last year?
✖ How would you describe our label?
✖ Who do you consider our competitors to be?
✖ What are your views on our newly launched junior range?

Example Question: What qualities do you consider a good pattern cutter needs?

==

✖ *Example Answer: To be a successful pattern cutter you need to have excellent technical knowledge in the construction of garments and the grading of sizes supported by a knowledge of fabrics. You also need to have an excellent eye for accuracy and detail.*

✖ *Advice: In your response to this question you should be able to explain your own understanding of the role of the pattern cutter (or other specific position). This question also provides you with an opportunity to explain how your present skills meet the criteria of the job specification.*

==

Aspirational Questions

✖ What are your career aspirations?
✖ How would you describe your career progress to date?
✖ What are your short-term/long-term ambitions?
✖ What do you hope to be doing in five or ten years' time?
✖ What are your long-term career plans?
✖ What are your life goals?
✖ Given the opportunity, what sort of training or experience do you require to achieve your ambition(s)?
✖ Why did you leave your last position?
✖ What was the most satisfying part of the job?
✖ Which other organizations have you worked for?
✖ What do equal opportunities mean to you?
✖ How important do you think qualifications are?
✖ Do you prefer to work in a team situation or on your own?
✖ What have you been doing to keep your knowledge up to date since graduating?

Example Question: Why are you considering leaving your present position?

==

✖ *Example Answer: I have worked for (company name) for two years and enjoyed the experience. However, I now want to work for a larger company, and this company has a good reputation. I want to utilize my present skills with the opportunity to learn new ones in an inspiring and challenging environment.*
✖ *Advice: In this question the interviewer is searching for information that may help them make a decision about your employability with reference to your motivation for leaving your present or previous position.*
✖ *There may be many reasons a candidate wants to leave a position within a company, for example: relocation, external commitments, an opportunity for promotion or career development, a career change or an increase in salary. Whatever your reason, it is important that you stress the positive points, outlining the advantages to the company of employing you.*

==

Personal Questions

✖ Why did you decide to go to college/university?
✖ What are your major strengths?
✖ What are your weaknesses?
✖ What is your greatest achievement to date?
✖ How would you describe yourself?
✖ What are your interests outside work?
✖ It states in your application that you enjoy reading: who are your favourite authors?
✖ What was the last exhibition you visited?
✖ What do you hope to achieve if appointed?

Example Question: What is your greatest achievement to date?

===

✖ *Example Answer: My greatest achievement to date is successfully completing my undergraduate studies in Fashion Design and presenting my fashion work on the catwalk at the university's fashion show. Alongside designing and showing my collection I was also involved in the fundraising, planning and organization of the event. Approximately 1,500 visitors attended the event over three shows. The show planning was very much a team effort, and we raised over £12,000 to fund the event.*

✖ *Advice: This question gives you the opportunity to explain one of your successes in greater detail and could be enhanced by adding that you really enjoy working in team situations to achieve a specific goal, but that you also enjoy working independently and benefit from the challenge of using your own initiative to complete a specific project.*

===

General Points About Answering

===

✖ *To answer the questions thoroughly it is important that you complete thorough research into the position, analyzing the role and responsibilities, as outlined in the job description. It is important that you give positive, enthusiastic answers identifying the reasons why you want the job and what you are able to bring to the company. Identify what your expertise, experience, knowledge and strengths are, listing your unique selling points and relating this information to the requirements of the original advert and job specification.*

===

Open-ended Questions

Open-ended questions offer you the opportunity to take charge of the interview situation, enabling you to give fuller and more informative answers. It is useful to have additional copies of your CV to hand that you can pass to each member of the interview panel, and relate some of the answers to the specific experiences listed on your CV.

✖ Tell me about yourself. (Often an interview will open with this question.)
✖ Tell me about your previous position.
✖ Tell me about your education.
✖ Tell me about your undergraduate studies.
✖ Give me an example of a problem you have had to deal with at work.
✖ Tell us about your greatest achievement to date.

Questions To Ask

After answering the interviewer's or panel's questions, to round up the interview the candidate is usually given the opportunity to ask questions of their own. Below is a short list of questions that you may consider asking:

✖ What are the opportunities for career development?
✖ What are the opportunities for promotion within the company?
✖ Does the organization offer a mentoring system?

✖ Where will the company be in five or ten years' time?
✖ How did the vacancy arise?
✖ When may I expect to hear from you?

Aptitude Tests/Psychometric Testing

Aptitude tests (psychometric tests) are frequently used by companies to gauge a candidate's intellectual potential and capacity to cope with situations. The tests usually consist of analytical, numerical and verbal reasoning. For example, an employer may want to test your maths ability if the position requires commercial awareness and the responsibilities include dealing with large sums of money, spreadsheets or involve any aspect of a company's financial planning. The verbal reasoning test may be applied if the candidate is going to be required to write reports, deal with written correspondence and plan schedules. Often these tests are used in the shortlisting process and are completed online before a formal face-to-face interview, or alternatively they may be completed in controlled conditions during the formal interview process. There are many websites that provide example aptitude tests to prepare you for interviews and these are worth investigating.

Creative Presentations

When you attend an interview it is often standard practice to be asked to give a formal presentation. This provides the employer with an understanding of your ability to gather and present information, your organizational and communication skills and your ability to give a presentation to an audience with confidence.

It is usual for the company to contact you in advance and ask you to give a presentation answering a specific question. For example: 'Complete a ten-minute presentation identifying what you can offer the company.'

Success is all in the planning. Always make sure you answer the question fully. A presentation should start with a brief introduction, main body and conclusion. The introduction should clearly identify what the presentation is about, outlining the main content. It is important that you identify who your audience is.

The length of time for the presentation is usually stated in the interview notes. (Usually about ten minutes.) It is important to stick to the time allocated; otherwise the interviewer may stop you midway through your presentation. Read the interview notes carefully, as they will state what is expected of you. Always check beforehand what equipment will be available to use during your presentation. (This is usually listed in the application pack or interview letter.) If you are still unsure, contact the company well in advance and check this out.

PowerPoint and Other Software Packages

To give a successful PowerPoint presentation you must know and understand your audience. From the interviewer's perspective, one thing that is very important is to engage with the audience which, if appropriate, could take the form of encouraging some interactivity and involvement.

Preparing the Presentation

Content: Keep this simple, to the point, and answering the question required, as stated in the interview literature.

Design: Keep the design of the presentation simple and don't overload it with transitional effects (created by the movement of one slide to the next). Use the screen as a tool to get the main points across. The information is the most important thing. See the sample presentation over the page.

Tips for PowerPoint Presentations

===

✖ *Keep the design of your PowerPoint presentation simple but effective and professional*
✖ *Use a standard style of font, for example Arial or Tahoma*
✖ *Use a minimum of 20-point font size, and larger for main headings*
✖ *Always check spelling and grammar*
✖ *Use around six to 12 slides for a ten-minute presentation*
✖ *Sequence of the slides – the slides should flow from one to another. The introductory slide should give the title of the presentation and your name. The last slide should summarize the presentation*
✖ *Visual imagery must be clear and of good quality*
✖ *Use bullet points*
✖ *Don't overload slides with information: include a maximum of four bullet points per slide*
✖ *Introduce one point at a time and allow your audience time to read each slide*
✖ *Practise giving your presentation, memorizing as much as possible and making the presentation flow. You may need to prepare additional notes for your reference*
✖ *Provide the interview panel with a printed copy of your PowerPoint presentation*
✖ *At the end of your presentation allow time for questions; keep the answers short and to the point*

===

Slide 1

WHAT CAN I OFFER THE COMPANY

Tanya Tryntja
May 2010

Slide 2

GENERAL

- BA (Hons) Fashion Merchandising
- Computer literacy skills: MS Office, Excel, Word
- Administration experience

Slide 3

PREVIOUS EXPERIENCE

- Responsibility for buying childrenswear
- Range planning and selection
- Helping the assistant buyer at all levels
- Dealing with suppliers and manufacturers

Slide 4

SPECIALIST KNOWLEDGE

- 2 years' experience as a Trainee Assistant Buyer

- 1 year of retail experience as a Junior Sales Assistant

- 2 years' part-time retail experience

Slide 5

SPECIALIST KNOWLEDGE

- Marketing skills

- Analytical skills

- Monitoring sales figures

- Accounting skills

- Knowledge of trends

Slide 6

PERSONAL ATTRIBUTES

- Creativity

- Enthusiasm

- Communication skills

- Motivation

- Time-management skills

Second Interview

If the company is interested in you, you may be asked back to the company for a second interview. The second interview will be more in-depth, so it is important that you prepare yourself fully. There may be a new panel of interviewers or more senior mangers to question you on a particular aspect of the position or the interview may take place off site in a relaxed setting, giving the interviewer an opportunity to talk to you on a more informal basis to review your interpersonal skills and how you communicate in a social situation. Beware of the 'free lunch', or when people invite you to dinner with colleagues and it all appears very sociable – don't drop your guard and be aware that they are assessing your attributes and attitudes as a potential colleague! It's a further opportunity for you to make a positive impression within the company. Be prepared for all eventualities and be aware that interviews can vary greatly from one company to another.

Salary

Never discuss salary during an initial interview (unless the interviewer brings it up). The initial interview provides you with the opportunity to find out what the job entails, if the job is what you want and if you want to work for the company. But at second interview the subject is likely to arise. Salaries are often negotiable – you do not have to divulge what your previous salary was, and the important thing to consider is what you are worth to the company. Often the salary is identified in the job advertisement and it is just a case of discussing and negotiating it if you are offered the job after the interview. When discussing the salary, it is also useful to ask questions relating to company benefits, pension schemes, bonuses, holiday entitlement, health schemes and relocation allowances.

It's important to know what you are worth but don't price yourself out of the market. Do thorough research and find out what similar positions offer.

General Interview Technique

Whether a first or second interview, and whatever form the interview takes, there are some rules you can follow to maximize your chances of success.

What to Wear

The initial impression of you that the interviewer will have will be based on your appearance. There are no hard and fast rules. The main consideration is to be smart and comfortable, to dress appropriately for the company and to use your common sense. Research into the company should give you an insight into the dress code for the position. A black or navy suit is a good choice for any interview. If the position is in design or retail there may be more flexibility, but if it is a corporate position a suit is recommended. A suit can be dressed up or down with the appropriate use of carefully selected accessories, adding individuality to your interview attire.

If you are applying for a university course, it's also a good idea to dress smartly, as if you were applying for a job in the career of your choice.

Avoid wearing shoes that you are unable to walk correctly in, as you may be given a tour around the company, which may include viewing several buildings a distance apart. Always make sure your shoes are clean and well heeled, and that they work with your interview outfit.

Combatting Nerves

Most people are very nervous before and during an interview. The more prepared you are, the less nervous you will feel. Try to stay calm – remember, it is a time for you to sell your skills and experience. Body language is very important. Smile and look people in the eye when they are talking to you. Try to moderate your voice, which will help you to keep calm and take control of your responses. Practise your handshake – a firm handshake gives the impression of confidence and will assure the interviewer that you are a suitable candidate to have been shortlisted. During the interview avoid fidgeting, playing with your hair or gesticulating too much while speaking. Sit forward during the interview, engage with the interview panel, be polite and friendly and try to create a rapport.

Things to Avoid

==

- ✖ *Dressing inappropriately*
- ✖ *Revealing heavy piercing and tattoos*
- ✖ *Heavy perfume or aftershave*
- ✖ *Heavy make-up*
- ✖ *Leaving your mobile switched on*
- ✖ *Chewing gum*
- ✖ *Smoking – never smoke, even if the interviewer offers you a cigarette*
- ✖ *Lying: never exaggerate your qualifications, knowledge or experience*
- ✖ *Talking negatively about your previous employer*
- ✖ *Drinking alcohol, especially if you are invited out to lunch*

==

Accepting the Position

If you are successful in the interview process and the company offers you the position, you may initially be contacted by phone to discuss the terms of contract. It is important that you subsequently receive full details in writing. Check all the contract details carefully and make sure you are happy with them. Give yourself time to read through all the details; don't rush into making a decision. Once you have decided to accept the position it is important to formally write to the company and accept the position. This letter should be short and to the point, professionally presented and typed on white paper. Salaries are negotiable, so if a company offers you a job with the understanding that the salary will be reviewed or increased in six months time, try to get this confirmed in writing.

Example Letter of Acceptance

Firm's Reference No.

Your address
Including postcode

6 May 2010

Browns & Co.
30-35 Finley Street,
Greater Manchester
UK

Dear Mr Brown

In reference to my interview on Thursday 6 May 2010. I would like to thank you for considering my application for the position of Trainee Merchandiser for Browns and Co.

I was very impressed by the organization of Browns & Co. and I am delighted to be able to accept the position of Trainee Merchandiser, as offered in your letter of 5 May 2010.

This position offers a wonderful opportunity for me to work with the team of merchandisers, contributing to the growth and development of the label within Browns.

As requested, I have signed the contract of employment, which I have enclosed. I am happy to accept the salary and benefits as outlined in the contract, with a salary review after my probationary year.

I look forward to starting work on *(date)* and working with you. If there is any additional information that you require please do not hesitate to contact me.

Yours sincerely

(Signature)

Mary Jo Sengal

Pre-employment Checks

Most companies will carry out pre-employment checks before making an offer of employment to an interview candidate. This ensures that all the information and data provided by the candidate is correct. This could include checking qualifications, educational and employment history and references. Occasionally a candidate is offered a position on the understanding that the employment checks are all correct.

New Job Checklist

Employment Checklist	Fill in details
Contract received	
Job description received	
Date of commencement of employment	
Salary	
Length of contract	
Type of contract - full time/part time/ temporary/permanent	
Probationary period and length	
Pension scheme	
Holiday entitlement	
Health schemes	
Relocation allowance	
Notice period	

Coping With Rejection: Reconsidering Your Options

If you are not appointed following an interview, it is worth approaching your interviewer and asking why. You may receive constructive comments that will help you in your job search. If you are not appointed send a brief thank you letter asking for your CV to be kept on file and considered if there are any further suitable openings within the company.

Example Letter

Firm's Reference No.

Your address
Including postcode

6 May 2010

Browns & Co.
30-35 Finley Street,
Greater Manchester
UK

Dear Mr Brown,

In reference to my interview on Thursday 6 May 2010. I would like to thank you for considering my application for the position as Trainee Merchandiser for Browns and Co.

I was very impressed by the organization of Browns & Co. and would be delighted to be given the opportunity to work in the company in the future. Would you please keep my CV and details on file for consideration if you have any further suitable vacancies within the company?

Thank you.

Yours sincerely

(Signature)

Mary Jo Sengal

Continuing the Job Search

If you are not successful in gaining employment it is important to persevere and to use your time productively while job hunting to gain further experience by completing work placements and additional training. This can then be added to your CV, making yourself a more suitable candidate for employment.

Consider the following:

Attend conferences, lectures and trade fairs to keep up to date with industry developments and extend your network of contacts. (See Resources, page 245.)

Update your skills, adding to your knowledge through practical experience.

Study additional short courses to add to your CV and meet likeminded people.

Use your local careers service for help and guidance and also a second opinion in checking through your CV, application forms, letters of application and personal statements.

Trained career advisors may be able to offer support, advice and guidance and will be able to suggest different types of work or training.

Review your career ideas. Are you aiming too high for your level of experience? (Alternatively, are you more capable and over experienced for the jobs for which you are applying?)

Improve your research into the job market and company profiles and extend your network base.

And, finally, never give up!

Chapter 10: Starting Your New Job

You have been offered a job within a company and made the decision to accept the position. This chapter discusses the importance of making a good impression, how to deal with colleagues at work, team building, career goals and development and your future prospects.

Making a Good Impression

Most people start a new job with a mixture of excitement and apprehension. Meeting people for the first time and working in a new environment can be exciting, but also daunting. Always make sure you are on time, and be positive in your approach to your work. After a few days working you will begin to settle down and understand more about what is expected of you, how you fit into the team and who's who in the company.

Things to Consider

Are there any unspoken rules in the department or company you are working in? Make sure you fully understand the nature of your position and what is expected of you on a daily, weekly and monthly basis. What projects are priorities? Are there any important deadlines looming?

Never be afraid to ask or check information – learn to listen carefully and act on the advice given. Get to know your co-workers, what their positions entail and how you fit into the team with your supervisor, line manager or your mentor. Whether this is your first job, a career move or a promotion to a senior position it is useful to have as much information relating to the company's business as possible.

Dress Code

It is most important that you feel comfortable when working and abide by any health and safety rules and regulations in relation to the dress code. If you are working in a laboratory working on fabric testing you may be expected to wear a white coat, but in a design studio anything may go. However, always be ready for the unexpected. One minute you are cutting patterns, the next you may be having a meeting with clients or an executive director of the company who is doing a quick tour of the design studios. Look at what others are wearing in the job and be aware of what is acceptable. You may have to compromise, but try to maintain your individuality and professionalism within whatever limits are acceptable in the company.

*Sourcing fabrics in industry,
Premiere Vision*

Job Description

Read your job description carefully and make sure you understand your roles and responsibilities. A job description should list your job title and outline the purpose of the job, listing your general and specific duties. It is useful to refer to your job description, particularly in the initial weeks of starting your new job, to provide a checklist of what you are responsible for.

Induction Programme

During the initial weeks of a new position, some companies will offer you a short induction programme, to welcome you and introduce you to the company. The induction programme usually provides a greater insight into the company, a brief history and details of the company ethos, company structure, policies, training and staff development, the availability of any internal staff development programme and a site tour and map. Some companies provide you with a staff handbook.

A good induction programme can often make all the difference to the performance and the effectiveness of staff, helping you to settle into the company, introducing you to the team that you will be working with and providing clear guidelines on what the company expects of their employers, but also what they are offering you. It provides an opportunity for you to ask any questions you still have about the company, your role and responsibilities and your contract.

Probationary Period

Most newly recruited staff complete a probationary period before being offered a permanent position. The length of this is usually identified in the job description and is generally between six months and one year. Once the probationary period has been satisfactorily completed, a probationary interview may take place discussing your contribution to the company, the progress you have made and the company's expectations of you in your new permanent position.

Colleagues at Work

Throughout your career you will encounter a variety of work colleagues, doing a range of jobs at many levels. In any organization there will be a diverse mix of personalities, offering a wide spread of skills. A good manager should be able to utilize their employees' full potential, pulling on the various personalities within a team and maximizing team dynamics to achieve the best results.

Team Building

Most employment in the fashion and textile industry involves working in a team, whether this is every day or sporadically, during staff development, training meetings, events and trade fairs.

Working in a team situation can be very enjoyable and rewarding; however, it can also present problems: group dynamics, the range of personalities, differing opinions and approaches to working practices and situations, pressurized deadlines, varying levels of ability and a different understanding of a common goal. All individuals within a team need to know their individual roles and responsibilities and also how they contribute to the team.

Communication is crucial to the team's success. Every team member has a responsibility to attend the required meetings and briefings. To work effectively in a team situation it is important to build strong collaborative skills, enabling you to talk, listen and interact with your colleagues in a positive and constructive way, getting the very best from each member of the team and avoiding any possible conflict.

When working for an organization, whether large or small, always make use of your line manager or mentor. Ask them when you do not understand something or require support. Some companies offer supervision meetings, providing a time for you to ask questions and set targets for the next few months.

Whatever area of the industry you enter, you'll be working with others in briefings, meetings and brainstorming sessions.

Successful Networking

Throughout your career in the fashion and textile industry, you will constantly meet new people through a variety of situations: conferences, trade fairs, exhibitions, fashion shows, internal or external staff development programmes, business meetings and business dinners. Always carry your business card with you and pass it to anyone who you meet and want to stay in contact with.

Annual Performance Review

Larger companies offer an annual performance review, which is sometimes known as an appraisal. In an ideal world an appraisal provides the opportunity for you and your line manager to meet on a regular basis (usually every 6-12 months) to discuss your progress and your performance within the company. It should give you the opportunity to discuss any issues or concerns.

It's also the time to discuss your progress, potential, staff development needs and career goals, and should be seen as a motivating experience. Usually paperwork is completed during the appraisal process, outlining the outcome, and a copy is given to the appraisee and the appraiser for future reference.

Career Goals

What are your future prospects? What do you want to achieve in your first or second employment position? What salary do you want in two years' time? Where do you want to be in five years' time? What do you want to achieve professionally? Having career goals will keep you focused and interested in your work. In your first position – working as a junior pattern cutter, for example – your aspirations may well be to develop competent skills in flat pattern cutting and gain greater understanding of the industry.

While in your second position it may be to work as a pattern cutter – using a combination of flat pattern cutting skills and modelling on the stand. Your ideal third position might be to work as a head pattern cutter, managing a small team of pattern cutters. Your aspirations will change constantly due to personal circumstances, developments within the industry, acquisition of new skills, and the opportunities and openings that are available to you.

Reassessing Your Career

It is perfectly healthy to periodically reassess your career. At times you may be looking for the next step up the career ladder. For example, you are appointed as a Trainee Assistant Designer and after two years you may want a career move and start looking for promotion within your existing company or with another. At other times you may find yourself reassessing as a result of a change in your own or the company's circumstances.

The fashion and textile industry is ever changing due to the economy, developments in technology and product advancements, and changes in the global marketplace. Some companies develop and expand quickly, growing in size and recruiting new staff, while others cannot compete – staff are made redundant and companies go into receivership. You may also find your circumstances changing after working for many years in one company and then finding your job title and description have changed following restructuring.

At such times it is best to take a positive attitude. It may just be time for a change, time for you to move on and work in a new environment, in a more senior position, or to consider an alternative career choice. Always be prepared, and keep your CV, skills and contacts up to date. Many agencies and services offer careers support and facilities to help you reassess your career. Changing your job may involve changing your approach to your present work situation or having the confidence to make bigger changes. This may include applying for new jobs or promotion, establishing your own business or working on a freelance basis.

__M__any graduates or employees will opt for self-employment (as opposed to being employed by someone else). Launching a fashion or textile business offers exciting opportunities to use existing professional and practical skills, and provides the opportunity to develop new entrepreneurial skills. The dream perception of running your own business is to be free of the constraints of working for someone else, to be able to work the hours you want to work and in the way that you want, resulting in greater independence, financial success and improved job satisfaction.

The Realities of Starting a Business

Every week, many new business start, but many also fold due to bankruptcy and other factors. It is vital to have a good business idea, which has been well researched and planned. Entrepreneurs have made millions through successful business ventures that have a unique selling point. It is useful to have worked for someone else in a similar set-up to gain the necessary knowledge, researching and assessing the strengths and weaknesses of your business idea as you do so.

Examples of Successful Business Ventures

==

- ✘ *Product based – manufacture and retail*
- ✘ *Skills based – running a workshop*
- ✘ *Consultancy*
- ✘ *Retail – outlet, online retail, party plan*

==

The fashion and textile industry lends itself to small businesses; many have been launched and received international recognition. Some entrepreneurs choose to operate as sole traders, enjoying the independence and freedom of operating and being in control of all aspects of the business themselves, while others aim to establish large businesses that employ many staff, sometimes internationally.

Design team working on an evening gown in the studio

To be successful, you need to be realistic and plan carefully, and understand what running a business entails. Starting your own business can be exciting and may be the realization of a lifelong dream, but it will also be extremely challenging and hard work. You must be prepared to put in long hours of hard work, be totally committed to your business and be exceptionally focused. You also need to be resilient enough to cope with knockbacks and pitfalls.

As well as the benefits of working for yourself, there are also disadvantages to consider. These include financial uncertainty, long hours, working in isolation, loneliness, no-one with whom to discuss new ideas, and no office banter. Many graduates and young entrepreneurs set up in business with insufficient experience or knowledge of their product, the service ethos, competitors, finance and what running their own business generally entails, leading to the business venture failing.

However, there are also many success stories with young entrepreneurs achieving success through having a great idea, a well thought-out business plan, fantastic contacts and being realistic in their ventures.

'Work hard, make friends, be decent… treat your suppliers, customers and staff well, think clearly when things don't go well, keep being creative even when financial pressures hit hard, don't get carried away by press coverage, be adaptable.'

Wayne Hemingway: Founder of Red or Dead

Entrepreneurial Skills

Every business needs a unique selling point. What makes your fashion and textile business different from what is already out there? Whether your business involves offering a service – from fashion or textile consultancy to a forecasting house predicting trends or an operation producing a range of bridalwear to sell exclusively from design studios – you will need to analyze the market: know who your clients and competitors are and understand the market value of your services.

SWOT Analysis

===

* ✘ **Strengths** – *do you have the necessary knowledge, skills, experience, business savvy and personal attributes?*
* ✘ **Weaknesses** – *is there anything you can identify that might create problems?*
* ✘ **Opportunities** – *what are the openings and the demands for your business?*
* ✘ **Threats** – *are there issues related to funds, competition, location, relevant contacts, market research into the product or service?*

It is worthwhile attending a short course designed for people who want to set up their own business. Usually local employment centres will be able to advise you on government schemes and short courses in your area. A well designed programme will guide you through all the stages from the initial business idea and writing a business plan, to negotiating financial and legal regulations and acquiring the marketing, promotion and administration skills to be successful.

Have You Got What it Takes?

Do you have what it takes to be successful running your own business? You will need to do much soul searching, questioning whether you have the personal qualities to make a go of it.

Essential Qualities

==

- ✖ *100 per cent focus*
- ✖ *Confidence*
- ✖ *Multiple skills*
- ✖ *Ambition*
- ✖ *Independence*
- ✖ *Organizational skills*
- ✖ *Dedication*
- ✖ *Ability to multi-task*
- ✖ *Capacity to work long hours*
- ✖ *Flexibility of working hours*
- ✖ *Adaptable in your approach to work*
- ✖ *Excellent communication skills*

==

Questions to Ask Yourself

- ✖ ***Is the time right for you to start your own fashion and textile business?***
  When is the right time to start your own business? This will depend in part on the individual. The world economy continues to fluctuate. However, there are many government initiatives being developed to support new young businesses. It may be through unemployment or redundancy, or through lack of promotion, striving for a new challenge or dreaming of success that makes you take the plunge into self-employment.

  Some people choose to start their own business while they are in employment, using their regular salary as financial security. Others choose to give up their paid employment to take the plunge, investing everything in setting up and establishing their own business.

✖ ***What are your personal commitments?*** Consider carefully your personal commitments and the type of business you want to launch. Is the business idea compatible with the time you have free to commit to the business? Is the timing of the launch of the business right for you or is this your busiest time of the year with the children on holiday and away from school, or other family commitments?

✖ ***Do you have sufficient time to spend in developing your idea?*** More and more people are setting up their own fashion and textile businesses and many of them are very successful. However, many also fail to achieve a successful business due to insufficient planning and lack of time to complete research and analyze the market, the business idea and the sources of financial support. Producing a realistic business plan is crucial to the success of the business.

✖ ***Do you have sufficient funds to start a business and make a realistic go of it?*** Insufficient funds to set up and establish the business will cause long-term problems. Researching and analyzing the start-up costs of the operation to achieve maximum success of your business venture is all-important. Be realistic, do your homework and research the costs thoroughly. Discuss your business plan with your bank manager, business and financial advisor, accountant and any business backers, drawing on as much advice and support as possible.

Type of Business

There are several types of business: you can operate as a sole trader, a partnership or a limited company.

Sole Trader
A sole trader is responsible for the entire running of the business and is also financially liable for any debts. This is one of the simplest ways to set up your own business. However, you need to have good practical skills and be very business-minded and focused to cope with the diversity of roles you'll need to take on.

Partnerships
A partnership is when two or more people enter into a business relationship. The advantages are that the business responsibilities and pressures are shared and partners can bring different skills and knowledge to the business. For example, there are many well-known business partnerships in the design world where one partner is the designer and innovator, and the other partner is in control of the promotion, marketing, accounting and book keeping. It is important to have a formal partnership agreement drawn up by a solicitor, which requires signing by all parties. The agreement will include details of the working relationship between the partners, the capital contributed by each partner, entitlements, salary and legal considerations.

Limited Company

A limited company is different from a sole trader or partnership in that this type of business is more complex to set up and the name needs to be registered with Companies House. A limited company has directors and shareholders, and the financing of the company is independent from the directors' personal finances, providing protection for personal assets. It is recommended that you seek advice in setting up a limited company, for example from company formation agents, local government business schemes and specialists such as solicitors and accountants.

Co-operative

A further type of business arrangement is a co-operative. A co-operative is a shared business that is managed by a group of people – for example they may share premises, facilities, equipment and clients. Everyone in the co-operative is involved in the decision-making, from the day-to-day running of the business to the ownership and the control of the business.

Whether you are considering operating as a sole trader, partnership, limited company or as a member of a co-operative, it is recommended that you seek the advice of a business advisor, particularly in the first few years of trading. There are also many well-written books that provide excellent business advice.

Business Preparation

When planning to start your own business it is important to have a strong business idea and be realistic, drawing up a comprehensive business plan. A business plan identifies your personal details: name, address and contact details; as well as the business title, the aims and objectives of the business and the type of business – sole trader, partnership or limited company. It also includes market research, information about the product or service, start-up costs, operational budget and cash-flow forecast, accounts, marketing and promotional strategy and analysis of your competitors.

Writing a business plan helps you to identify what you want to achieve through your business, highlighting the motivation behind the dream. It helps you answer some questions: How realistic is your idea? How do you intend to develop your idea into a thriving business? What return should you expect and what are the realistic costs of starting up your own business?

Start-up Costs

Most people who start up their own fashion and textile business require additional money to finance their idea. Your business plan will help you to establish how much money you require to make your idea work by analyzing all the costs, from start-up costs, to daily, weekly and monthly budgets, within the context of a realistic financial forecast of the overall feasibility of the business over a period of years.

Start-up Costs Checklist

Start-up costs	Yes	No	Summary of costs
Premises			
Design equipment			
Office equipment			
Stock			
Consumables			
Stationery and printing			
Transport			
Additional training			
Accounts and banking			
Income protection and liabilities			
Business support			
Promotion of business			
Memberships			

Premises

Where are you going to work from? You may choose to work from home, depending on the type of business you are running, which may be very convenient and cost effective. However, if this is not the case you will need to find a suitable studio to work from or a retail outlet to trade from. Important factors to consider include: location, rent/mortgage, annual costs, rates, buildings insurance, and cost of alterations to the property to make it safe and fit for purpose.

Design and Office Equipment

Consider carefully what equipment you will need to set up and run your business smoothly. Do you need office equipment – a computer, software, printer, fax machine, photocopier, telephone, mobile phone, filing cabinet, desk and office chair? Will you buy new or second-hand, or can you lease the equipment at competitive rates? Do you need all the equipment immediately to function properly or can some be purchased at a later date? Do you require design and/or manufacturing equipment – mannequin, sewing machine, lockstitch equipment, garment press, weaving loom, knitting machine, print table or drawing board?

Stock and Consumables

Consider carefully what stock and consumables you require to start your business. Consumables include items that you use on a daily basis and will need replacing, for example photocopier paper, pens, pencils, notepads and ink cartridges. These items appear to be relatively cheap to purchase initially, but will need replacing regularly at a cost that soon adds up and which must be counted in your business costs. For example, a business with direct mail marketing uses thousands of envelopes each week along with the cost of postage, the cost of a franking machine and the cost of travel to the post office if the mail is not automatically collected. All costs need to be calculated in a business plan.

Stationery and Printing

Every new business needs a good marketing strategy. Business cards, printed letterheads, printed brochures, catalogues, promotional postcards, advertising flyers, delivery notes and promotional printed bags can all be used to give your company a corporate identity (you also need a logo). These items are relatively cheap. However, the quantities that are required once the business is up and running can be surprising, and this all adds up in reducing your profit margins.

Transport

Will you need a vehicle for the business? What type and size of vehicle? How much will it cost to purchase, or does renting a vehicle make more sense? What will the general costs of upkeep and maintenance be? How much will you pay in weekly fuel bills, tax and insurance? In addition, will your business require national or international travel to trade fairs and exhibitions, for business meetings or to attend business seminars?

Training

To successfully set up and run your own business, will you require more training in the near or distant future? Consider whether any additional training is required, the type of course – full time or part time – what the training costs are and what the benefits would be to your business.

Accounts and Banking

It is important that all your accounts are kept up to date in an accounts book identifying all monetary transactions. It is very useful to employ an accountant to prepare your annual accounts and to advise on financial matters relating to the business. A good accountant should be able to help a business with cashflow, sorting out your accounts, providing advice relating to tax benefits, tax relief, insurance, capital allowances, pensions, business expenses and business rates.

When sourcing finance, make appointments with the business managers at several banks and building societies to discuss all the options available, get the best banking deals and the support you require. Many high street banks and building societies offer deals and incentives to business start-ups to encourage their custom. However, it is important to look at the bigger picture. Do your homework and be prepared to talk through your ideas with the manager, presenting your business plan, giving as full a picture as possible. Know what you are asking for and compare the options each bank or building society offers before making any final decisions. Consider the convenience of the bank's location, availability of online and telephone banking, types of accounts and incentives on offer, access to your account, free banking periods for new businesses, interest charges and any other relevant factors. It is important that you establish a good working relationship with your bank manager, keeping him or her informed if there are any problems with or changes and developments to your business.

Cash Flow

Be prepared for unforeseen costs, unpaid bills, late payments, money for equipment repairs and upgrades, postage, printing, materials, service bills, cost of training and development, sampling, exhibiting at trade fairs and exhibitions and costs incurred for promotion material and marketing.

Grants and Funding

Grants are available, both nationally and internationally, that provide funding for small businesses, the regeneration of businesses and support for new and innovative community projects. Some funding is available through government schemes and regional enterprise schemes, organizations and associations. There are websites that identify sources of funding, listing the latest information and providing regular updates on successful fund applications and also advice on completion of the funding application forms. See Resources, page 249. Many sites are well worth viewing, giving you an indication of successful previous applications.

Income Protection and Liabilities

As with any business, it is important to take out insurance to cover various risks, including loss of stock through fire and theft, health insurance to cover any ill health and loss of earnings and shop, office and property insurance to cover other contingencies.

Be aware of legal issues such as copyright, employment laws, import and export regulations in the clothing and fashion sector, labelling regulations, safety legislation, insurance cover and intellectual property rights. Keep up to date with changing policies and health and safety issues. This is important from the viewpoint of the public profile of the company, as well as to prevent lawsuits that could be potentially damaging to its financial viability.

Business Support

Membership of a specialist business association may offer you invaluable information and support. See Resources, page 240, for details of relevant international fashion and textile associations.

Promotion of the Business

There are many different ways of marketing and promoting a business from advertising and editorials in local and national newspapers and journals, trade association newsletters and bulletins to radio, television, cinema, the internet, trade fairs and exhibitions, flyers, press releases, mail-shots, promotional postcards, billboards and word of mouth. It is important to plan a marketing strategy. Consider where the best place for you to advertise is, and promote your business at the optimum time.

For example, someone who sets up a fashion publishing business would find that, rather than take out expensive advertising space in glossy journals, it is far better to send out promotional packs to editors of selected journals and receive publicity through editorial coverage, which is free. However, a service industry may benefit from taking out advertising space in a journal to ensure good coverage.

Networking is also crucial to the development and promotion of your business. Often people who start their own business work in isolation, which can be very lonely. A good network of like-minded people who understand your business can offer help and support, encouraging you through the more difficult times when you feel like giving up. Attending trade shows and exhibitions will provide industry updates, knowledge of competitors, market research and the chance to establish new contacts.

Managing and Developing Your Business

You should regularly assess the performance of your company. Make sure that the infrastructure and staffing is commensurate with the nature and scale of the market – and that any potential opportunities for expansion or increased profits are taken advantage of.

As your business grows, it is important to ensure that staff roles in your company become appropriately differentiated with a suitable skill mix – covering such functions as finance, human resources, marketing and sales – and that they work in a team to develop and realize your business goals.

Marty Stevens-Heebner:
Accessories Designer and Online Retailer

Marty Stevens-Heebner from New York, USA launched Rebagz™ in 2007, producing colourful tote bags from recycled materials such as rice sacks and woven juice bags. As Marty states: 'Style comes first to us; our "eco" focus is the icing on the cake.' Rebagz™ is a business that has grown from strength to strength due to Marty's ability to be aware of an ever-changing market and her astute business sense and strong marketing skills. Her designs are sold internationally and also through her website.

An Interview with Marty Stevens-Heebner

How did you get into this line of work?

I made jewellery with my friend, Christine Calla, who had grown up in the Philippines, and she suggested I head there with my ideas for handbags. I originally made samples out of fabric, but discovered recycled weave and started the rice sack line, literally roaming the markets and trying to convince the rice sellers to sell their used sacks to me to make handbags.

When did you first become interested in recycling issues?

I did humanitarian work in Mexico following the Zapatista rebellion and my mama was a serious recycler, so working with recycled materials was an obvious choice.

What is the concept behind the Rebagz™ label?

Rebagz™ handbags are made from recycled rice sacks and woven juice packs. My aim is to create handbags that are as varied and versatile for stylish women of all ages. We believe you can't call yourself eco-friendly without being human-friendly as well, so we ensure the people who make our bags are paid and treated fairly.

Can you describe your design process in a few sentences? What is the procedure for producing a Rebagz™ design?

I sketch ideas out in detail, produce samples, then travel to the Philippines to supervise the revisions of the samples. I usually start out with between 12 and 14 ideas, and end up introducing about six new designs per season.

What is the key to the success of the Rebagz™ label? What skills and attributes are required to successfully set up your own design label?

I didn't go to design school, so forget that as a necessity! You need to know how to draw and sketch, but I have taught myself. There are two things vital to success – hard work and being a good listener. You need a feel for colour and dimension, proportion and trends, but working hard is the only way to succeed.

Part of working hard is listening to what people tell you and then acting decisively on the suggestions and ideas. I have never, ever forgotten it's a business. You can run your design business professionally and still be eco-friendly and human-friendly.

Top: *Limited edition Rebagz™ rice sage bag designed by Marty Stevens-Heebner*

Top right: *'Unige' woven shoulder bags designed by Marty Stevens-Heebner*

Above: *Marty Stevens-Heebner with Virgie, the head weaver at The Foundation, which makes the woven line, in*

Marketing has also been vital to Rebagz' success. We've been very effective at telling people the story behind our bags – and they love it!

Finally, I celebrate every small inch of success. We've had a lot of extraordinary opportunities that have fallen into our laps, but I've also acted on them immediately and let those responsible know how grateful I am.

Where can your bags be purchased?
We have a web store at www.rebagz.com, but we also sell in a lot of stores and boutiques.

What was the greatest challenge in setting up your own business?
My father, who's my best business advisor by far, has a saying: 'Things are never as bad or as good they seem.' I've had my designs copied and that was infuriating at first. But that's when I learned to rely on my own ingenuity and I came up with new designs that surpassed the old ones in terms of originality and style.

My father was president of a company that he took from bankruptcy to top-ranked profitability over the course of 17 years and he makes me keep my numbers straight. I loathe accounting, but I sit down and deal with it because I have to.

What advice can you give to a designer who wants to launch his or her own business?

Lisa Jayne Dann:
Independent Fashion Designer

Lisa studied Fashion Design at Dewsbury College of Art and Design before a short stint in retail. While working part-time, dressmaking for a local designer, she formed a friendship with the team at Aqua Couture, who at that time were launching a new shopping outlet at the Corn Exchange in Leeds.

Lisa Jayne Dann the label has never looked back. Now stocked in numerous independent boutiques across the country, Lisa Jayne Dann can be seen worn by celebrities and the fashion elite from all over the UK. Described as the as 'Queen of Leeds Independent Fashion' she uses influences from both current and future trends on the catwalk to dictate her own unique style.

An Interview with Lisa Jayne Dann

What is the concept behind your company?
The concept behind the Lisa Jayne Dann label is to create innovative, wearable fashion with vintage references, designed for the immaculately stylish. My collections are wearable garments and are a must for all the cool girls who like to party out on a Saturday night.

How would you describe your style?
My style constantly changes with my mood for that day; my look is definitely interchangeable, but overall it's thought out but with a relaxed edge! My collections need to be wearable but with up-to-the-minute detail... statement pieces.

You have been awarded Leeds Independent Designer of the Year, what is the key to your success?
Hard work and perseverance. The fashion industry is a constant battle to better yourself and your designs, but it is extremely rewarding.

How many people work in your company?
I work independently.

How do you manage the production of your collections?
I tackle most of the work myself; however I now have some good connections

with some production factories, so I can ship work out to them when it gets too much for me alone.

Which trade fairs and exhibitions do you attend?
Pure, London

Is there anything about your role as a designer that has surprised you?
My strength and determination to continue when the going gets tough – it's vital to hold and keep that passion for what you do and believe in.

What are your future aspirations for the Lisa Jayne Dann label?
An online shop.

What advice would you give to an aspiring fashion designer?
Push yourself each day and your return for your work will be worth it. Believe in your ideas; don't be scared to put yourself out there.

What advice can you give to designer that wants to launch his or her own business?
If you believe in something, go for it, but be sure to get some working capital behind you. Most independent designers struggle and go under because they do not have sufficient finance to keep afloat; you must keep your finances in order to keep buying fabrics, trims and to keep the business up and running, whilst awaiting invoices and money that's owed to you for previous work to be paid… it's a waiting game.

Bria Phillips: Online Fashion Retailer

Bria Phillips launched her online fashion retail business, Le Train Bleu, in 2003. In 2006 she expanded her business, opening an independent fashion boutique, Le Train Bleu, but then returned to online trading, expanding her online store to sell many international design labels, womenswear and accessories.

An Interview with Bria Phillips

What is the concept behind your company – Le Train Bleu?
Le Train Bleu was inspired by some of the pioneering online fashion magazines such as *Showstudio, Dresslab* and *Hintmag.* These were sites that were really exploring the new media of the internet and how it could be used to present fashion in new ways: movies, live content, fashion illustration that was animated through the use of Flash, viewer participation, and so on. I saw them as fashion magazines coming alive. With Le Train Bleu I strive to create that same personal and experiential shopping experience but within a new medium.

Where did the name Le Train Bleu originate?
Le Train Bleu is the name of a Ballet Russes production based on a story by Jean Cocteau, with costumes by Chanel and a backdrop by Picasso. To me, the ballet is a symbol for a really vibrant and creative time in the early twentieth century when artists from different disciplines, media and cultures worked in collaboration. With the growth of the internet I see the creative industries of today having that same exciting mix of cultures, disciplines, fine art and commercial art.

How did you get into this line of work?
The idea evolved slowly. There was a period of about a year where I was just researching and writing the business plan. I had no background in retail and no prior knowledge of how the fashion industry functioned, so there was a lot of study involved.

What labels does Le Train Bleu stock?
Although we have carried some more established brands such as Cacharel, Karen Walker and APC, our focus is more on under-the-radar designers, so our roster changes quite a bit from season to season. There has always been a focus on international designers.

Which trade shows and exhibitions do you attend?
I do all of my buying from my desk. In the beginning this was a necessity; I couldn't afford to travel or to hire somebody to run Le Train Bleu whilst I was away. Now that online stores are a dime a dozen, I really have to stay ahead of the pack with my buying. Plus, I buy internationally and with the shows occurring all around the world I could just about spend all year travelling and buying.

Being an online retailer allows me to take more risks, since my market is not reliant on one region or country. We have a lot of customers in Australia and Western Europe, which has been really important, as the economy in the US has suffered.

Describe a typical working day.
I usually start my day at home around 8am and spend two or three hours

Bria Phillips, online Fashion Retailer

catching up with people in Western Europe and on the East Coast. After that, I am usually at the studio helping with customer service, processing orders, meeting with designers, buying merchandise, following up on press requests, having photo shoots, writing copy for the website, working on photo editing and cleaning the toilet! Then I go home and eat and work some more!

My work is really integrated into my life. My husband is a strategic planner at an ad agency, so we talk a lot about the internet, media and popular culture, but it's just part of my life and my interests.

What makes a successful online fashion retailer?
Adaptability is key. I actually started out selling active wear as fashion. I had a phenomenal turnover, but I quickly realized that it wasn't really a feasible business in the long term. Seeing that it took the same amount of man-hours to sell a $300 dress as a pair of $30 legwarmers, I quickly switched into a more high-end market, but still selling things that would appeal to the same customer.

What is the key to your success?
Le Train Bleu has always been a creative endeavour rather than just a store. I think people remember Le Train Bleu because of the unique visual identity that we create through our own graphic design, photography and styling, as well as the idiosyncratic voice.

What is the most rewarding aspect of working for yourself?
The amount of control you have to shape your destiny and dramatically affect the business. When there are bumps in the road I can always fix them through sheer hard work. The solution might mean a lost weekend or two, but it's nice to have that ability to sort the problems out.

I've had to learn new things out of necessity. For instance, early on I would hire professional photographers and stylists for each photo shoot. I quickly realised that was going to be too expensive to keep up since we have new deliveries arriving every week. I taught myself some basic photography and have become the sole photographer for Le Train Bleu, which is now my favourite role in the business.

What advice can you give to someone who wants to launch his or her own business?
Don't use a lot of money upfront, and have fun. My advice is to start small and let demand dictate your growth. The best thing about online retail is that it afforded me the opportunity to start on a shoestring budget in a studio apartment, far away from the major fashion centres of the world, and yet immediately reach a global market.

Chapter 12: Moving Onwards and Upwards

*T*here are many employment opportunities in the fashion and textiles industry: many successful entrepreneurs who have established their own businesses and design labels; many graduates who have completed their studies and made a significant mark in the world of fashion and textiles; many people who work quietly backstage holding everything together doing very challenging jobs; and still others who have been successful working from the shop floor up through the ranks of a company.

This final chapter examines some of the new names within the industry who are making a mark, both nationally and internationally. The profiles and interviews provide an insight into their careers and successes to date.

Contemporary, feminine womenswear design by Laura Figueras – Bambi by Laura – Barcelona, Spain

Christopher Raeburn
Fashion Designer

Christopher Raeburn, a graduate of the Royal College of Art in London, is director of Raeburn Designs, whose men's and women's collections focus on 'functional beauty in the 21st century cityscape'. As a designer, he creates ethically intelligent garments from re-deployed military fabrics which are innovative in design and 'address the needs and concerns of a forward-thinking, modern society'. His inspirational work has been recognized for its creativity and attention to detail.

Christopher's past experience is varied from working for the Royal College of Art, structuring and running a 'Design Camp' to working freelance on design projects, producing capsule collections for the high street, drafting patterns and size grading, and also producing concept illustrations for trend forecasts. Clients have included Carmel Clothing, Wintle Menswear, Carolyn Massey, Rapha Cycles, Yesnomaybe, Austin Reed and JLD International.

Raeburn's designs have been well received by the press, in journals, and on websites, including: *Elle* (UK); WGSN; the *Weekend Mail*, Fashion-Era.com and Style Bubble. Showcases within 'New European Fashion Designers' and Hywel Davies' book *100 New Fashion Designers* (Laurence King) have helped to boost his profile. Due to his innovative approach to design he has received many awards for his work: Umbro 'Fashion. Kit. Lifestyle' award 2005, semi-finalist in the Fashion Fringe Competition in 2005 – working in collaboration with his brother Graeme Raeburn – winner in the Pommery Champagne Design Competition 2005, finalist in the Swarovski & the Costume Society Fabric and Gem Competition in 2004, and has also exhibited his work in the Camouflage Exhibition at the Imperial War Museum, UK.

Top: *Casual styling combines with intricate yet functional detailing to create a relaxed silhouette, with nylon parachute bomber jacket. Menswear collection by Christopher Raeburn*

Left: *Heavy wool bomber jacket constructed from vintage military battledress jacket with emphasis on the integrated original detailing. Womenswear collection by Christopher Raeburn*

The Raeburn Design label continues to grow in strength with the establishment of a vibrant multi-disciplinary studio, producing seasonal collections, and he also continues to work on collaborative projects with industry and independent artists and designers. Upcoming work includes a short film for Nick Knight's SHOWStudio.com, the expansion of London-based stockists and an exclusive reversible range for Design Week.

An Interview with Christopher Raeburn

What is the concept behind your label?
Raeburn Design constructs ethically intelligent garments from the materials of war. As a London-based company we are proud of our city and its history – our garments reflect this heritage, whilst incorporating a modern design outlook. Above all we are unique, innovative, British and proud.

Can you describe your design process in a few sentences?
Thoroughly researched chaos with a sprinkling of happy accidents.

Who or what are your biggest inspirations artistically?
Poster art, Nick Cave, second-hand books, battered leather bags, snow parkas, BBC documentaries, trips to the south coast, semaphore, Slavomir Rawicz, instructional design and long walks along the canals of East London have all helped to inspire garment and print concepts for upcoming work.

What is your greatest career challenge to date?
Pulling together catwalk shows and fashion shoots are certainly challenging but that's also part of what makes them so exciting; getting work published or exhibited at the Imperial War Museum was a challenge – but again success has been incredibly rewarding.

What is the most difficult challenge in establishing your own label?
Having to learn about every area of business from scratch. Education gives you a cocooned environment in which to experiment, but once you're out in the real world there are a lot of other factors that influence your daily activities.

You produce garment collections; do you also get involved in other projects?
Absolutely. At any one time I have four or five projects on the go: I work with product designers, illustrators, filmmakers, teachers and photographers. Collaboration and multi-disciplinary briefs have always inspired me; as a result I now have an upcoming film to be launched at London Fashion Week, a new section in the book *100 New Fashion Designers*, a spot during Design Week, and lots more to come…

What is the key to your success?
It's still early days but I think my work has a unique selling point: the fact that the original fabrics are finite means each garment that leaves our studio already has a history beyond its own.

What advice can you give to a designer who wants to launch his or her own business?
Winston Churchill failed sixth grade. He was subsequently defeated in every election for public office until he became prime minister at the age of 62. He later wrote, 'Never give in, never give in, never, never, never, never – in nothing, great or small, large or petty – never give in except to convictions of honour and good sense.' Never, never, never, never give up.

Sarah Handy
Assistant Buyer/Merchandiser

Sarah Handy, Assistant Buyer/Merchandiser, DKNY, London

Sarah Handy studied a BA (Hons) in Fashion Studies in the UK, achieving a first-class honours degree. During her three years of study Sarah completed several work experience placements at Burberry, London and Milan, and also worked alongside TV presenters Trinny Woodall and Susannah Constantine at a charity event in Selfridges, London.

On completion of her studies Sarah immediately gained a position as a Buyer's Administration Assistant with Freeman's, London, and was responsible for all the administration of orders, compiling and maintaining the sample library, assisting on photo shoots, liaising with suppliers and attending fit sessions and UK buys.

After a year working at Freeman's, Sarah moved to Club 21, an international retail and distribution company, working as an Assistant Buyer/ Merchandiser on the DKNY Jeans ladieswear brand. The company has over 30 designer labels including the Armani brands, DKNY, Luella and Mulberry. Sarah's work is varied, with responsibilities for buying and merchandising the main ladieswear jeans collection including DKNY accessories – watches, shoes, bags, fragrance and underwear.

An Interview with Sarah Handy

What did you enjoy most about studying fashion at university?

I enjoyed learning new skills and developing my own individuality within my ideas. I feel it was a great platform for me to explore what direction I wanted to go in. I enjoyed the design work and discovering my own creative process but I also enjoyed learning about the business side to fashion and how to behave as a professional outside of university.

How did you get into this line of work?

I have always thought that fashion came to me very naturally. I have always been creative and this is what led me to choose fashion as a career. During my final year of university I concentrated a lot on getting my foot in the door. I worked hard, completing several work placements and making sure I had a professional CV.

How important was completing work placements in industry during your studies?

I honestly feel that without the work placements that I did, it would have taken me longer to find a position within the industry. The course that I chose did not include a year out in industry, so I had to find my own work experience. I knew it would be what made me stand out from the other graduates. In all the interviews I have been to, they always ask more about my work placements than they do anything else! It was difficult at the time, with the expense and time away from my studies but it was more than worth it. I also think it is really good to spend time away from the 'bubble' of university, as it prepares you for life afterwards and you have more knowledge about what to expect in the industry.

What advice would you give to someone who wants to work in buying?

I would say do some work experience in a buying office, even if it is only for a week, and make sure that you like the kind of work it involves. The first year is the hardest because you do a lot of administration and don't get too involved in product development, which is the area where you get to be the most creative.

The hours can be long, as with any job I'm sure, but it's important to have stamina and enjoy the job. Some days you might be photocopying or typing all day so you have to have the right attitude to stick it out. The next day you might be shopping, so that's the fun part!

It's also important to like working with numbers. I come from a very creative background, but I also don't mind working with numbers and have learnt to enjoy it. Buyers work very closely with merchandisers, and understanding the figures shows you how to make better selections when buying. There is also some travel involved, so it's important to have the freedom to work away from home sometimes.

What are your short-term ambitions?

Short-term ambitions are to gain more experience in my new role as Assistant Buyer, and take on the accessories department as my own and try to grow the department and brand. I am still learning all about the retail industry and I just want to take on board as much as I can. I also have a buyer's administrative assistant starting with me soon, so I have to learn all about being responsible for someone else. It's important for me to be a good role model to other team members.

What are your long-term career ambitions?

Long term, I would like to think I would become a buyer at some point. I would still like to work within ladieswear or accessories and I really enjoy working within the luxury market. You never know what's going to happen, but at the moment I am so busy in this role that I don't think much further than two seasons ahead!

Caroline Mitchell
Milliner

Caroline Mitchell successfully completed a BA (Hons) Fashion Studies course followed closely by an MA in Design, specializing in millinery and accessories. During her postgraduate studies Caroline set up her own label, Caroline Mitchell Millinery, designing fascinators, millinery and accessories. Her work is bespoke, producing one-off original pieces that are handcrafted and detailed. Her achievements have included designing stage headpieces for burlesque performers Gwendoline Lamour and Immodesty Blaize, along with seasonal collections produced for individual clients. She has exhibited her unique designs and has received editorial coverage in many prestigious UK fashion journals.

An Interview with Caroline Mitchell

How did you get into this line of work?
It all started back when my cousin was getting married. I was elected to make her tiara, which was quite an honour. About that time, I won a competition to have one of my pieces displayed in a millinery store. After that, I started talking to the owner about whether I could sell some of my other work, and one thing led to another…

What projects are you working on right now?
'Lamour' collection, working with Gwendoline Lamour to design and produce a more wearable collection of millinery with a 1930s touch of glamour. I think vintage items hold a certain glamour that's often lost today. I like items that have a unique quality to them, with almost their own personality. I am also working on next season's collection and a bridal collection.

Where do you see yourself in five years' time?
In five years' time I would like to have established a name for myself, selling throughout the UK and also having international recognition for my work. Through the growth of the business I would like to employ a team of in-house designers and be confident there is a continued and growing demand for my work.

What advice would you give to someone setting up their own label?
Do your market research, make sure your designs are unique to the market and grab people's attention; otherwise the business will fail quickly. Get a range of people's opinions, gaining positive views and comments on how to strengthen your work.

Make a concerted effort to understand all the legalities of running a business, for example accountancy, finance, legal issues and copyright issues. There's plenty of advice out there. Have a good book of contacts for networking, which will help you to meet people who may be able to advise you, potential customers and clients.

Japanese-inspired fascinator designed by Caroline Mitchell

David Steinhorst
Fashion Designer

David Steinhorst studied pattern cutting in Berlin, Germany, moving to the UK to study Fashion Design, Fashion Womenswear on the BA (Hons) and Masters course at Central St Martins, London, successfully graduating in 2008. Throughout his studies David worked on many freelance projects, which included: visual merchandising for Louis Vuitton, Paris; working as an assistant during London Fashion Week for Preen by Thornton Bregazzi, London; producing print-textile and graphic design for Feote, Karlsruhe, Germany; designing garments for game characters for CDV Software Entertainment AG, Karlsruhe, Germany; and trend scouting for WGSN.

David's work has been featured in many international publications: the *Observer*, the *Mail on Sunday*, *Senken* newspaper (Japan), *Vogue* (UK), *International Textile Fashion Forecast* (UK), *Grazia* (UK), *Gazeta*, *Obcasy* supplement (Poland), the *Berliner Zeitung* newspaper (Germany) and WGSN.

David has won many prestigious awards for his design work, including winner of the Harrods Design Award, UK. Other awards include the Leonardo Da Vinci Bursary Award, Germany; winner of the Lancôme Colour Design Award, UK and the International Talent Support's Fashion Collection of the Year Award.

Top: *Womenswear design, soft, elegant and feminine in silhouette with adventurously exaggerated detailing from the autumn/winter 2009 collection by David Steinhorst*

Above: *Design development exploring the draping and detailing of neckline ideas by David Steinhorst*

An Interview with David Steinhorst

You initially studied pattern cutting in your home country of Germany; how important was your move to London to study fashion design?
Whilst living in Berlin I acquired the technical knowledge and developed my ideas into garments. It was a very formative time and although I remain very fond of the city, its people and the friends I made there, I wanted to push myself further on an artistic and creative level. In that respect, moving to London has been very important, as it is closer to industry and good for networking. I have benefited from the city's high velocity; diving into such a holding centre of creativity and inventiveness from people from all over the world was exactly what I was seeking.

What were the benefits of and were there any difficulties with working freelance while completing your studies?

The benefits are obviously experience within the industry, working with other designers, dealing with suppliers and clients, possibly finding a specific niche or a special aspect of my work that can sustain real-life conditions, meaning criticism and competition outside of the university-realm.

Who or what have been your biggest inspirations artistically?

My family has always been a major influence and inspiration to me. If it was a few sketches or a 10 foot canvas, my father always brought work home; it was everywhere. I believe truly creative people take their work wherever they go. You cannot choose to leave it at the office or in the studio; it surrounds you and follows you...

My parents taught me patience, accuracy, passion, determination and how to celebrate their outcomes. I learned that the more effortless things look, the harder they have been worked on.

What inspires and influences your work?

I admire craftsmanship, in whatever form. I always respect a well-made, good piece of craftsmanship, as it will always be timeless to the audience; however, it entails such a vast amount of time, paired with knowledge and skill of its maker. I always find the dualistic correlation at the essence of things fascinating and very inspiring. On a more visual level I greatly admire Gottfried Helnwein's work, for his attention to detail, his perfectionist manner and dimmed aesthetic. I enjoy clever pattern cutting and I am inspired by Heinz Schulze Varell's and Helmut Lang's work, and Horst Egon Kalinowski's pieces, for their dimension and tactile quality.

What is the most difficult part of designing a collection?

Letting go of good ideas.

What makes a successful fashion designer?

I am yet to find out.

You have won many awards; what is the key to your success?

Receiving awards is wonderful recognition of my work, providing a level of exposure to the industry and media which has provided other experiences. However, attention is only a good thing when you have something to say. So for that you need fresh experiences, inspiration and to move on. The chimney has to smoke.

What is your biggest fashion achievement to date?

I am very thankful for the recognition my work has received to date. On a more personal level I enjoy inventive pattern cutting and structural fabrics. In most of my work repetition forms a part-decorative device in the exaggeration of elements, creating abundance. I am excited about defining my own style through the use of repetition, as an aesthetic concept, which is an achievement in the development of my work.

What is your vision for your work?

Fashion for me lives in comforting elegance, a casual wearability paired with a substantial exquisiteness, craftsmanship and a certain portion of surprise. Fashion can be very loud, very large-lettered; however, a truly modern and desirable piece of clothing can be merely a whisper.

I would like to continue creating clothes that people can relate to and that are inspirational; clothes that people actually want to wear. I know the desirable feeling when I see a beautiful piece, so ultimately being able to create that in others would be very nice.

What advice would you give to an aspiring fashion designer?

Sometimes it is hard not to get lost in the immediate gratification of the process, so staying critical – most importantly towards oneself – is very important. Apart from that, stay fresh and work your socks off.

Lene Toni Kjeld
Textile Designer

Danish textile designer Lene Toni Kjeld successfully completed her MA in Textile Design at the Designskolen Kolding, Denmark, in 2004. During her studies she completed an internship, working as a print designer at the Pepper Corn Print Studios in Denmark and the Faro Disegni Design Studios in Italy. In 2004 she was awarded the Interior Innovation Award, Germany.

In 2005, Lene launched her own business – Lene Toni Kjeld – producing decorative transition wallpapers, using 'limited batch production'. Through her business she has worked on many exciting commissions and several collaborative projects with architects and interior design projects.

Lene's work is gaining an international reputation and has appeared in many international exhibitions, including the Coda Museum, the Netherlands; the Dansk Design Centre, Denmark; IMM Milano Furniture Fair, Italy; Helsinki; and in Finland and China. Her designs sell in the UK, France, Denmark, Norway, Hong Kong, Japan and New Zealand. Her work has been featured in many design magazines, journals and books, including *Metropolis* (US), *Elle Decoration* (Hong Kong), *Case da Abitare* (Italy), *Elle Décor* (Italy) and *Spaces* (UK/international).

An Interview with Lene Toni Kjeld

How did you get into this line of work?
Since I was very little I have always enjoyed sewing, printing and playing with fabrics, which I later realized was actually a profession. I realized that as a textile designer there are no limits, I can mix all kinds of materials together, which is a very playful approach to my work.

Who were your early influences?
My mom is a creative person and was my earliest influence. She was always using her hands, sewing, knitting and printing.

Who or what are your biggest inspirations, artistically?
I like to use photography as an inspiration, producing and exploring compositions with small details, forms, shapes and a special colour combination that, when you see the whole picture, doesn't stand out.

Hanna Werning is a wallpaper designer whose colourful and complicated patterns I love.

How would you define your style?
My style is a mixture of many techniques, which makes my work complex and personal. I never compromise on quality.

Can you describe your design process in a few sentences?
When defining the subject it's very chaotic. I brainstorm ideas not knowing where to start or where my work will end and what the results will be. All words are analyzed and grouped so I can move onto the sketching phase: hand drawing, scanning, computer drawing, using collage and stencil prints. I use many different mixed techniques during the design process before finalizing my designs on computer, and then I am able to work on the production.

What is the concept behind your company?
All my work is based on the key words: transformation, individualism, functions mixed with decoration and tradition. My work focuses on visual storytelling. I create patterns with changing atmospheres.

What is your greatest career challenge to date?
An interesting challenge is learning to work together with architects, like I did with Dorthe Mandrup Architects on a decoration project in Copenhagen.

What advice can you give to a designer that wants to launch his or her own business?
Always do what feels best and is the most fun. When you enjoy your work and it makes you happy, the result is also satisfying.

'Lace Rose' transitional wall decoration; a hybrid combining two different repeat patterns, designed by Lene Toni Kjeld

Sandra Backlund
Knitwear Designer

Sandra Backlund studied Fashion Design, graduating from Beckmans School of Design, Sweden in 2004. On completion of her studies she immediately set up her own company, Sandra Backlund, designing knitwear. She has received many exciting commissions, including a collection commissioned by *Vogue Italia*, a collaborative project with Louis Vuitton and special knit pieces for Printemps in Paris. Sandra has also been presented with awards for her outstanding work, including winner of the Swedish Elle Awards 2008, British Fashion Council New Generation 2008 and winner of Future Design Days Award in Sweden.

An Interview with Sandra Backlund

How would you describe your work?
With the human body as the main starting point I improvise on a tailor's dummy or on myself to discover ideas of shapes and silhouettes that I could never come to think about in my head. I do not sketch, instead I work with a three-dimensional collage method; I develop some handmade basic 'bricks' that I multiply and attach to each other until they become a garment. My clothes are always quite sculptural with strong silhouettes, but I also put a lot of time into the finish and fit. They are not made with the purpose of pleasing everyone. Actually, I try not to think so much about trends and wearability when I design my collections. I do this to satisfy myself. Whilst others write poems or something to express themselves, I create fashion.

In your opinion, what makes a successful fashion designer?
Everyone who thinks of fashion more as an expression of art rather than an industry, who has their own voice and brings something unique to this business.

What is the key to your success?
I try to keep an open mind and not worry too much about the future, but on the other hand I am not the kind of person who rushes for the stars either. I work very hard, protect my origins and what I am good at, but also continue to actively investigate

Top: *Knitwear design by Sandra Backlund, exploring traditional knit techniques to create 'heavy wool collage knitting' – improvising, distorting and transforming the natural silhouette of the body*

Above: *Portrait of Sandra Backlund, renowned in Sweden for her award-winning, creative, structural knitted garments*

how I can develop my designs and my company.

What inspires and influences your designs?
Apart from the handicraft techniques and the materials I work with, I am really fascinated by all the ways you can highlight, distort and transform the natural silhouette with clothes and accessories. I like to consciously dress and undress parts of the body.

I am kind of introverted and lock myself in my studio when working, so in that sense I guess I find inspiration from everything that is going on in my own life privately, as a designer and as a founder of my own company.

What is the most difficult part of designing a collection?
When I start on a new collection I always take off from just a diffuse idea. One thing leads to another, one garment breeds the next one and in the end the collection is almost like a three-dimensional personal mind map. For me the last part of the process is the most difficult, when I have to make everything fit together and 'accept' what I have done.

What is a typical working day in your life as a designer?
I get up early in the morning and answer my emails. Then I work with my collection all day and half the night, then try to get a short sleep.

What advice would you give to an aspiring designer?
From my experience, go to fashion school. Learn and explore the basics of tailoring and traditional handicraft techniques and be aware of any mistakes and ideas along the way. I think that many concentrate too hard on just living up to the image of being a new fashion designer, instead of actually working as one. In the beginning it is important that you try not to worry about what other people might expect from you and instead spend a lot of time experimenting on your own to find what is special about you and what you are good at.

What is your vision for your work?
I am a searcher, without set goals, so that means I will never reach a finishing line, but I would of course like to be able to live off my work.

What is your greatest achievement to date?
For the last four years I have put everything into establishing my own company, which I am very proud of. I have stuck to my original plan to do my own thing and I am still standing. Being selected as the grand prix winner of Festival International De Mode & De Photographie in Hyères 2007, is of course also a major highlight for me.

Cecilia Sörensen
Fashion Designer

Fashion designer Cecilia Sörensen was born in Finland, where she studied tailoring in Helsinki, before moving to Spain to study fashion design in Barcelona. After graduating she showed her collections at Pasarela Gaudí – Barcelona Fashion Week – and they were well received. Her womenswear and menswear collections are ecology-conscious with strong emphasis on recycling. Her collections are sold in many international retail outlets in Spain, Italy, Finland, Japan and the USA.

An Interview with Cecilia Sörensen

How did you get into fashion design?
As a teenager I started to experiment, making clothes for myself and my friends. I first studied fine arts, then tailoring and finally I chose to study fashion design.

What or who are your biggest inspirations artistically?
It's not someone specifically, it has more to do with my life and what I am experiencing and living at a certain time. For example, when I got my first company studio I designed a collection entitled 'my room', which was based on all the rooms that I had during my life from my childhood playroom and student apartments to my first studio.

What is the concept behind your label?
The style is clean, feminine and wearable. I guess it also has to do with my Scandinavian origins, combined with living in the Mediterranean.

Can you describe your design process in a few sentences?
My design process – research, experiments and manipulations, design, patterns and prototypes. I have an intuition and feeling-based approach to my research. Many times I investigate themes that are

Top: *Pintucked detailed blouse by Cecilia Sörenson*

Left: *White feminine ruffle blouse with emphasis on detailing by Cecilia Sörenson*

in some way linked to my family, my life, my past or me personally.

What is the vision for your business?
I am keeping my company very small at the moment, growing slowly and securely to keep it under control. With every season I set myself new goals, to move forward, developing the company further. I am now involved with a government-aided production programme that provides me with a product manager, who is in charge of all the production procedures. This gives me a lot more time to be able to concentrate on developing my designs more thoroughly. I also want to develop my company, producing the garments in as environmentally friendly a way as possible, which is not so easy with a limited budget.

What are the advantages of setting up your own business and working for yourself?
Obviously the freedom! I am able to do exactly what I want and how I want to, respecting fabric, production and financial limitations. Having my own business gives me a lot of freedom but there is also an overwhelming amount of responsibility.

Which trade events do you attend and do you exhibit at any exhibitions or shows?
I have done all possible shows and fairs in Barcelona, starting from MerkaFAD to Circuit, Pasarela Gaudí, Bread & Butter and 080 Barcelona Fashion. At the moment I am showing at Rendez-Vous in Paris with ten other Catalan designers showcased by the Catalan government.

What is your greatest career challenge to date?
Production, production and production. I want to produce locally but it's an incredible struggle to achieve good quality fabrics, finishings and garments. I would never have thought it would be so difficult, but it is something I really believe in. I think the direction to go for now is stepping away from the 'use and throw' society with the superficial 'every two months' trends.

All the cheap retail chains have over-produced in the world, producing cheap and short-lived trash. I hope we can go back to the incredible pieces of clothing that last from one generation to another. I hope that we learn to appreciate good quality design and craftsmanship and are also prepared to pay for it. Less is more!

What advice would you give to an aspiring fashion designer?
Study, experiment and work as much as possible. Do internships in different companies from the first day of your studies and participate in the course as much as possible. Create and develop an authentic personal style. With enthusiasm and a lot of hard work, it's possible!

Laura Figueras
Fashion Designer

Left to right:

Sweet, nostalgic, feminine womenswear collection from Bambi by Laura

Young contemporary womenswear design by Laura Figueras, Bambi by Laura

Fashion designer Laura Figueras was born in Barcelona in 1980 and is one of Spain's young directional designers. Laura studied fashion design at Escuela des Artes y Técnicas de la Moda in Barcelona, Spain. On completion of her studies she presented her collection at Graduate Fashion Week in London, UK.

In 2002 Laura completed a work placement in the design studio with the London fashion label Preen. This gave her valuable experience and in 2003 she was offered the position of Head Designer for 'Women's Secret', a lingerie and corsetry label creating collections being sold in stores in Europe and Asia. In 2003 Laura set up her own label, Bambi by Laura, and in 2004 showed her first collection at Circuit – the alternative fashion catwalk event. Her work was well received and she achieved rave reviews in the national and international press, and has continued to launch seasonal collections that sell internationally.

An Interview with Laura Figueras

When did you first discover you had a flair for fashion?

I guess I was always interested in clothes and the way people looked, but what really made me realize that was what I wanted to do was visiting Japan when I was 16. It was the first time I'd been to Asia and I was amazed by the way the women dressed – always looking perfect and also looking very cool. There just weren't people dressing like that in Spain, and that's when I knew that I wanted to be a fashion designer.

How important was completing a work placement with Preen?

It was really important. I really admired Preen's work (still do). I admired their way of making a deconstructed image and working with complex patterns; it's something I've developed in my own work. What was really important about the work placement was that, by learning how the business of fashion worked, you could start a small label and it was possible to make it work.

What or who are your biggest inspirations artistically?

There are too many inspirations to list, but I guess the ones that inspired me when I was growing up were people like Egon Schiele, Oscar Wilde, De Chirico and of course Dalí and Picasso, but later on, people like Yves Klein or Guy Bourdain. Also photographers like Diane Arbus and, of course, William Egglestone.

Can you describe your design process in a few sentences?

I normally start thinking about a new collection immediately after I have shown the last collection! Like most designers I am quite eclectic in where I take inspiration from, I guess. On a practical level I normally start with colours and fabrics, make sketches, make the samples with the atelier and start to work with them on the mannequin before finalizing each piece.

How important was showing your first collection at Circuit?

Let's say if I hadn't done that, I probably wouldn't be doing this now. It was great, my first show was a big success, I made a lot of sales and also gained a sponsor for my next show. I thought it would always be that easy. Sadly, it's not!

What is the vision for your label, Bambi by Laura?

I want to make the leap from 'young designer' to established brand; I want to make it a real luxury brand, with a full range of products – shoes, accessories, and so on. My one specific ambition is to create a fragrance.

What is the key to your success?

Work hard and be nice to people.

What advice would you give to an aspiring fashion designer?

Get a proper job...!

Tanis Alexander
Costume Designer

Above: *Costume design by Tanis Alexander*

Right top: *Tanis Alexander on set*

Right bottom: *Costume and set design by Tanis Alexander*

Tanis Alexander studied fashion design at Baylor University and Columbia College, Chicago, then moved from Texas to Los Angeles to study as a costume designer and successfully completed the 'Costume for Television' course at CBS Studios in 2006. She has since worked on many productions for PathFinder Productions, Stormfront Films and Sunswept Productions, holding various positions including Costume Production Assistant, Costume Designer and Costume Supervisor.

An Interview with Tanis Alexander

What made you go into costume design?
I wish I could say that I 'have dreamed of being a costume designer' since I was a child. Unfortunately, that isn't the case. Actually, when I first began my college education at Baylor University in Waco, Texas, I was a biology major,

intending to go on to medical school. In my heart I knew that biology and medical school were not for me. After (several) long, intense, emotional phone conversations with my parents my dad asked me one simple question: 'What do you want to do for the rest of your life? If you could do anything, every day, for the rest of your life – what would it be?' My answer was 'something with clothes'.

The next week I changed my major to Fashion Merchandising and transferred to Columbia College in Chicago to continue my fashion education. I then went to Los Angeles for a six-week 'semester in LA'. In a matter of days I knew that costume design was exactly what I wanted to do. I had a passion for it. It made me happy and it was fun! And not just costumes; I realized that I had a passion for every aspect of filmmaking. After the semester ended, I made the decision to stay in Los Angeles and pursue my new dream and career; and I've been here ever since.

How important is it to have formal training?

I have worked with some very accomplished and amazingly talented costume designers, and they all come from different backgrounds. Some have undergraduate and graduate degrees from highly respected institutions; whereas others 'fell into' the position without any formal training. Some have filmmaking degrees; some have backgrounds in theatre. I think that regardless of a person's educational background, it's their inner drive and passion that is most important. If you truly love what you do and pursue it with integrity and determination; then formal education becomes less relevant.

What is the most difficult part of designing a costume?

Maintaining the balance of what is right for the character and what looks good on the actor. Sometimes aesthetics and current trends have a way of swaying your focus from the true analysis of a character. So you occasionally have to step back and assess that.

What are the most important aspects of designing and producing costumes?

Trying to juggle the expectations of the directors/ producers with the comfort and request of the actors and the accuracy of the characters with your own artistic vision to achieve the final costume.

Can you describe your design process in a few sentences?

I read the script the first time to familiarize myself with the characters and story. I then read it a second time to learn the characters. Age? Sex? Job title? Pre-existing clothing dictated in the script? I then really analyze the characters and research my ideas, collecting photos or magazine clippings. I will sketch out my costume ideas and present them to the director, producers and actors. If we are all on the same page, I begin the process of gathering the clothing (purchase, made-to-order or rental).

What is the most challenging part of your job?

This varies project to project: sometimes it's time, sometimes it's budget, sometimes it's knowing exactly what you want for a character for their costume.

What is your dream project?

Period shows. I seem to have a personal love for the 1930s and 1940s. Although I also enjoy working on contemporary shows with a strong emphasis on the clothing telling the story, which is quite fun as well.

Where do you see yourself in five years' time?

Happy. Whatever it is in five years that makes me excited to get up each day and that I have a strong, connection with, that's what I intend to be doing.

What advice would you give to someone seeking employment as a costume designer?

If you really want to pursue it, pursue it with your whole heart. Immerse yourself in a city that has film, television, and/or theatre resources and culture. Research the industry. Network, network, network! Find a mentor. Learn about fabrics and materials. Don't be afraid to express yourself.

Mark Liu
Fashion and Textile Designer

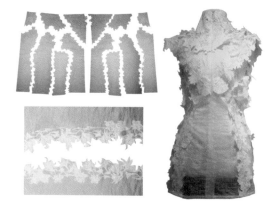

Top: 'Eco-aware and eco-responsible' fashion designer Mark Liu's innovative 'Zero Waste' fashion collection

Above: The 'Zero Waste' fashion collection combines the traditional techniques of print design and tailoring with laser cutting techniques and digital printing

Mark Liu, fashion and textile designer, trained at the University of Technology in Sydney, Australia, successfully completing a BA in Fashion and Textile Design, and then continued his studies at Central St Martins, London, UK. He completed work placements with Alexander McQueen, Ghost and Miss Selfridge. He now works freelance in the Australian fashion industry. His work involves innovative printing and pattern cutting techniques that challenge garment construction with new technologies, producing collections of innovative womenswear. His work has received excellent reviews in *Crafts* magazine, *ETN Textile Forum* and many other journals.

An Interview with Mark Liu

What is the concept behind your label?
My label challenges conventional methods of producing fashion and textiles by creating garments that do not produce any waste in the cutting process. We aim to design waste and inefficiency out from the very beginning of the production process. It is our hope that sustainability will inspire innovations in fashion. At the end of the day we want to create desirable fashion which is environmentally sustainable.

How would you describe your work?
My designs hybridize fashion and textiles, creating new possibilities in fashion design. By designing garments which will fit within a certain size of fabric it forces the designer to come up with new creative solutions that may not have been considered before.

What techniques do you apply to your work?
I combine pattern making and textile design.

What or who are your biggest inspirations, artistically?
In fashion my greatest influences are probably Issey Miyake, Rei Kawakubo and Yohji Yamamoto. However, I now find most of my inspiration no longer comes from art and design, but from science and philosophy. I'm really inspired by the physicist Michio Kaku and how he makes complex scientific concepts fascinating and tangible in his books.

Can you describe your design process in a few sentences?
I see the vision of what I want and usually have the silhouette in my head. Then I imagine building the dress, visualizing the inside out while moving flat pattern pieces around. The trick is to design in 3D while also visualizing the 2D flat pattern. It is like sculpting whilst playing Tetris at the same time.

What is your greatest challenge to date?
Putting together the next collection – with every collection the level of sophistication increases.

What is your greatest achievement to date?
Putting together the last no-waste collection – when I first started it I honestly didn't know if it would be possible.

What is your dream project?
I have so many dream projects it is hard to keep track of them. At the moment writing a book or designing a zero-waste building would have to be one of them.

What is the most difficult challenge in establishing your own label?
The hardest task is keeping the label running. There are so many roles to juggle besides just designing.

Designing is probably the easiest part compared to the more mundane aspects of the business.

You produce garment ranges and collections; do you get involved in other projects?
I always have many projects. I sometimes teach and lecture about fashion and textiles. I am also the textile designer for the label Asudari. At the moment I am putting together a book of illustrations and experiments about the nature of the creative mind.

What is the key to your success?
I think keeping an open mind, being open to change and not being complacent are key to success.

What advice can you give an artist or designer who wants to launch his or her own business?
Remember that the relationships with the people you work with are going to reflect in the quality of the work you produce. Make sure you have enough money to survive. Small businesses can be like gambling; a situation which is normally not important can become heightened with emotions when money is at stake. Learn to balance your emotions and ego so you can make clear decisions.

Nicoline Patricia Malina
Fashion Photographer

Nicoline Patricia Malina was born in Indonesia and moved to the Netherlands, where she studied Fine Art and Fashion Photography at the Utrecht School of the Arts.

In 2004 Nicoline established her own business as a fashion photographer, working for clients in Amsterdam, Paris and Antwerp. In 2007 she was awarded first prize in the Iconique Societás Excellence in Fashion Photography. Her website showcases her expanding portfolio of styles, which are all very individual, inspiring and innovative in concept.

In 2008 she moved to Jakarta, Indonesia, where she now lives and works as a fashion photographer, receiving commissions and working for clientele in Indonesia, Singapore and China. Her work is internationally recognized and commissions have included photographic work for: *Harper's Bazaar*, *Elle*, *Esquire*, *Cosmopolitan*, *Amica*, *Lace*, *Parisian*, *Maxim* and Young Designers United.

An Interview with Nicoline Patricia Malina

How did you get into this line of work?
While I was studying fashion design in Beijing I was also a model; that took me to Europe, where I continued my studies in design and fine art. Photography seemed to be a natural progression, and a new challenge, so I bought a small digital SLR four years ago. I read the manual and started by shooting street scenes – basically I'm an autodidact. In 2005, I shot my first fashion/model shoot and got really hooked. I continued shooting models' portfolios for almost a year, then I got my first magazine assignments. From that moment, I've been shooting for magazines, print ads, model comp-cards and my own personal work.

Top: *Nicoline Patricia Malina at a fashion studio shoot*

Above: *Fashion photography from the Fashion 01 series by Nicoline Patricia Malina,* Clora *magazine (Indonesia)*

I moved to Jakarta, Indonesia early 2008 to join an agency and started shooting for fashion commercials, while still doing magazines here.

What or who are your biggest inspirations artistically?

There are several genius photographers and film directors. I would put Peter Lindbergh and Ellen von Unwerth on top of my list because of their technical abilities and the way they can give true depth and life to the characters in their work.

How would you describe your work?

My photos are portraits inside a fashion scene; I enhance the character of my models, so they're not just mannequins wearing nice outfits.

What photographic techniques do you apply to your work?

I experiment with all kinds of lighting: the sun, flash strobes, movie lights; even candle lights. My photo shoots are always relaxed, intimate and fun. I love capturing that one second of perfect glimpse, wink and emotion.

What sort of camera and equipment do you use?

I use all kinds from digital and film SLRs (Canon/ Nikon), medium format (assembled h3) to Polaroid; also different kinds of lighting. On favourite equipment, I love fixed 50mm and 85mm lenses.

How influential are your photographs to fashion?

I hope my work inspires.

What makes a successful fashion photographer?

When he or she can capture the sense of fashion and art, and find the balance of beauty, order and chaos.

What is the key to your success (in winning first prize in the Iconique Societás Excellence in Fashion Photography, 2007)?

Hard work, spirit and love. I was so lucky and grateful to have such a fantastic team. They were excellent, and they are my good friends. We shot the story in one day, with a major concept change in the middle because we were shooting outside and it started raining. Nobody complained, and we continued the shoot inside my make-up artist's house. We had great fun, and it really made winning or losing not matter (that much!).

What is your greatest career challenge to date?

To lose my ego.

What advice would you give to an aspiring fashion photographer?

Learning about every aspect of fashion is really important, from make-up to styling. During my teenage years I experienced a lot from modelling, make-up classes and fashion design school, and right now I would say all of that experience is key to what I do now.

Always listen to people who have been around longer than you, because faces change, but the things they do stay the same. Learn to work closely with other people, keep your team working hard, and your clients well fed.

Akari Inoguchi
Artist, Illustrator and Designer

Left to right:

Fashion illustration, mixed media: 'Pink' 2007 by Akari Inoguchi

Fashion illustration: 'Pretty' 2007 by Akari Inoguchi

Akari Inoguchi trained as an artist, illustrator and visual designer, and produces work for a range of specialist areas, which include illustrations for magazines, designs for t-shirts, textiles and also television commercials. Her work has appeared in *ELLE Girl* magazine, *Vogue* and *Trace* and her clients have included Lippe Taylor, Boskov and Diesel. She has exhibited her work in both solo and international group exhibitions, including in Japan and the USA.

An Interview with Akari Inoguchi

Did you have any formal training in art and design?
In 1999 I received A.A.S in Fine Arts, Parsons School of Design, New York, and in 2006 I received a B.F.A. in Studio Arts from Hunter College, New York.

You worked as a graphic designer and a visual artist; how did you get into this line of work?

I started my career as a painter. Every time I have an exhibition there are all different kinds of creative people, such as fashion photographers, fashion magazine editors and curators who are interested in my artwork and ask me if I am interested in collaborating with them. My work has grown organically; I started my work in the field of illustration and designing.

What makes a successful graphic designer/visual artist?

The most important thing to be a successful designer/artist is to have a passion for improvement. You must take each project as an exercise in creativity; always trying to make something better than before. Needless to say, it is also very important to listen to your clients' needs and complete the work on time.

Which clients and companies have commissioned your work?

Vogue, *ELLE Girl*, *WWD*, *Trace*, Elite *Traveller*, *Brutus*, *Tokion*, Bloomingdales, Mavi, Diesel, Isetan, 4°C, St. Ives, Aussie Haircare, Lippe Taylor, Boscov, Guayaki, And A, Graniph and Freddy & Ma.

Do you work with an agent?

US: Traffic Creative Management www.trafficnyc.com; Europe: ZeegenRush www.zeegenrush.com; Japan: Taiko & Associates Co., Ltd. www.ua-net.com/taiko.

How would you describe your work and what media techniques do you use?

My work expresses an organic sensuality I feel is peculiar to women. It also shows aesthetic derived from my nostalgia for my own Japanese culture.

I like painting both on paper and using Photoshop. I go back and forth between analogue and digital formats.

Who or what is your biggest inspiration artistically?

My core inspiration comes from my personal experience as a Japanese woman and the private emotions that accompany that experience.

The artist that has most inspired me is Takashi Murakami. He was the first Japanese artist who became successful in the Western fine art market. I feel he created a platform for subsequent young Japanese artists. I feel very close to his philosophy of making no border between high and low art (fine and commercial art).

What is your greatest career challenge to date?

My greatest challenge as an artist was moving to New York City from the suburbs of Tokyo. I spoke no word of English, but wanted to study in the centre of the art world.

What is your dream project?

I would like to make a beautiful mural painting to cover the walls of a big room, which survives for a minimum of a hundred years.

What advice can you give to an artist or designer who wants to launch his or her own business?

Never give up. Talk about your dreams and aspirations; there are always people who might be interested in your work and give you an opportunity in the future. Also, speaking aloud gives you a higher motivation. Be close to the people who are already doing what you want to do. Listen to those people's opinions and advice.

Glossary

accessory designer – person whose main focus is designing accessories such as footwear, millinery, gloves, belts, bags, glasses or jewellery.
apparel – generic term for clothing.
archivist – person responsible for the restoration, preservation and conservation of artefacts.
art therapist – person who works in the healthcare sector helping those with physical or mental difficulties through experimentation with art and design.

bespoke tailor – person who creates individually custom-made clothing.
boutique – small shopping outlet specializing in elite and fashionable items.
buyer – person responsible for purchasing product to sell to the consumer.

CAD – computer aided design.
cash flow – measure of a company's financial health.
chain store – one of a number of retail stores under the same ownership and dealing in the same merchandise.
CMT – manufacturing terminology for Cut, Make, Trim.
colourway – one of a range of colours or colour combinations used to create a garment or range.
community artist – artist or designer who promotes the arts in schools and community groups.
comparative shopping – researching current products on the market offered by competitors.
concession – outlet store trading under its own name but located within a larger department store.
conservationist – person who cleans, restores and repairs textiles and garments.
co-operative – shared business owned and controlled by a group of people.
copyright – exclusive legal right to reproduce, publish, sell or distribute artistic work.
corporate wear designer – person who designs garments for the corporate sector, from air stewards' uniforms to catering staff overalls.
costing sheet – list of all the elements needed to make up a garment (fabric, trims, cost of manufacture), which are then used to calculate the manufacturing, gross margin and selling price of a style.
costumier/costume designer – person who creates outfits for TV, film and stage productions.
cottage industry – business or industry in which goods are produced primarily in the home of the producer.
cutting ticket – exact details for an actual order set for production otherwise know as the production run.

department store – large retail store offering a variety of merchandise and services.
distribution – supply and delivery of fashion goods to warehouses, shops and other outlets.

eco fashion – fashion that is designed to be environmentally friendly.
editorial shoot – photographic spread that tells a story and creates an atmosphere.

events planner – person who manages and organizes trade and corporate events, from fundraisers to fashion shows.

fabric technologist – person responsible for all issues relating to fabric, from sourcing to quality checks.
fit model – model with standard proportions who tries on samples to get fit right.
forecaster – person who predicts trends in styles and colours ahead of new fashion seasons.
franchise – right to market a product or provide a service as granted by a manufacturer or company.

garment technologist – person responsible for monitoring the production process, ensuring that standards of fit and quality are maintained.
gross profit – profit before overhead (fixed operating expenses) has been deducted.

haute couture – exclusive clothes individually designed for private clients.
high end – expensive designs below haute couture level, often produced in limited numbers.

lay planner – person employed to make sure there is minimum fabric waste in the garment cutting process (most often done by computer these days).
limited company – registered company with directors and shareholders.
line sheet – sales document presenting information such as style, colours, fabrics, order quantities, delivery period, manufacturing and selling prices along with garment sketches to wholesale buyers. Also called a range sheet.
look book – a designer's or manufacturer's portfolio presenting a season's range; can include technical drawings, catwalk shots and illustrations.

merchandiser – person who works with a buyer to develop a product range.
merchandising plan – graphic representation of a store floor area in 2D or 3D used to plan the display of garments prior to the collection arriving in store.
milliner – designer whose main focus is on creating headwear.
model booker – person responsible for managing a fashion model's profile and work.
model scout – model agency representative responsible for discovering and recruiting new models.

outworker – home machinist who manufactures small production runs.

partnership – shared ownership and control of a business.
pattern cutter – person who produces patterns from designers' original sketches and spec sheets.
pattern grader – person who alters a pattern to fit different sizes, either manually or using CAD.
personal shopper – person who advises clients on trends and selects items to suit their requirements.
picture researcher – person who sources and supplies visual material to the publishing and media industries.

prêt a porter – clothing that is bought straight 'off the peg' from shops, rather than specially created 'bespoke' or high-end 'haute couture' items.

production manager – person who oversees a garment's production, from prototype sample to finished garment.

prototype – initial garment sample created prior to going into full production.

psychometric test – often given at interviews to gauge a candidate's intellectual potential and aptitude to cope with various situations.

public relations officer – person who promotes a company through the publication of press releases and dealing with queries.

rag trade – industry slang term for the fashion and garment business

range – collection of garment styles created for a particular season or occasion (e.g. summer range, bridal range). Also called a 'line'.

range board – presentation of a collection of co-ordinating garments showing individual styles and colourways.

range sheet – sales document presenting information such as style, colours, fabrics, order quantities, delivery period, manufacturing and selling prices along with garment sketches to wholesale buyers. Also called a 'line sheet'.

ready-to-wear – clothing that is bought straight 'off the peg' from shops, rather than specially created 'bespoke' or high-end 'haute couture' items.

sample machinist – person who produces prototype garments prior to them going into full production.

shop floor – main selling area of a retail space.

sole trader – person responsible for entire running of a business, and financially liable.

specification sheet (or 'spec') Includes a technical drawing (with front and back views and, if necessary, a side view and internal views), plus all detailed measurements required to produce the garment.

story – a themed fashion collection.

stylist – person who creates strong fashion images and looks to promote trends in the media, advertising, and events.

swatch – fabric sample, usually available in books from fabric manufacturers.

technical drawing – also known as 'flats', 'working drawings' or 'line drawings', technical drawings are an accurate representation of a garment.

toile – trial garment created during the early design stages so the garment can be seen three-dimensionally and fit and drape assessed. Usually made in calico cotton.

trend books – industry publications that can contain mood photographs, swatches and technical drawings, which are intended to provide a forecast of new ideas for future seasons.

visual merchandiser – person who creates window and in-store displays to promote retail brands.

wardrobe assistant – person who assists the costume designer in creating and maintaining the costumes for theatrical, TV or film production companies.

Resource Directory

This comprehensive resource directory lists international professional trade associations, exhibitions, trade fairs and events, trend forecasting services, recruitment agencies and internet resources.

For easy reference each section is divided alphabetically by country within the following regions:

✖ **Europe:** UK, France, Germany, Italy and Spain
✖ **Asia and the Pacific:** Australia, China, Hong Kong, India, Japan and Taiwan
✖ **North America:** USA and Canada

Useful Websites

www.gradunet.co.uk – Careers advice and jobs for graduates

www.drapersonline.com – Fashion news and jobs from *Drapers Record*

www.companieshouse.gov.uk – Listing of all UK companies

www.fashion.net – Fashion portal with job listings

www.fashioncapital.co.uk – Job listings and industry information

www.prospects.ac.uk – Advice and jobs for graduates

www.lamodefrancaise.org – Professional associations and industry information

www.onisep.fr – Information for graduates

www.fashionlive.com – Fashion search engine

www.andam.fr – Association for the development of fashion

www.parisfashion.org – Paris Fashion Institute

www.textile-fr.com – French textile industry

www.apparelsearch.com – Fashion and textile industry directory

www.fashion-career.com – Job listings

www.fashioncareercentre.com – Job listings

www.stylecareers.com – International job listings

www.fashioncentre.com – Job listings

www.infomat.com – Fashion industry search engine

Associations

Europe

UK

British Apparel and Textile Confederation (BATC)
5 Portland Place, London W1N 3AA
Tel: +44 (0)20 7636 7788 Fax: +44 (0)20 7636 7515
Email: batc@dial.pipex.com
Website: www.apparel-textiles.co.uk

British Clothing Industry Association (BCIA)
5 Portland Place, London W1B 1PW
Tel: +44 (0)20 7636 7788 or +44 (0)20 7636 5577
Fax: +44 (0)20 7636 7515
Email: contact@5portlandplace.org.uk
Website: www.5portlandplace.org.uk

British Fashion Council (BFC)
5 Portland Place, London W1B 1PW
Tel: +44 (0)20 7636 7788 Fax: +44 (0)20 7436 5924
Email: emmacampbell@britishfashioncouncil.com
Website: www.londonfashionweek.co.uk

British Glove Association
32 Park Hill Road, Harborne, Birmingham B17 9SL
Tel: +44 (0)121 2422602 Fax: +44 (0)121 4275358
Email: info@gloveassociation.org
Website: www.gloveassociation.org

British Hat Guild
PO Box 48664, London NW8 6WS
Tel: +44 (0)7932 678003 Fax: +44 (0)1582 481821
Email: info@britishhatguild.co.uk
Website: www.britishhatguild.co.uk

British Interior Textiles Association
5 Portland Place, London W1B 1PW
Email: enquires@interiortextiles.co.uk
Website: www.interiortextiles.co.uk

British Knitting and Clothing Export Council
5 Portland Place, London W1B 1PW
Tel: +44 (0)20 7636 5577 Fax: +44 (0)20 7636 7515
Email: contact@5portlandplace.org.uk
Website: www.5portlandplace.org.uk

British Menswear Guild
5 Portland Place, London W1B 1PW
Email: director@british-menswear-guild.co.uk
Website: www.british-menswear-guild.co.uk

Chartered Society of Designers (CSD)
1 Cedar Court, Royal Oak Yard, Bermondsey Street,
London SE1 3GA
Tel: +44 (0)20 7357 8088 Fax: +44 (0)20 7407 9878
Email: info@csd.org.uk
Website: www.csd.org.uk

Crafts Council
44a Pentonville Road, Islington, London N1 9BY
Tel: +44 (0)20 7806 2500 Fax: +44 (0)20 7837 6891
Email: crafts@craftscouncil.org.uk
Website: www.craftscouncil.org.uk

Design Council
34 Bow Street, London WC2E 7DL
Tel: +44 (0)20 7420 5200 Fax: +44 (0)20 7420 5300
Email: info@designcouncil.org.uk
Website: www.designcouncil.org.uk

Designer Forum
EMTEX LTD (DESIGNER FORUM)
Designer Forum Studio
69–73 Lower Parliament Street, Nottingham NG1 3BB
Tel: +44 (0)115 9115339 Fax: +44 (0) 115 911 5345
Email: info@design-online.net
Website: www.design-online.net

Design Trust
41 Commercial Road, London E1 1LA
Tel: +44 (0)20 7320 2895 Fax: +44 (0)20 7320 2889
Email: info@thedesigntrust.co.uk
Website: www.designnation.co.uk

Fashion and Design Protection Association Ltd.
69 Lawrence Road, London N15 4EY
Tel: +44 (0)20 8800 5777 Fax: +44 (0)20 8880 2882
Email: info@fdpa.co.uk
Website: www.fdpa.co.uk

Graduate Teacher Training Registry (GTTR)
Rosehill, New Barn Lane, Cheltenham, Gloucestershire
GL52 3LZ
Tel: +44 (0)871 468 0469
Email: enquires@gttr.ac.uk
Website: www.gttr.ac.uk

Shell LiveWIRE
Unit 3, Ground Floor, 7–15 Pink Lane, Newcastle NE1 5DW
Tel: +44 (0)191 423 6229 Fax: +44 (0)191 423 6201
Website: www.shell-livewire.org
Email: enquiries@shell-livewire.org

Northern Ireland Textile and Apparel Association Ltd
5C The Square, Hillsborough BT26 6AG
Tel: +44 (0)2892 68 9999 Fax: +44 (0)2892 68 9968
Email: info@nita.co.uk

The Prince's Trust
Head Office, 18 Park Square, London NW1 4LH
Email: webinfops@princes-trust.org.uk
Website: www.princes-trust.org.uk

Register of Apparel & Textile Designers
UK Fashion Exports, 5 Portland Place, London W1N 3AA
Tel: +44 (0)20 7636 5577 Fax: (+44) (0)20 7436 5924
Email: contact@5portlandplace.org.uk
Website: www.5portlandplace.org.uk

The Scottish Textile Association
Scottish Textiles, Scottish Enterprise, Apex House,
99 Haymarket Terrace, Edinburgh EH12 5DH
Tel: +44 (0)131 313 4000 Fax: +44 (0)131 313 4231
Email: scottish.textiles@scotnet.co.uk
Website: www.scottish-textiles.co.uk

Skillsfast UK
Head Office, Richmond House, Lawnswood Business Park,
Redvers Close, Leeds LS16 6RD
Tel: +44 (0)113 2399 600 Fax: +44 (0)113 2399 601
Email: enquiries@skillfast-uk.org
Website: www.skillfast-uk.org

The Textile Institute
1st floor, St James Building, Oxford Street, Manchester
M1 6FQ
Tel: +44 (0)161 237 1188 Fax: +44 (0)161 236 1991
Email: tiihq@textileinst.org.uk
Website: www.texi.org

UK Fashion Exports (UKFE)
5 Portland Place, London W1B 1PW
Tel: +44 (0)207 636 7788 or +44 (0)207 636 5577
Fax: +44 (0)207 636 7515
Email: contact@5portlandplace.org.uk
Website: www.5portlandplace.org.uk

France

**Association pour la Formation Professionnelle des
Industries du Cuir (AFPIC)**
178 Rue Paul-de-Kock, 93230 Romainville
Tel: +33 (0)1 4810 2700 Fax: +33 (0)1 4810 0005

Chambres Syndicale de la Couture Parisienne
45 Rue Saint-Roch, 75001 Paris
Tel: +33 (0)1 4261 0077 Fax: +33 (0)1 4286 8942
Email: ecole@modeaparis.com
Website: www.modeaparis.com

Fédération Francais du Prêt-à-Porter Féminine
5 Rue Caumartin, 75009 Paris
Tel: +33 (0)1 4494 7030 Fax: +33 (0)1 4494 7004
Email: contact@pretparis.com
Website: www.pretaporter.com

Fédération Française des Industries du Vêtement Masculin
8, Rue Montesquieu, 75001 Paris
Tel: +33 (0)1 44 55 66 50 Fax: +33 (0)1 44 55 66 65
Website: www.lamodefrancaise.org.fr

Fédération Nationale de L'Industrie de la Chaussure
51 Rue de Miromesnil, 75008 Paris
Tel: +33 (0)1 44 717171 Fax: +33 (0)1 44 710404
Email: presse@midec.com
Website: www.midec.com
Website: www.chaussuredefrance.com

Germany

Confederation of the German Textile and Fashion Industry
Frankfurter Strasse 10–14, D-65760 Eschborn
Tel: +49 6196 9660 Fax: +49 6196 42170
Email: info@textil-mode.de
Website: www.textil-mode.de

European Textile Network (International Membership)
ETN Secratariat, PO Box 5944, D-30059, Hanover
Email: etn@etn-net.org
Website: www.etn-net.org

Texere
Buchenstrasse 20, 52076 Aachen
Email: pchristy@talktalk.net
Website: www.texere-u.net.dk

Italy

**Associazione Italiana della Filiera Tessile
Abbigliamento SMI**
Federazione Tessile e Moda
Viale Sarca 223, 20126 Milano
Tel: +39 (0)2-641191 Fax: +39 (0)2-66103667/70
Website: www.smi-ati.it
Email: info@sistemamodaitalia.it

Centro di Firenze per la Moda Italiana
Via Faenzan, 111, 50123, Florence
Tel: +39 (0)553 6931 Fax: +39 (0)5536 93200
Email: cfmi@cfmi.it
Website: www.cfmi.it

**Assoconfezione Association of Suppliers of the
Garment Industry**
Via Eritrea 21, 20157 Milano
Tel: +39 02 39090301 Fax +39 02 39090331
Email: info@assoconfezione.it

Spain

Association of New and Young Spanish Designers
Segovia 22, Bajos CP 28005 Madrid
Tel: +34 915 475 857 Fax: +34 915 475 857
Email: nuevosdisenadores@telefonica.net

Spanish Federation of Clothing Manufacturers
Alvarez De Baena, 7–2806 Madrid
Tel: +34 915 158 180 Fax: +34 915 635 085
Website: www.fedecon.es

Spanish Association of Knitwear Manufacturers
Av. Diagonal, 474-08006 Barcelona
Tel: +34 934 151 228 Fax: +34 934 160 442
Email: aegp@agrupaciontextil.org
Website: www.knitting.org

Asia and the Pacific

Australia

Australian Fashion Council
Showroom 16, 23–25 Gipps Street, Collingwood VIC 3066
Tel: +61 (0) 38680 9400 Fax: +61 (0) 38680 9499
Email: info@australianfashioncouncil.com
Website: www.australianfashioncouncil.com

Cotton Australia
Suite 4.01, 247 Coward Street, Mascot, NSW 2020
Tel: +61 (0) 29669 5222 Fax: +61 (0) 29669 5511
Email: info@cottonaustralia.com
Website: www.cottonaustralia.com.au

Council of Textiles and Fashion Industries Australia Ltd (TFIA)
Level 2, 20 Queens Road, Melbourne, VIC 3004
Tel: +61 (0) 38317 6666 Fax: +61 (0) 38317 6666
Email: info@tfia.com.au
Website: www.tfia.com.au

Design Institute of Australia
486 Albert Street, East Melbourne, VIC 3002, GPO Box 4352
Tel: +61 (0) 38662 5490 Fax: +61 (0) 38662 5358
Email: admin@design.org.au
Website: www.dia.org.au

The Melbourne Design and Fashion Incubator (MDFI)
Shop 238, Level 2, Melbourne Central Shopping Centre,
211 La Trobe Street, Melbourne 3000, Victoria
Tel: +61 (0) 39671 4522
Email: info@fashionincubator.com.au
Website: www.fashionincubator.com.au

China

China National Textile and Apparel Council
China Textile Network Company, Rm 236, No 12,
Dong Chang'an Street, Beijing 100742
Tel: +86 10 85229 100 Fax: +86 10 85229 100
Email: info@ml.ctei.gov.cn
Website: www.ctei.gov.cn

China Fashion Designers Association
Room 154, No 12, Dong Chang'an Street, Beijing, 100742
Tel: +86 1085 229427 Fax: +86 1085 229037

China National Textile Company
12 Dong Chang'an Street, Beijing, 100742
Tel: +86 1085 229089 Fax: +86 1065 135947
Email: b2b@ml.ctei.gov.cn
Website: www.cntextile.com

Hong Kong

Federation of Hong Kong Garment Manufacturers
Room 401–403, Cheung Lee Commercial Building,
25 Kimberely Road, 4/F, Tsimshatsui, Kowloon, Hong Kong
Tel: +852 2721 1383 Fax: +852 2311 1062

Email: info@garment.org.hk
Website: www.garment.org.hk

The Hong Kong General Chamber of Textiles Ltd.
Unit 708–709, Trade Square, 681 Cheung Sha Wan Road,
Kowloon, Hong Kong
Tel: +852 2357 9978 Fax: +852 2191 7271
Website: www.textileschamber.org

Hong Kong Research Institute of Textiles and Clothing
R906-08, Shirley Chan Building, The Hong Kong Polytechnic
University, Kowloon, Hong Kong
Tel: +852 2627 0180 Fax: +852 2364 2727
Email: info@hkrita.com
Website: www.hkrita.com

Hong Kong Trade Development Council (HKTDC)
38/F Office Tower, Convention Plaza, 1 Harbour Road,
Wanchai, Hong Kong
Tel: +852 1830 668 Fax: +852 2824 0249
Email: hktdc@tdc.org.hk
Website: www.hktdc.com

Textile Council of Hong Kong
Room 401–403, 4/F, Cheung Lee Commercial Building,
25 Kimberely Road, 4/F, Tsimshatsui, Kowloon, Hong Kong
Tel: +852 2305 2893 Fax: +852 2305 2493
Email: sec@textilecouncil.com
Website: www.textilecouncil.com

India

Apparel Export Promotion Council India
Email: info@texprocil.com
Website: www.texprocil.com

The Clothing Manufacturers Association of India
902 Mahalaxmi Chambers, 22 Dhulabhai Desai Road,
Mumbai 400026
Tel: +91 2353 0245 Fax: +91 2351 5908
Email: cmai@vsnl.com
Website: www.cmai.in

The Textile Association of India (TAI)
Ahmedabad Unit, Dinesh Hall, Ashram Road, Ahmedabad
380009, Gujarat
Tel: +91 79 265 82123, Fax: +91 79 265 86311
Email: taia1@dataone.in
Website: www.taindia.com

Japan

Japan Fashion Association
Fukushima Building, 1-5-3 Nihonbashi – Muromachi,
Chuo – ku, Tokyo, 103-0022
Tel: +81 33242 1677 Fax: +81 33242 1678
Email: info@japanfashion.or.jp
Website: www.japanfashion.or.jp

Japan Association of Specialists in Textile and Apparel
Jasta Office, 2-11-13-205, Shiba – koen, Minato – Ku,
Tokyo 105-0011
Tel: +81 03 3437 6416 Fax: +81 03 3437 3194
Email: jasta@mtb.biglobe.ne.jp
Website: jasta1.or.jp/index_english.html

Japan Fashion Colour Association
Fukushima Building 6F, 1-5-3 Nihonbashi – Muromachi,
Chuo-ku, Tokyo 103-0022
Tel: +81 33242 1680 Fax: +81 33242 1686
Email: jafca@japanfashion.or.jp
Website: www.jafca.org

Pakistan

Pakistan Cotton Fashion Apparel Manufacturers Exporters Association
5 Amber Court, 2nd Floor, Shaheed-e-Millat Road,
Karachi, Sindh
Tel: + 92 (21) 454 3183
Fax: + 92 (21) 454 6711
Website: www.textileconnexion.com

Pakistan Hosiery Manufacturers Association
PHMA House, 37-H, Block 6, PECHS, Karachi
Tel: +92 214 544 789
Fax: +92 214 543774
Email: info@phmaonline.com
Website: www.phmaonline.com

Pakistan Readymade Garments Manufacturers and Exporters Association
18 A Shaheen View Building, Mezzanine Floor, Block – 6,
PECHS, Shahra-E-Faisal, Karachi 75400
Tel: +92 21 454 9073
Fax: +92 21 453 9669
Email: info@prgmea.org
Website: www.prgmea.org

Taiwan

Taiwan Textile Federation, Textile and Fashion Design Centre
13F TTF Building, 22 Aikuo East Road, Taipei 100
Tel: +886 2 2341 7251 Fax: +886 2 239 23855
Email: service@textiles.org.tw
Website: www.textiles.org.tw

North America

USA

American Apparel and Footwear Association
1601 N Kent Street, Suite 1200, Arlington VA 22209
Tel: +1 703 524 1864
Fax: +1 703 522 6741
Website: www.apparelandfootwear.org

Brazilian–American Fashion Association (BRAMFSA)
PO Box 83-2036, Delray Beach, Florida 33483
Email: bramfsa@bramfsa.com

The Color Association of the United States
315 West 39th Street, Studio 507, New York, NY 10018
Tel: +1 212 347 7774 Fax: +1 212 594 6987
Email: caus@colorassociation.com
Website: www.colorassociation.com

Council of Fashion Designers of America
1412 Broadway Suite 2006, New York, NY 10018
Tel: +1 212 302 1821
Website: www.cfda.com

Fashion Group International New York
8 West 40th Street, 7th Floor, New York, NY 10018
Tel: +1 212 302 5511 Fax: +1 212 302 5533
Email: cheryl@fgi.org
Website: www.fgi.org

International Textile and Apparel Association
ITAA 6060 Sunrise Vista Drive, Suite 1300, Citrus Heights,
CA 95610
Tel: +1 916 723 1628
Email: info@itaaonline.org
Website: www.itaaonline.org

Society of Illustrators
128 East 63rd Street, New York, NY 10065
Tel: +1 212 838 2560 Fax: +1 212 838 2561
Email: info@societyillustrators.org
Website: www.societyillustrators.org

Wool Bureau Incorporated
330 Madison Ave, 19th Floor, New York, NY 10017
Tel: +1 212 986 6222 Fax: +1 212 953 1888

Canada

Canadian Apparel Federation
124 O'Connor Street, Suite 504, Ottawa, Ontario K1P 5M9
Tel: +1 613 231 3220 Fax: +1 613 231 2305
Email: info@apparel.ca
Website: www.apparel.ca

Canadian Textile Institute
222 Somerset Street West, Ste.500, Ottawa, Ontario K2P 2G3
Website: www.textiles.ca

Montreal Fashion Network
5 Place Ville Marie, Suite 140, Montreal,
Quebec H3B 2G2
Email: info@montrealfashionnetwork.com
Website: www.montrealfashionnetwork.com

Exhibitions, Trade Fairs and Events

Europe

UK

Knitting and Stitching Show – Harrogate/London
Creative Exhibitions Ltd
Exhibition House, 8 Greenwich Quay London SE8 3EY
Tel: +44 (0)20 8692 2299 Fax: +44 (0)20 8692 6699
Email: mail@twistedthread.com
Website: www.twistedthread.com

London Fashion Week
British Fashion Council
5 Portland Place, London W1B 1PW
Tel: + 44 (0)20 7636 7788 Fax: +44 (0)20 7436 5924
Website: www.londonfashionweek.co.uk

London Edge and London Central
Londonedge Ltd., Hazel Drive, Leicester LE3 2JE
Tel: +44 (0)116 289 8249 Fax: +44 (0)116 263 1269
Email: info@londonedge.com
Website: www.londonedge.com

New Designers
Upper Street Events, 58 White Lion Street, Islington,
London N1 9PP
Tel: +44 (0)20 7288 6738
Email: nd@upperstreetevents.co.uk
Website: www.newdesigners.com

Pure Womenswear, London
EMAP Direct, Greater London House, Hampstead Road,
London NW1 7EJ
Tel: + 44 (0) 20 7728 5000 Fax: +44 (0) 20 7728 3900
Email: pure.enquiries@emap.com
Website: www.purewomenswear.co.uk

France

Expofil
20 Boulevard Eugene Deruellic, 69432 Lyon, Cédex 3
Tel: +33 (0) 472 60 65 00 Fax: +33 (0) 472 60 65 09
Email: info@premierevision.fr

Indigo
7 Rue du Pasteur Wagner, 750111 Paris
Tel: +33 (0) 170 38 70 10 Fax: +33 (0) 170 38 70 11
Email: e.v.raluy@indiogo-salon.com

Intersélection
Website: www.interselection.net

Paris Fashion Week
Federation Francais de la Couture du Prêt-à-Porter des
Couturiers et des Créateurs de Mode, 100–102 Fauborourg
Saint-Honoré, 75008 Paris
Tel: +33 (1) 42 66 64 44 Fax: +33 (1) 42 66 94 63
Websites: www.modeaparis.com, www.parisfashionshows.net

Prêt à Porter, Paris
Sodes, Paris Prêt à Porter, 5, Rue De Caumartin, 75009 Paris
Tel: +33 (1)-44947000Fax: +33 (1)-44947034
Website: www.pretparis.com

Première Vision
20, Boulevard Eugène Deruelle, 69432 Lyon Cédex 03, France
Tel: +33 (0) 472 60 65 00 Fax: +33 (0) 472 60 65 09
Email: info@premierevision.fr
Website: www.premierevision.fr

Texworld, Paris
1 Avenue de Flandres, 75019 Paris
Tel: +33 0155 268 989, +33 0140 350 900
Website: www.texworld@france.messefrankfurt.com

Tissu Premier
37–39 Rue de Neuilly, BP121, 92113 Clichy Cédex, Lille-Europe
Email: tissue-premier la-federation.com
Web: www.tissu-premier.com

Germany

Body Look
Messeplatz, Dusseldorf, Germany.
Tel: +49 211 439601/439601 Fax: +49 211 4396345/4396345

CPD: Düsseldorf Womenswear
Messeplatz, Stockumer Kirchstrasse 61 D404 74, Düsseldorf
Tel: +49 211 439601 Fax: +49 211 4396345
Website: www.igedo.com

Igedo, Fashion Fair, Düsseldorf, Germany
Messeplatz, Stockumer Kirchstrasse 61 D404 74, Düsseldorf
Tel: +49 211 439601 Fax: +49 211 4396345
Website: www.igedo.com

Interstoff: Fabrics/Colour
Website: www.interstoff.messefrankfurt.com

Italy

IdeaComo: Fabrics/Colours
IdeaComo, Via 5 Giornate 76h, 22012 Cernobbio (CO)
Tel: +39 031 513312 Fax: +39 031 340022
Website: www.ideacomo.com

Milano Unca International Trade Fair
Head Office, Viale Sarca 223, 20126 Milano
Tel: +39 02 66 101 105 Fax: +39 02 66 111 335
Email: info@milanounica.it
Website: www.milanounica.it

Pitti Immagine Bimbo: Childrenswear, Florence
Email: bimbo@pittimmagine.com
Website: www.pittimmagine.com

Pitti Immagine Filatti, Florence
Email: filati@pittimmagine.com
Website: www.pittimmagine.com

Pitti Immagine Uomo, Florence
Email: uomo@pittimmagine.com
Website: www.pittimmagine.com

Spain

Bread & Butter, Barcelona (Directional Casualwear)
S.L, Paseo de Gracia 25, Pral 2A 08008 Barcelona
Tel: +34 93 272 6763 Fax: +34 93 272 6770
Website: www.breadandbutter.com

Moda Barcelona
Moda Barcelona, Escoles Pies, 1 2, 08017 Barcelona
Tel: +34 932 093 639 Fax: +34 932 021 378
Email: info@barcelonabridalweek.com

SIMM: Semana Internacional de la Moda, Madrid (Womenswear, Menswear and Childrenswear)
Email: simm@fema.es
Website: www.ifema.es

TextilModa, Madrid
Textilmoda, UL. Traktorowa 128, 91-204 Lodz, Poland
Tel: +42 252 9955 Fax: +42 252 9956
Email: textilmoda@interia.pl
Website: www.textilmoda.cabanova.com

Portugal

Modtissimo
Rua Roberto Ivens, no 1314, Sala 18, 4450-251 Matosinhos
Tel: +351 22 938 06 10 Fax: +351 22 937 48 16
Email: modtissimo@mail.telepac.pt
Website: www.modtissimo.com

Asia and the Pacific

Australia

Fashion Exposed
PO Box 82, Flinders Lane, Melbourne, VIC 8009
Tel: +61 (0)3 9654 7773 Fax: +61 (0)3 9654 5596
Email: fashion@aec.net.au
Website: www.fashionexposed.com

Mercedes Australian Fashion Week
Website: www.afw.com.au

Rosemount Australian Fashion Week (RAFW)
IMG Fashion, Level 4, 263 Clarence Street, Sydney, NSW 2000
Tel: +61 2 9285 8000 Fax: +61 2 9260 2333
Email: rafw@imgworld.com
Website: www.rafw.com.au

China

China (Dalion) International Garment and Textile Fair (CIGF)
Contact Mr Andy Liu/Miss Rella Dong
F3, World Expo Center, N10 F, Zone Xing Bay, Dalion (116023)
Tel: +86 411 8489 2907 Fax: +86 411 8489 2900
Email: dl@cigf.com.cn
Website: www.cigf.com.cn

China International Trade Fair for Apparel and Accessories
Tel: 010 85 229 440, 85 229488 Fax: 010 65 121732
Website: www.ccpittex.com

China International Trade Fair
Shanghai International Convention Centre, Shanghai
Tel: +852 2238 9983 Fax: +852 2238 9921
Email: arosia.tong@hongkong.messefrankfurt.com
Website: www.messefrankfurt.com.hk

Hong Kong

Hong Kong Fashion Week
Exhibitions Department, Hong Kong Trade Development Council, Unit 13, Expo Galleria, Hong Kong Convention and Exhibition Centre, Wanchai, Hong Kong
Tel: +852 1830 668 Fax: +852 2824 0249
Email: exhibitions@tdc.org.hk
Website: hkfashionweekfw.hktdc.com

Taiwan

International Textiles and Apparel Show
Tel: +886 2 23417251 Fax: +886 2 23923855
Email: service@textiles.org.tw
Website: www.textiles.org.tw

Taipei Innovative Textile Application Show
Taiwan Textile Federation
Tel: +886 2 2341 7251 Fax:+886 2 2394 3245
Email: titas@textiles.org.tw
Website: www.titas.com.tw

India

Connecting Asia
811 Tower B Hung Hom Commercial Centre, 37–39 Ma Tau Wai Rd, Hung Hom, Kowloon, Hong Kong
Tel: +852 29549133
Email: info@EDLasia.com
Website: www.ediasia.com

North America

USA

The International Fashion Fabric Exhibition, New York
Magic International, 6200 Canoga Avenue, 2nd Floor,
Woodland Hills, CA 91367
Tel: +1 818 593 5000 Fax: +1 818 593 5020
Email: cs@MAGIConline.com
Website: www.fabricshow.com

New York Fashion Week
The Waldorf Astoria, 301 Park Avenue (between 49th and
50th Street) New York
Tel: +1 212 202 4604
Email: info@ucsafashionshows.com
Website: www.couturefashionweek.com

Canada

Fashion Week Canada
Email: info@fdcc.ca
Website: www.lorealfashionweek.ca

Trend Forecasting Services

Europe

UK

Fashion News
www.vogue.co.uk

Jill Lawrence Designs (Fashion and Colour)
JLD International, Studio 2, 64 Southwood Lane, London N6 5DY
Tel: +44 (0)20 8340 9122 Fax: +44 (0)20 8340 9244
Email: jill@jldintl.com
Website: www.jldintl.com

Mudpie
Unit 21–23 Home Farm Business Centre, Lockerley,
Hants SO51 0JT
Tel: +44 (0)1794 344040
Email: website@mudpie.co.uk
Website: www.mudpie.co.uk

Trendzine
Fashion Information Ltd, Gainsborough House, 81 Oxford
Street, London W1D 2EU
Email: info@fashioninformation.com
Website: www.fashioninformation.com

Trendstop
Trendstop Ltd, 28–39 The Quadrant, 135 Salisbury Road,
London NN6 6RJ
Tel: +44 (0)870 788 6888 Fax: +44 (0)870 788 6886
Website: www.trendstop.com

WGSN (Worth Global Style Network)
Email: eduinfo@wgsn.com
Website: www.wgsn.com

France

Carlin International
79 Rue de Miromesnil, 75008 Paris
Tel: +33 (0) 1 53 04 42 00 Fax: +33 (0) 1 53 04 42 08
Email: style@carlin-groupe.com
Website: www.carlin-groupe.com

Nelly Rodi, Paris, France
28 Avenue De Saint Ouen, 75018 Paris
Tel: +33 (0) 1 42 93 04 06
Email: info@nellyrodi.com
Website: www.nellyrodi.com

Peclers, Paris, France
23 Rue Du Mail, 75002 Paris
Tel: +33 (0) 1 40 41 0606
Email: peclers@peclersparis.com
Website: www.peclersparis.com

Promostyl
Head Office, 31 Rue de la Folie Méricourt, 75011 Paris
Tel: +33 (0) 1 49 23 7600 Fax: +33 (0) 1 43 38 2259
Website: www.promostyl.com

Sacha Pacha
16 Rue du Faubourg St Denis, 75010 Paris
Tel: +33 (0) 1 42 46 15 15
Email: style@sachapacha.com
Website: www.sachapacha.com

Germany

CPD, Düsseldorf
Igedo Company, GM6H8 co. KG – Messeplatz/Stockumer
Kirchstrase 61, D 40474 Dusseldorf
Tel: +49 211 43 96 01 Fax: +49 211 43 96 01
Email: info@igedo.com
Website: www.igedo.com

Mode Information
Pilgerstrasse 20, 51491 Overath
Tel: +49 2206 6007-0 Fax: +49 2206 6007-17
Email: info@modeinfo.com
Website: www.modeinfo.com

Italy

A R Studio
A R Studio, Via Broggi 7, 20129, Milan
Tel: +39 022 6822730
Email: info@fashioncampus.it

Moda Trends
Modatrend SRL, Via Emilia 8, 56125, Pisa
Tel: +39 050 99 11 935 Fax: +39 050 99 11 937
Email: info@modatrends.com
Website: www.modatrends.com

Asia and the Pacific

Australia

Fashion Forecast Service
18 Little Oxford Street, Collingwood, VIC 3066
Tel: +61 3 9415 8116 Fax: +61 39415 8114
Email: info@fashionforecastservices.com.au
Website: www.fashionforecastservices.com.au

USA

Committee for Color and Trends
60 Madison Avenue, Suite 1209, New York 10010
Tel: +1 212 532 3555 Fax: +1 212 447 1628
Email: colortrends@earthlink.net
Website: www.color-trends.com

Doneger Group Associates
The Doneger Group, 463 Seventh Avenue, New York,
NY 10018
Tel: +1 212 564 1266
Email: tburns@doneger.com
Website: www.doneger.com

Trends West
8425 West 3rd Street, Suite 301, Los Angeles, CA 90048
Tel: +1 323 622 2200 Fax: +1 323 655 2203
Email: office@trendswest.com
Website: www.trendswest.com

Recruitment Agencies

Europe

UK

Denza International Ltd
11 St George Street, London W1S 2FD
Tel: +44 (0)20 7499 5047 Fax: +44 (0)20 7629 8376
Email: denza@denza.co.uk
Website: www.denza.co.uk

Fashion and Retail Personnel
Circus House, 21 Great Titchfield Street, London W1W 8BA
Tel: +44 (0)20 7436 0220 (Fashion) Tel: +44 (0)20 7637 0220
(Retail) Fax: +44 (0)20 7436 0088
Email: info@fashionpersonnel.com
Website: www.fashionpersonnel.com

Freedom Recruitment
Tel: +44 (0)20 7734 9779 Fax: +44 (0)20 7734 1101
Email: drapersjobs@freedomrecruitment.com
Website: www.freedomrecruit.com

People Marketing
4 Bowden Drive, Boulevard Industrial Park, Beeston,
Nottingham NG9 2JY
Tel: +44 (0)115 922 3335
Email: sales@peoplemarketing.co.uk
Website: www.peoplemarketing.co.uk

Prolink-Europe Ltd
Irene House, Five Arches Business Estate, Maidstone Road,
Sidcup, Kent DA14 5AK
Tel: +44 (0)20 8309 2700 Fax: +44 (0)20 8309 7890
Email: enquire@prolink-europe.com
Website: www.prolink-europe.co.uk

Success Appointments
York House, 23 Kingsway, London WC2B 6UJ
Tel: +44 (0)20 7759 7337 Fax: +44 (0)20 7759 7338
Website: www.successjobs.co.uk

Quest
3rd Floor, 9 Argyll Street, London W1F 7JT
Tel: +44 (0)20 7440 5990 Fax: +44 (0)20 8222 0556
Website: www.questsearch.co.uk

France

Januou Pakter
4, Rue du Fbg St. Honoré, 75008 Paris
Tel: +33 (0)1 45 23 18 54 Fax: +33 (0)1 42 66 04 55

Italy

Moda Research
San Polo, 2580, 30125 Venezia
Tel: +39 (0) 415237402 Fax: +39 (0) 415200390
Email: info@modaresearch.it

North America

Arts CounSEL, Inc.
Email: info@artscounselinc.com

Adkins & Associates
PO Box 16062, Greensboro, NC 27416
Website: www.adkinsassociates.com

Designer Resource International
450 7th Avenue, New York. NY 10123
Tel: +212 564 6505 Fax: +1 212 564 6183

24 seven
120 Wooster Street, 4th Floor, New York, NY 10012
Tel: +1 212 966 4426 Fax: +1 212 966 2313
Email: candidates@24seventalent.com

Australia

Permanser Pty Ltd.
174 Victoria Parade, East Melbourne, 3002 Victoria
Tel: +613 9654 5988 Fax: +613 9650 7329
Website: www.permanser.com.au

Further Reading

Chapter 1

Blackman, Cally, *100 Years of Fashion Illustration*. London: Laurence King Publishing, 2008

Braddock Clarke, Sarah and Marie Mahony, *Techno Textiles 2: Revolutionary Fabrics for Fashion and Design*. London: Thames and Hudson, 2007

Brannon, Evelyn L., *Fashion Forecasting: Research, Analysis, and Presentation*. New York: Fairchild Publications, 2005

Davies, Hywell, *Modern Menswear*. London: Laurence King Publishing, 2008

Jenkyn Jones, Sue, *Fashion Design*. London: Laurence King Publishing, 2005

Rhodes, Zandra, *The Art of Zandra Rhodes – A Lifelong Love Affair with Textiles*. London: The Antique Collectors' Club Ltd. and Zandra Rhodes Publications Ltd., 2005

Chapter 2

Aldrich, Winifred, *Metric Pattern Cutting for Women's Wear*. Oxford: Blackwell Publishing, 2008

Alvardo, Judith, *Computer Aided Fashion Design Using Gerber Technology*. New York: Fairchild Publications, 2007

Hayes, Steven Georges, and John Mc Loughlin, *Introduction to Clothing Manufacture*. Oxford: Blackwell Publications, 2006

Joseph-Armstrong, Helen, *Pattern Making for Fashion Design*. New Jersey: Pearson Prentice Hall, 2006

Joseph-Armstrong, Helen, *Draping for Apparel Design*. New York: Fairchild Publications, 2000

Kadaolph, Sarah Jane, *Quality Assurance for Textiles and Apparel*. Oxford: Berg Publishers, 1988

Von Elberlt, Hannelore, Hermann Hermeling and Marianne Hornberger, *Clothing Technology – From Fibre to Fashion*. Germany, Verlag Europa-Lehrmittel, 1999

Chapter 3

Davis Burns, Leslie, and Nancy O'Bryant, *The Business of Fashion: Designing, Manufacturing and Marketing*. New York: Fairchild Publications 2008

Diamond, Ellen, *Fashion Retailing*. New Jersey: Prentice Hall, 2005

Dickerson, Kitty G., *Inside the Fashion Business*. New Jersey: Prentice Hall, 2003

Easey, Mike, *Fashion Marketing*. Oxford: Blackwell Publications, 2008

Kunz, Grace L., and Myrna P N Garner, *Going Global*. New York: Fairchild Publications, 2006

Morgan, Tony, *Visual Merchandising*. London: Laurence King Publishing, 2008

Regan, Cynthia L., *Apparel Product Design and Merchandising Strategies*. New Jersey: Prentice Hall, 2007

Solomon, Michael, and Nancy Rabolt, *Consumer Behavior in Fashion*. New Jersey: Prentice Hall, 2008

Sternquist, Brenda, *International Retailing*. New York: Fairchild Publications, 2007

Chapter 4

Dingeman, Jo, *Mastering Fashion Styling*. Basingstoke: Palgrave, Macmillan, 1999

Everett, Judith C., and Kristen Swanson, *Guide to Producing a Fashion Show*. New York: Fairchild Publications, 2004

Keeble, Richard, *Print Journalism: A Critical Introduction*. London: Routledge, 2005

Swanson, Kristen, and Judith C Everett, *Writing for Fashion Business*. New York: Fairchild Publications, 2008

2010 Writers' and Artists' Yearbook. London: A&C Black 2009

Chapter 5

Forrester, Susan, and David Lloyd, *Arts Funding Guide*. DSC, 2002

Griffiths, Susan, *Work Your Way Around the World*. London: Crimson Publishing, UK, 2009

Directory of Grant-Making Trusts, DSC, 2003–4, 18th edition

Manser, Sally, *Artists in Residence: A Teachers' Handbook*. London Arts Board, 2001

The Voluntary Agencies Directory. London: National Council for Voluntary Organizations (NCVO), 2008

Wilkinson, Christine, *Art & People: A Practical Guide to Setting Up and Running Arts Projects in the Community*. Slough Borough Council, 2003

Withers, Alison, *Gap-Year Guide*. London: John Catt Educational Ltd., 2008

Chapter 6

Fagan, Angela, *Brilliant Job Hunting: How to Get the Job You Want*. New Jersey: Prentice Hall, 2007

Williams, Lynn, *The Ultimate Job Search Book: Invaluable Advice on Networking, CVs, Cover Letters, Interviews, Psychometric Tests and Follow-up Strategies*. London: Kogan Page Ltd., 2008

Chapter 7

Bright, Jim, and Joanne Earl, *Brilliant CV: What Employers Want to See and How to Say It*. New Jersey: Prentice Hall, 2007

Byers, Ann, *Great Resume, Application, and Interview Skills*. Rosen Publishing Group, 2008

Cottrell, Stella, *Skills for Success*. Basingstoke: Palgrave Macmillan, 2003

Chapter 8

Blackman, Cally, *Fashion Illustrator*. London: Laurence King Publishing, 2006

Bubonia-Clarke, Janace, and Phyllis Borcherding, *Developing and Branding the Fashion Merchandising Portfolio*. New York: Fairchild Publications, 2007

Centner, Marianne, and Frances Vereker, *Fashion Designer, Handbook for Adobe Illustrator*. London: Blackwell Publishing 2007

Morris, Bethan, *Fashion Illustrator*. London: Laurence King Publishing, 2006

Chapters 9 & 10

D'Souza, Steven, *Brilliant Networking: What the Best Networkers Know, Say and Do*. New Jersey: Prentice Hall, 2007

Hall, Richard, *Brilliant Presentations: What the Best Presenters Know, Say and Do*. New Jersey: Prentice Hall, 2007

Tomsho, Greg, *Guide to Networking Essentials:* Course Technology Inc, 2006

Williams, Lynn, *The Ultimate Interview*. London: Kogan Page, 2008

Chapter 11

Barrow, Colin, *The Business Plan Workbook: The Definitive Guide to Researching, Writing Up and Presenting a Winning Plan*. London: Kogan Page, 2008

Coates, Caroline, *A Guide to Setting Up a Designer Fashion Business*. London: British Fashion Council, 1997

Finch, Brian, *How to Write a Business Plan*. London: Kogan Page, 2006

Gehlar, Mary, *The Fashion Designer Survival Guide: An Insider's Look at Starting and Running Your Own Fashion Business*. Kaplan Business, 2005

Chapter 12

Cole, Drusilla, *Patterns*. London: Laurence King Publishing, 2008

Davies, Hywell, *100 New Fashion Designers*. London: Laurence King Publishing, 2008

Hidalgo, Marta R., *Young Fashion Designers*. Taschen, 2007

Jones, Terry, and Susie Rushton, *Fashion Now 2*. Taschen, 2005

Index

Page numbers in **bold** refer to illustrations

Picture Credits

5 Courtesy breadandbutter.com; 8&10-11 Courtesy Antonio Berardi; 14 Irene De Caprio; 15 Courtesy Simon Jersey; 16 Tuc Tuc, www.tuctuc.es; 17 Courtesy Adidas; 18-19 Courtesy O'Neill; 20 Courtesy Initimissimi; 22 Courtesy Ian Stuart; 25 Courtesy Shreenie J. Vasan and Susan Ritchie; 27 Courtesy Sophie Steller; 28 Othello De Souza Hartley; 28 Courtesy Antonio Berardi; 30 Clive Arrowsmith © Zandra Rhodes; 30 Norman Eales © Zandra Rhodes; 31 © Zandra Rhodes; 32-33 Kim Parker; 32 Felipe Porto; 36-37 Irene De Caprio; 38 © Andreea Angelescu/Corbis; 39 © MARCOS BORGA/ Reuters/Corbis; 40 Courtesy Gemma Valance/DeMontfort University; 40 Kevin Guildford/DeMontfort University; 42 Courtesy Céline Robert/G. Aresteanu; 43 Courtesy Céline Robert/G. Durand; 44 Courtesy Peclers, Paris; 47 Mudpie; 48-49 David Steinhorst; 50-51 Anna Kiper; 52 Stefanie Grewel/ Corbis; 55 Adam Verity; 57 Courtesy Robins & Wrights Ltd.; 58 © LECTRA, Lectra.com; 59 Bettmann/Corbis; 59 © LECTRA, Lectra.com; 60 Adam Verity; 63 Courtesy Consorzio Tela di Penelope+ www.teladipenelope.com; 64 Romilly Lockyer/Getty Images; 66 © breadandbutter.com; 69 Amy Sussman/Getty Images; 70 Jen Siska/Getty Images; 72-73 Courtesy Agatha; 76 Eugenio Recuenco/LeBookMaker. com; 79 Courtesy ELLE Italia; 79 Courtesy Silvia Brandi; 83 Courtesy Tony Glenville; 87 Courtesy Faulhaber PR; 89 Liam Wycherley and Krishan Palmer; 89 © breadandbutter. com; 90 Liam Wycherley and Krishan Palmer; 94 Julia Albee; 95 Sue Leland; 96 Peter Chin; 97 Shaun Cloud; 98-101 Eugenio Recuenco/LeBookMaker.com; 104-105 View Management www.viewmanagement.com;106 Courtesy Kamal Dollah www.kamaldollah.com; 109 Laura Pledger; 111 David Overton; 115 Lois Blackburn; 116 Courtesy Kamal Dollah www. kamaldollah.com; 118 Carol Brown; 121 Annalaura Palma; 122 David Overton; 140 Pure London August 2008 www. purewomenswear.co.uk; 149 Pure London August 2008 www. purewomenswear.co.uk; 150 © Premiere Vision; 151 Courtesy Pitti Bimbo/Grant; 151 © breadandbutter.com; 154 David Steinhorst; 155 Alice Binns; 160 David Steinhorst; 161 Laura Pledger; 161 Keighley Hines; 163 Christopher Moore; 163 David Steinhorst; 163 Alice Binns; 164 Daniel Clark; 165 Alice Binns; 165 Alice Binns; 165 Courtesy Parveen Chana/De Montfort University; 165 Courtesy Mike Brown/De Montfort University; 166 Sarah Handy; 166 Sarah O'Hara; 167 David Overton and Caroline Mitchell www. carolinemitchellmillinery.com;168 Courtesy Lene Toni Kjeld; 169 Siobhan Noon;169 Courtesy Lene Toni Kjeld;190 © Premiere Vision; 196 Reggie Casagrande/Photographer's Choice/Getty Images; 207 Courtesy Half the Sky Designs; 208 Courtesy Lisa Jayne Dann, photographer Kerry Harrison; 211 Matt Kelley, Le Train Bleu www.letrainbleu.com; 212 Quentin de Briey www.quentindebriey.com; 214 Courtesy Christopher & Graeme Raeburn; 216 Sarah Handy; 219 Steven Haddock www.stevenhaddock.co.uk and Caroline Mitchell www.carolinemitchellmillinery.com; 220 Christopher Moore; 220 David Steinhorst; 223 Courtesy Lene Toni Kjeld; 224 Courtesy Denise Grünstein; 226 Lina Persson; 226 Nacho Alegre; 228 Quentin de Briey www.quentindebriey.com; 230 Eric Billman; 232 Mark Liu; 234 Nicoline Patricia Malina; 236 Akari Inoguchi

Acknowledgments

I would like to thank everyone who has supported this project. In particular I would like to thank Antonio Berardi for writing the foreword and for his other contributions to this book. In addition, grateful thanks go to the following people:

Tanis Alexander; Sandra Backlund; Lois Blackburn; Sally Jane Botwright; Cinzi Brandi; Lisa Jayne Dann; Christina Faulhaber; Laura Figueras; Tony Glenville; Cristy Guy; Sarah Handy; Wayne Hemingway; Akari Inoguchi, Carl Jacklin; Fiona Jenvey; Anna Kiper; Lene Toni Kjeld; Alicia Lawhon; Jo Little; Mark Liu; Nicoline Patricia Malina; Maria Manning; Caroline Mitchell; Dave Overton; Sacha Pacha; Krishan Palmer; Kim Parker; Bria Phillips; Enzo Pirozzi; Marie Thérèse Pumfrey; Christopher and Graeme Raeburn; Eugenio Recuenco; Zandra Rhodes; Céline Robert; Cecilia Sörensen; David Steinhorst; Sophie Steller; Mary Stevens-Heebner; Ian Stuart; Adam Verity; Liam Wycherley.

I am also grateful to the many companies who have given their support to this project and offered advice and guidance, in particular Adidas; Agatha; Debenhams; Mudpie Ltd.; mywardrobe.com; Blake Simms at LECTRA, www.lectra.com; Peclers; Sacha Pacha; Tuc Tuc; View Management.

A special thank you goes to Anne Townley, my development editor, for all her kindness and encouragement in the planning and preparation of this book, as well as to Jo Lightfoot, Gaynor Sermon and all involved with this book at Laurence King Publishing. I would also like to acknowledge the support provided by Annalaura Palma, the picture researcher, for her persistence in sourcing images and her enthusiasm throughout the project, and Jon Allan at TwoSheds Design.

In addition, I would like to thank the following students and recent graduates at the University of Lincoln who supplied images of their work and quotes for the book: Amy Barrass; Alice Binns; Daniel Clark; Gemma Clews; Keighley Hines; Sarah O'Hara; Joanne McKenna; Sophia Miller; Siobhan Noon; Stacey Richards; Laura Smith; Cindy Yuen and John Mukusha.

A huge thank you also goes to all my friends and colleagues at the University for their enthusiastic support throughout this project.

Finally, heartfelt thanks go to my parents, George and Margaret Brown, for their fantastic encouragement and continuing support. This book is dedicated to them.